LIVING & WORKIN

A selection of other How To Books

Applying for a Job
Applying for a United States Visa
Choosing a Package Holiday
Doing Business Abroad
Doing Voluntary Work Abroad
Emigrate
Find Temporary Work Abroad
Finding Work Overseas
Getting a Job Abroad
Getting a Job in America
Getting into America
Getting a Job in Canada
Getting a Job in Travel & Tourism
Manage Your Career

Master Languages
Obtaining Visas & Work Permits
Passing that Interview
Planning Your Gap Year
Retire Abroad
Setting Up Home in Florida
Spending a Year Abroad
Study Abroad
Teaching Abroad
Travel Round the World
Using the Internet
Working Abroad
Working As an Au Pair
Working on Contract Worldwide

Other titles in preparation

The How To series now contains nearly 250 titles in the following categories:

Business & Management
Computer Basics
General Reference
Jobs & Careers
Living & Working Abroad

Personal Finance
Self-Development
Small Business
Student Handbooks
Successful Writing

Please send for a free copy of the latest catalogue for full details (see back cover for address).

LIVING & WORKING ABROAD

LIVING & WORKING IN AMERICA

How to gain entry and how to settle when you are there

Steve Mills

5th edition

How To Books

British Library Cataloguing in Publication Data
A catalogue record for this book is available from the British Library.

© Copyright 1998 Steve Mills.

The author asserts the moral right to be identified as the author of this work.

Published by How To Books Ltd, 3 Newtec Place,
Magdalen Road, Oxford OX4 1RE, United Kingdom.
Tel: (01865) 793806. Fax: (01865) 248780.
email: info@howtobooks.co.uk
www.howtobooks.co.uk

First published in 1988
Second edition 1992
Third edition 1995
Fourth edition 1997
Reprinted 1997
Fifth edition 1998
Reprinted 1999

Note: The material contained in this book is set out in good faith for general guidance and no liability can be accepted for loss or expense incurred as a result of relying in particular circumstances on statements made in the book. The laws and regulations are complex and liable to change, and readers should check the current position with the relevant authorities before making personal arrangements.

Produced for How To Books by Deer Park Productions.
Typeset by PDQ Typesetting, Stoke-on-Trent.
Printed and bound by Cromwell Press, Trowbridge, Wiltshire.

Contents

Preface
to the Fifth Edition

This book, like its sister volumes on US jobs and visas, is for anyone who has ever thought about spending some time in the United States. Millions of Europeans continue to go to the United States, whether for business or for pleasure, to visit or to stay, for anything from a long weekend to forever. Increasingly, though, the choice is not between a Concorde weekend break and emigration. Millions continue to visit the USA for a period longer than their annual holiday but without ever finally settling down there. This further revised and updated edition is for anyone who has ever thought of living or working in the USA for anything from a few weeks to many years. It is particularly geared to those who would like to experience the USA for more than just a few days' holiday.

What follows results from living and working backwards and forwards across the Atlantic for the last 25 years, travelling from coast to coast by plane, hitching, driving a van, by hired car, and even at times on foot. It's the result of visiting some 30 different states and living for years in and around the federal capital as much as of teaching American history, cultural geography and urban studies to Britons and Americans at Keele University and the University of Maryland. It follows from entering the USA by plane, by car, and even on foot, on three totally different kinds of visa, crossing sometimes alone, sometimes with family, on holiday and on business. It's a little bit of what has become American within me, even while I live and write in the UK.

I hope you will find the lessons of my own experience enable you, the reader, to enjoy your own visits to the USA with just a little more emphasis on the fun and a little less on the hassle for having been that little more prepared than I ever was. Friends and colleagues have often said that I should pass on my experience: so here it is. With the incredible bits cut out so that you don't think this is another Tom Sharpe novel, here is a guide to living and working in the USA. May you enjoy your own experience as much as I've enjoyed mine.

SO WHAT DOES THIS BOOK DO?

It's a guide to the USA, providing hints and suggestions that may help you gain just that much more from your decision to visit or even to live in the USA. Many aspects of being in the USA come as a shock even for those who think they are well prepared. When I first arrived with a newly minted American Studies degree in my pocket I thought I'd arrived in the wrong country, so little did I recognise or understand in my first few weeks. So bad was the *experience* I could have cheerfully hijacked a plane out and away (in any direction!) if only I'd have known how. Nothing *bad* happened at all: no muggings, no illness, nothing specifically traumatic. But the experience overwhelmed me as I tried to cope with the reality of a new job, looking for somewhere to live, no car, no pay yet though my savings were fast ebbing away, and I'd arrived in one of the hottest and most humid Augusts for years. The only guides had been my textbooks and guidebooks for those visiting the sights. I didn't even know that all the paper money was the same colour and size, that I'd have to pay a month's rent in advance plus a month's rent as deposit, that my pay wouldn't be paid directly into my account but that I'd have to do that myself every other Friday. Traffic on the right-hand side of the road was the least of my problems. That I'd expected!

So this guide will start by asking you to consider what you expect from the USA, for what you want will be the most significant factor in how the USA measures up to your expectations. Anyone expecting a Big Mac in a vegetarian restaurant is going to get a nasty surprise! Be honest with yourself as to what you want to do, and, just as importantly, what you don't want from a holiday, a family reunion, an American business market or a new start in life, and you'll be able to explore precisely what opportunities the USA does indeed hold for you.

Once you've decided you're off to the USA there's the whole question of the paperwork. The US is not an easy country to deal with even once you've been let in. Many people expect US bureaucracy to be more efficient, or at least less convoluted than in Britain. They often find that the truth is far from pleasant. Don't forget that everything governmental is duplicated: a State income tax may well be payable as well as the Federal one. Income tax liability is by self-assessment, but it's usually so complex, and the penalties threatened so dire, that most people pay a tax specialist to fill out the annual forms for them. Just thinking of your local tax inspector in

Britain may bring a warm glow to your heart (but only while you're in the USA!).

But what opportunities exist? These are discussed in terms of the various groups – such as students, business people, entrepreneurs, professionals and artists. Read widely here, for though all face different problems all share similar problems as outsiders trying to get on the inside.

Throughout there is a wealth of information, outlining where best to go for further advice, with addresses and phone numbers for contacts both in Britain and in the USA. A careful use of the telephone can be a great time saver, especially in such a complex and potentially overwhelming matter as going to the USA.

CAVEAT

I have tried to update all UK phone numbers and Web addresses listed here, but some old ones are sure to have lain low and escaped detection. And to phone abroad remember the international access code is 00, so to call the USA dial 001 before the US seven digit number.

Whilst every attempt has been made by the author to ensure that the information presented in this book is accurate at the time of going to press neither the author nor the publishers can accept any responsibility for any errors or omissions.

Steve Mills

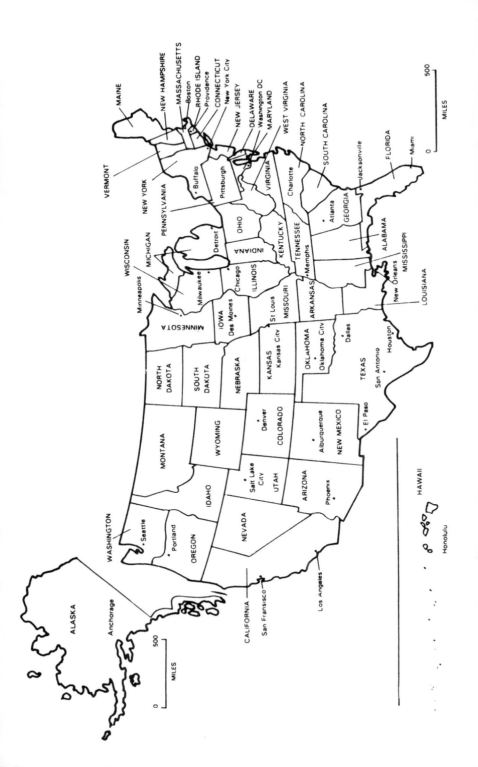

1
Considering the USA

WHY CONSIDER GOING TO THE USA?

The appeal of the United States is as varied as the country is vast.
Millions have traditionally gone there to settle down. Nowadays more
and more people visit the USA whether on holiday, to visit family or
friends, on business or to study, as the 747s ply backwards and forwards
across the Atlantic. For many people a particular visit has been greatly
enhanced by combining a business trip with a holiday, a family reunion
with travelling around, or using an initial holiday as the way to sample
American life before making a commitment to stay longer. The country
is so large and varied that a lifetime of visits would hardly exhaust its
potentials; the USA is more a continent than the kind of country found
in Europe.

British associations
The British have a long association with the United States. The eastern
(Atlantic) coast states were once British colonies, though they broke
away from the empire in the late eighteenth century. English is still

---

American or English?

In Illinois the State language is deemed American, but more
usually, as in a California language referendum, 'English' will do.

---

the main language, long since adopted as America's own. The initial
settlers of the north-eastern States were English Puritans (and the states
they founded are still together called New England). English and Welsh
Quakers founded Pennsylvania further down the coast. Inland the
mountains were first settled by Ulster folk tired of defending Ireland for
the Crown. In the south the English landowners and Scots soldiers,
pioneers and convicts laid the foundation of a distinctively Anglo-
Saxon, almost pro-British society, but one quite unlike that back in
Europe, for here a plantation economy was directly based upon the
labour of African slaves.

European immigrants

The Founding Fathers of the American Republic were essentially English gentlemen in rebellion, paradoxically, to protect their English rights against a despotic government far away in Britain. To the west their descendants carved out an empire dedicated to individual freedom, corporate growth and the Protestant work ethic, sweeping aside the native societies (and most other European settlers). When millions of Europeans then arrived at the end of the nineteenth century, not at first speaking English, a nation based firmly upon American experience was already in place, echoing only faintly its British origins. These immigrants created an urban and industrial society almost obliterating the rural British landscape and so recasting the language and the political system that the links with Britain became even more obscured. Even as immigrants learned in school that their new country spoke English and used the common law, their numbers and the needs of their new surroundings brought about a continual reworking of vocabulary and syntax, whilst their strident demands for action and protection recast both the legal and government systems. The British link became ever more submerged: the United States becomes ever more foreign.

A shared language

The British and the Irish, alone amongst Europeans, are uniquely able to ignore the foreignness of America if they choose to do so. Though America remains a very distant foreign country whose ethnic variety is today more firmly rooted in Africa or eastern Europe than in Britain or Ireland, the shared language opens up the USA to English-speaking Europeans as for no others from the Old World. Add the considerable number of such people with friends already in America and the British and Irish can retain their links with the USA even while the USA at large looks elsewhere, particularly today across the Pacific.

A familiar place

Even as the USA nowadays looks far beyond Britain and Ireland the British and Irish look ever more avidly at the USA. Hollywood movies first brought the rich variety of US life across the Atlantic. Today television continues that tradition. The very quantity of TV movies, documentaries and situation comedies brings both fantasy and daily life into everyone's homes. The USA is a country we visit passively every day, year in, year out. No wonder it often seems more familiar than even unvisited parts of our country, and beckons with the promise of exotic parts where the locals reassuringly speak English. The educated and skilled middle classes already speaking English, can consider settling down in the USA, melting into the background as quickly or as slowly as they want, like East German refugees did in West Germany; no language barriers to put off all but the most stout-hearted as happens when the French and German middle classes look across the Atlantic. No wonder it is to the USA that so many British people turn for holidays, business, or to start a new life.

THERE'S SOMETHING FOR EVERYONE IN AMERICA

This may sound like little more than an ad man's copy, like a Texan boast, or just a piece of wishful thinking. The size, the physical contrast, the ethnic variety, the particular rural-urban mix, the wealth and poverty and 400 years of European history (resting upon thousands of years of earlier people's!) means that whatever your interest, from landscape painting to railway trains, from ornithology to folk music, there is indeed something for everyone. And millions of British people have families over there, sisters and aunts who went over as GI brides in the 1940s, or brain drain scientists from the days of the space race.

It's amazing how many people have never visited their families in the USA but have always thought they'd like to, always able to find a 'reason' for not going.

HAVE YOU EVER THOUGHT...?

- **I haven't the time**
  Well, save up your annual leave. Most of us now get two weeks, and three can usually be arranged if planned far enough ahead.

- **I couldn't afford the money**
  It's not all the QE2, caviare and dressing for dinner now. Wide-bodied jets fly across in eight hours for only a couple of hundred pounds if you can book a month or so in advance.

- **They've never asked me over**
  They probably did years ago, or thought they did. Why not ask if they'd like to come visit you? That would get the ball rolling!

- **I don't like all that violence you see on TV**
  Though Washington DC is more violent than Belfast at its worst, most visitors never see anything more violent than a repeat episode of *Blott on the Landscape* on American TV. If you are sensible and are staying with family or friends, visiting the USA is less dangerous than staying at home. And US sports crowds are very well behaved!

- **I couldn't stand all the junk food**
  Fast food isn't the only food the US is famous for. Every kind under the sun is available (even fish and chips, from equipment made in

Britain!). This is hardly surprising given all the different people (from Albanians to Vietnamese) who have settled there over the years.

- **I wouldn't like the heat**
  The US has taken central heating in winter and air conditioning in summer to its heart. You need only be hot (or cold) if you want to.

- **I hate motorway travel**
  Well fly, or take the train (yes, long distance trains still connect the main cities with some degree of civilisation). Also, believe it or not, driving an air-conditioned mid-size hired car can be almost relaxing at a continuous 60 mph over the gently graded freeways of the south and west, with a comfortable motel at the day's end (including a swim in the pool followed by a steak supper and a film on the TV movie channel in your room).

NO RELATIVES IN THE USA?

- **Well find some!**
  Didn't a cousin go over, marry and stay? Now's the chance to visit that aunt you've not seen since Christmas 1973 to ask her about her daughter in Seattle. Doesn't someone have a US penfriend from days in the Scouts?

- **Old school friends?**
  Ring around and find who's gone abroad. An old school friend now in Alberta would give you somewhere to aim for as you drive westwards from Chicago. A trip just across the border would be quite interesting, and a worthwhile detour en route for Seattle!

- **Ask around...**
  for people at school, college, work or sports club who have been to the USA. They may have US friends who keep open house to visiting stamp collectors, squash players, local historians, bird watchers and so on. How would you respond if an American couple who shared your passion for bees or real ale wrote saying they were passing through your area on their next holiday? Wouldn't you get the spare room ready and take the risk of inviting in strangers on the basis of a mutual friend and a shared hobby?

- **Ask at your school, college, rotary or town twinning meeting...**
  about people who have gone on sponsored visits, scholarships and exchanges. Track them down and ask them how they arranged to go over, what it cost, who they stayed with. They'll probably be only too pleased to share their experiences with you. And many towns are twinned with their US namesakes.

Most of us can get to visit the USA one way or another if we are employed (or students with job prospects). It may take a year or so of overtime saving up the money or a couple of long vacations pulling pints in a holiday resort, and if you want to give up smoking or drinking a trip to the USA would be a worthwhile target to save for, and something to get you through the cravings. Some people have even taken to entering competitions as a hobby, and once into the swing of things, they start to recognise what's required of entries and tie-breaking slogans, winning prizes that can include holiday trips abroad. It's a long shot, but someone's going to win that trip by Concorde for two to Disneyland. It could just be you!

LISTING YOUR INTERESTS IN THE USA

Make your own list, for example:

- touring the sights
- going on a resort-based family holiday
- visiting friends or relatives
- going on a speciality trip (battlefields, bird watching, old cars)
- making a business trip
- having a look around prior to emigrating.

All are excellent reasons for going to the USA. But if you can make it clear in your own mind why you are interested in the USA then it'll be easier to answer the essential question:

What do I/we want from our trip to the USA?

You may well be able to combine several concerns:

- visiting family then touring
- family holiday after a business visit
- family resort plus personal speciality
- touring between business visits.

Beware!

Mixing your trips together could ruin the whole thing:

- What would happen if the children got sick while you are all hurrying to the next business appointment?

- Will the children be able to enjoy anything on a rapid, long distance chase between business appointments?

- What will you do if friends not seen for years now chain-smoke, wife swap, play bridge all the time, are workaholics or can't stand children?

However, some considerations can work out just fine:

- If you are geared up to tour you can make your excuses and leave any disastrous reunion.
- If militant chain-smoking friends have now mellowed with children and exercise you can always stay a night longer than planned, or even visit again on your way back to the airport.

WHAT KIND OF VISIT DO YOU WANT?

For some people holidays are action-packed, for others relaxed and gentle. Where you go depends upon how you feel about holidays:

	like	*so-so*	*don't like*
Big cities like New York			
Resorts such as Disneyworld			
Famous sights or battlefields			
Spectacular landscapes			
Lakes and forests			

Using a different coloured pen, go over and make the choices again, this time thinking how your children might respond. Then ask your children to fill in *their* choices: did you get their choices right? Did they like the choices you'd already made for them?

Would you gain relaxation from visiting the following:

	like	*so-so*	*don't like*
Manhattan's shops			
Niagara Falls			
Washington's museums			
Virginia's battlefields			
Casinos of Las Vegas			
Disneyworld			

If you've built up a column of no answers, then for a relaxing holiday you may need to go elsewhere, or perhaps concentrate upon some US version of what you've done successfully before:

- If you like walking in the Lake District...
  try walking in the Rocky Mountain National Park.

- If you like the Costa del Sol...
  try the Florida coast around Miami.

- If you like Blackpool and Alton Towers...
  try Disneyworld.

- If you like the British Museum...
  try Washington DC's Smithsonian Institute.

- If you like the Normandy battlefields...
  try the Civil War battlefields.

- If you like European Spa towns...
  try Saratoga in New York, White Sulphur West Virginia or Hot Springs Arkansas.

- If you like salmon jumping in Scotland...
  try Minke Whales in a New England summer.

To know what kind of visit you want you must sort out your priorities in your own mind. Remember, people who like the Lake District often like Blackpool too. But such a person might find one day at a resort quite enough, a week in the hills not enough. If you want mountains with a day off in a resort then don't go to Florida, for unlike Britain the drive from resort to mountains isn't an hour up the motorway, but two whole days! If you make a mistake in the USA you may well be stuck with it, through no more perhaps than if you'd flown off to the Mediterranean.

GETTING MARRIED

The USA has long cornered the market in speedy weddings (and 6-week divorces). In Nevada a wedding licence is easier to acquire than a rented car. You need your passport and $45 for the paperwork. The Elvis Experience in Las Vegas is open 24 hours a day for the ceremony. In Florida ceremonies can be arranged at Disneyworld (licences $88.50 require passport and birth certificate). Nuptial packages exist from Hawaii to Key Largo. **Kuoni** do Hawaii and Florida (01306 742222), **Airtours** do California and Florida (01706 830130).

FURTHER THOUGHTS ON STAYING WITH FRIENDS OR RELATIVES

It's worth thinking how well you relax with friends and relatives *back home* before you visit overseas.

- Do you dread visiting your wife/husband's school friends?
- Do you now find your old college friends boring?
- Do you leave Aunty Flo's as soon as possible?
- Do you leave your in-laws vowing never to return?

If family visits are fraught with suppressed anger at home perhaps you ought to reconsider such an option overseas?
Also consider:

- **How well** do you know your old friends and relatives?
- Have your **holiday demands** changed since you all last met?
- What **options** do you have if their welcome sours?
- Can you afford to **risk** your family holiday or business trip?

A leisurely week on a canal boat on North Staffordshire's Cauldon Canal with a couple of days at the Alton Towers leisure park plus canalside real ale and cream teas would be a more relaxing way to spend your hard-earned holiday if family and one-time friends simply get you het up rather than help you relax.

But you can always keep your options open. If there's any doubt about staying with family or friends in the USA make them just one part of a tour abroad. Knowing that you'll be off and away in a couple of days can help you relax and may make all the difference between a successful and a disastrous trip.

FAMILY REUNIONS

Family reunions can be short or long. A short stay with friends or relatives in Britain can turn out to be little short of disaster. Imagine how awful it would be to leave Britain to spend the rest of your days with your family already long settled in the USA only to find out after a few weeks that you can't stand each other. If you intend to live with, or even nearby, younger family it's essential that:

- it's been thought through carefully by all concerned

- you've visited and seen what accommodation is available

- everyone knows what the financial implications will be (will grandparents' pensions from Britain be sufficient to keep them, or will a family subsidy be necessary?)

- you have talked over and experienced each other's lifestyles in case the clash is too loud

- each side should know and understand their responsibilities (from paying rent to babysitting).

Initially the most crucial thing is for the Europeans to visit and stay with the Americans. And stay beyond the holiday couple of weeks. Anyone can put up with almost anyone for a few weeks. But how about after three months? What is it like in the middle of a midwestern winter? – a Florida summer? Parents do go overseas to be with their grown-up children, and it can be the start of a very successful new life. But it can also be a recipe for disaster. But then staying at home never seeing children and grandchildren isn't always much fun either.

A word of warning
A family holiday in, say, Florida can be quite expensive, even though you may get value for money and a holiday to remember. But if you dwell too much on how much it's costing you may be driven to cram in too many people and places to get your money's worth.

- Just think of a generation of US visitors that have done precisely that. ('If it's Tuesday it must be Belgium.')

- Trying to see everything, even in one State, will mean an awful lot of time will be spent on the motorway (whether on the bus or in a hired car). Would you advise Americans to see as much of Britain as possible by way of keeping to the M4, M5, M6, M74, A1(M) and M1 circuit? And yet Britain is smaller than most US States!

- If you visit a Florida relative it doesn't mean you will be able to drive to visit others in New Orleans, Chicago and New York City, even though on a map that looks like a reasonable drive around. Would you spend a continental holiday driving from home to Moscow and back again by way of Athens? If this visit to the USA is indeed the trip of a lifetime and you really must see everyone then consider flying instead. **Multiple destination tickets** can be arranged before leaving home, often in conjunction with your transatlantic carrier, at very advantageous rates. If you must drive either take as long as possible so that you can leave the motorways, visiting as you go along, or better still, plan to come back again to visit the rest of the family.

TRIP OF A LIFETIME?

It is a great temptation to try to do too much on an initial visit to the USA. If for reasons of health you know this is a one-off visit *focus* your trip.

- What is the primary object of your visit:
  - to get away from it all?
  - to visit relatives?
  - to visit a specific site or resort?

- Maybe your relatives should visit you where you want to stay (such as Disneyworld or the Grand Canyon) rather than you rush around central Florida and then dash on to Chicago?

- Be firm in your own mind as to why you are in the USA.

- Be explicit with your relatives as to where and what you want to do.

- Be up front about who is paying:
  - if you are paying, relatives visit you;
  - if relatives are offering hospitality, careful negotiations may be necessary so you aren't at their beck and call.

But remember: most visitors can return if they want to, even if not the following year:

- Focus on your main interest during an initial visit.
- Dare to leave other areas or people for next time.

During my first visit I planned to tour nationwide with a Greyhound Bus Pass I'd bought in Britain. Instead I cashed it in for a focused trip around the North East. I have never regretted that. I'm still returning to complete my original travel plans.

BEING IN THE USA FOR THE MILLENNIUM

Though most Brits will probably celebrate at home or in a local hostelry, some will seek out a dream destination such as the islands of the South Pacific. But many who have already visited the USA may well look across the Atlantic for first footing, even though by being away from home US visitors will be postponing the big moment for at least five hours. For ideas world-wide see *The Rough Guide to the Millennium* now available from Penguin (£5).

New York's **Times Square** *is* New Year's Eve for most Americans, even if they would usually rather die than actually visit downtown New York in the middle of the night. Times Square is not actually a square.

Rather it is a strange intersection of 5th Avenue, part of that great North-South grid pattern of streets and avenues, with Broadway, the far older track that once crossed the island from Manhattan's southern tip to Harlem. The modern tradition began as recently as 1904 when *The New York Times* at One Times Square started sponsoring rooftop parties. In 1907 someone had the bright idea of lowering a reflective ball down the flagpole atop the building as a visible countdown to midnight. The rest, as they say, is history. With the coming of television millions across the USA and even overseas now time their festivities with the goings on in Times Square just as people in Britain do with the party in Trafalgar Square.

For the Millennium, Times Square's bash will be bigger and better: Times Square 2000 – the Global Celebrations at the Crossroads of the World. Giant video screens will broadcast footage of celebrations from around the world, beginning with Fiji (7.00am New York time). Given that it will probably be below freezing in New York at the time, Miami is trying to wrest the US focus to celebrate within more lazy climes. South Beach Miami is already asking people where they would rather be: in frigid Manhattan or on a warm Florida beach. Of course, that may not be the choice: fans of *Get Shorty* will no doubt recall the less than tropical winter with which the film opens. So California is planning to exploit its desert location with the party to end all parties out on the road to Palm Springs, where the organisers hope to attract 2.5 million people for a three-day, five-band extravaganza. Watch your Web browser for further details.

For **Miami Millennium** ideas contact the Greater Miami Convention & Visitors Bureau: (0171) 734 1427.

For **Miami travel** details try:

- American Airlines (0181) 572 5555
- Virgin Atlantic (01293) 747747
- Laker Airways (01293) 789000.

For **Miami hotels** with UK contact numbers there's:

- Island Outpost with 6 trendy hotels: 0800 614790
- Leading Hotels of the World: 0800 181123
- Sheraton: 0800 973106.

For **New York City** start with the New York Visitors Bureau: 00 1 212 484 1200, plus:

- Four Seasons Hotels: 0800 526648
- Sheraton: 0800 973106
- Westin Hotels: (0171) 408 0636
- Ritz-Carlton: 0800 234000.

ALTERNATIVE DESTINATIONS

If you want to experience life in another part of the English-speaking world, the United States is not the only country you might like to consider, whether for a visit or to live. Consider perhaps Australia, New Zealand, even South Africa. But the best and most appropriate comparison is probably with Canada just north of the border.

Just considering an alternative to the USA may help sort out precisely what you're looking for in going abroad. You may end up knowing that the USA *is* for you after all!

CANADA

Larger than the USA, but with only about half Britain's population, Canada is a bilingual country where English and French are equal in the eyes of the law. The British-settled Maritime provinces on the Atlantic coast are today far from economically buoyant particularly as fishing declines, and they now rely upon federal aid and tourism. The dynamic areas of English-speaking Canada are further inland, from Toronto on the Great Lakes westwards to Vancouver on the Pacific Coast, especially the rich farmlands and oil of the prairies around Calgary. French-speaking Canada, once restricted mainly to the farmland along the St Lawrence River, is now both urban and industrial, based upon Montreal and its massive iron ore fields and electrical generating stations to the north.

After a prolonged visit to the USA, English-speaking Canada may appear very British, though if arriving directly from Europe it'll probably appear very American with its sprawling cities, freeways, high summer humidity and deep winter chills. Increasingly cosmopolitan Canada retains for many visitors and residents alike the benefits of the old world in the new. Does it really have all the benefits of the USA but with few of the problems?

Getting there
- Similar air packages exist as for the USA.
- A full British Passport is needed (and a valid US visa is necessary for cross border trips to the USA).
- No visas are required for tourists up to 90 days.
- For long stays first contact the Canadian authorities *before* leaving home.

Staying there
- As the recession tightened in the late 1970s immigration restriction

became more stringent. Permission to live in Canada, 'landed immigrant status', became available only to certain people with specific skills needed but not locally available. This principle is rigorously applied.

• Temporary work for foreign visitors is generally not allowed. Male students are, however, permitted to apply for a permit to work on tobacco farms in southern Ontario. (Contact **British Universities North America Club**, 16 Bowling Green Lane, London EC1 for details. Early application is essential.) Casual jobs for cash are likely to be in fruit-picking in the Okanagan Valley of British Columbia, or in the bars of the Rocky Mountain resorts.

• Immigration and visa enquiries should be made initially at the **High Commission**, 38 Grosvenor Street, London W1X 0AA. Tel: 0891 616644 (a premium rate call).

Considering Canada?

	yes	no
I don't mind no sub-tropical or desert areas		
Speaking in French would be fun		
I quite like the British heritage		
I like cities that aren't dangerous		
I'd enjoy harsh winters 'with all mod cons'		

If you've answered *yes* to three or more then further consideration of Canada seems a good idea. But you could be based in Canada and drive to sub-tropical or desert areas. You could ignore, depending upon where you are, either the French or the British heritage, or even both! You could also enjoy Canada-like conditions (social, economic and climatic!) across large parts of the USA, for instance in the harsh but anticipated winters of Minnesota.

Reconsidering the USA
• Don't think the USA is all New York City, Miami and Los Angeles. Small town America has been making a come back these last few years, with some very high growth rates. It isn't all *NYPD Blue* and *ER*.
• If you settle in the USA, Canada is there as a great place to visit.
• The US economy is generally more vibrant, and for the real go-getter

the USA remains the place to be in certain fields such as the movies or rock music.

Perhaps the phrase should be 'There's something for everybody in North America'?

Beware: if your US stopover is in Los Angeles don't expect relatives from Canada to come to visit you. Would you go to greet a visiting American relative on their arrival in Rome, never mind Istanbul!

OTHER OVERSEAS OPPORTUNITIES
In order to place the US in a wider context you might also consider the following:

Teaching English as a Foreign Language (TEFL)
If you want to use your native grasp of English, taking this qualification could well be a worthwhile investment in time and money. These courses are not grant-aided. If you already have a teaching certificate and a degree in English this added qualification could be profitable. The broadsheet newspapers, such as the *Guardian*'s Tuesday education section, have adverts for colleges offering TEFL (postgraduate) courses. Any of the good colleges attempt placements for their successful students.

For those with a degree or teaching qualification plus a recognised TEFL qualification plus at least one year's TEFL experience, details of overseas posts can be obtained from **Overseas Educational Appointments Department**, The British Council, 10 Spring Gardens, London SW1A 2BN. Tel: (0171) 930 8466. Fax: (0171) 839 6347.

Voluntary Services Overseas (VSO)
Despite the old gap year image, for the most part VSO prefers graduates with practical skills like home economics, animal husbandry or intermediate technology. Contracts can be for several years so that worthwhile projects can be undertaken. Contact: **VSO** at 317 Putney Bridge, London SW15 2PG. Tel: (0181) 780 2266.

Voluntary work
There are endless possibilities:

- *Kibbutz Representatives* (0181 458 9235) are the official recruiters. Expect to pay your airfare and stay for at least 2 months.

- *The Project Trust* (01893 230444) places volunteers aged 17½–19 on application in developing countries such as Cuba. Expect to have to raise about £300 in sponsorship beforehand.

- *GAP Activity Projects* (01734 594914) charges a substantial arrangement fee, plus airfare and insurance (board and lodgings provided) for 6 months overseas.

For other possibilities see *International Directory of Volunteer Work*, Vacation Work, annually, or Mark Hempshell *Doing Voluntary Work Abroad*, How To Books, 2nd edition 1997.

Paid employment

At your next job interview ask what opportunities exist for overseas work. At least it'll give you something to say when the interviewer asks 'Any questions?'.

Some useful books

- Roger Jones, *How to Get a Job Abroad*, How To Books, 4th edition 1995.

- G. Golzen, *Working Abroad*, Kogan Page, 1987 (still useful for general ideas).

- D. Leppard, *The Directory of Jobs & Careers Abroad*, Vacation Work (periodically updated).

For those of you thinking further afield try:

- Jeremy Gough, *Living & Working in Hong Kong*, How To Books, 1996.

- Jonathan Hayter, *Working in Japan*, How To Books, 1996.

- Hamid Atiyyah, *How to Live and Work in the Gulf*, How To Books, 1995.

Then there's always working your way around from country to country:

- Susan Griffith, *Work Your Way Around the World*, Vacation Work 1997

- Nick Vandome, *How to Travel Round the World*, How To Books, 1995.

The Central Bureau for Educational Visits & Exchanges annually publishes *Working Holidays* (£8.99 including postage and packing) dealing with paid and voluntary work in over 70 countries for people aged 12–70 with advice on visas, insurance and health precautions. Call (0171) 486 5101 for details, or Fax (0171) 935 1017.

2
What's It Like in the USA?

GETTING RID OF MISCONCEPTIONS

Americans know an awful lot about Britain and Ireland. They have seen the royal weddings on breakfast television and bombed RUC police stations on the nightly news. Avidly they watch the Dickensian horrors of *Our Mutual Friend*, delight in the decadent affluence of *Brideshead Revisited* or *The Buccaneers* and thrill to the period pieces of Agatha Christie's rural detective mysteries. The Sherlock Holmes stories forewarn a further generation about London fog while *Blott on the Landscape* confirms stereotypes of a perverted, class-conscious old world. No wonder they loved *Four Weddings and a Funeral*! It's hardly surprising the real Britain often comes as a great surprise to American visitors.

• All US television is endless soap operas, commercials and cop shows.	*But*	• Many stations are free of commercials within specific programmes – especially cable channels and publicly financed stations.
• America is just too violent to visit let alone live in.	*But*	• Sport is family entertainment with spectator violence almost unheard of.
• The New York City subway system is dangerous and very difficult for visitors to understand.	*But*	• The Washington DC metro system is one of the world's safest and cleanest, and it's easy to use.
• Everything is so much more expensive in the USA. Everyone knows that!	*But*	• Petrol is 35p a litre.

European misconceptions about the USA may be just as misleading, for our images come from a steady diet of musicals and horror films, cop adventure shows and such modern yarns as the *New Adventures of Superman* or *Quantum Leap*. Unfortunately these media images repel as many people as they attract. Endless violence, materialism, urban sprawl and drugs seem to cloud many people's views, as do equally misleading images of easy wealth, limitless opportunity and beautiful weather.

Of course, each stereotype can be substantiated. Commercial television can seem impossibly overloaded with adverts, the USA is considerably more violent than Britain or Northern Ireland, and though cheap the New York city subway is as chaotic and under-capitalised as London's underground. But if you are prepared to look more widely the stereotypes can be put into some kind of perspective. After all the USA is almost a continent, with some 250,000,000 people of every kind. Knowing a little about where to go and what to avoid, what to buy and what not to, can make all the difference.

For most would-be visitors the outstanding feature will probably be the USA's great variety of people and places, plus the incredible extremes of wealth.

THE USA: DISCOVERING PEOPLE AND PLACES

The USA is about half of North America, one of the world's major continents, over 9 million square kilometres (some 3 million square miles). Today the USA stretches beyond the mainland 48 states to the Arctic wastes of northern Alaska and the tropical forests of Hawaii. There is also one Federal district (Washington DC), plus the Caribbean Commonwealth of Puerto Rico and assorted island colonies. Being mostly temperate but with little of the polar or equatorial extremes found in other countries such as Canada or Russia on the one hand or Brazil or Zaire on the other, the USA is one of the most fertile slices of any continent anywhere.

North–South v. East–West

During the nineteenth century the newly independent USA spread westwards from its original colonial toe-hold along the Atlantic coast, over the mountains and rivers of the continental interior to the Pacific. This produces an essential feature of American geography: the mountains, rivers, weather systems and even migrating birds tend to move north and south, but the USA spreads against and across the grain. The attempt to forge a great north–south trading system to exploit the lay of the land and the southward movement of the main river system failed when the Mississippi River lost out to the growing east–west railway networks last century. Nevertheless, the overall physical structure of the USA remains north–south.

Physical, social and economic variety

Despite the superficial similarities of a common currency, a federal constitution, and one legal tongue, English, the physical (geographical) variety is compounded by a social variety and economic variety. The native peoples spoke many languages. The variety of lifestyles echoed that of the physical environment within which they lived. But the great eras of European settlement imposed a degree of variety far beyond that of the natural order. Imperial Spain moved in from the south-west, Russia from the north-west, Britain and France from the north-east. As in Africa their territorial carve-up paid scant regard to the original inhabitants. Territories were swapped for reasons of big-power politics. France was defeated by its British rival, but left behind a French-speaking, Roman Catholic population to the north of the USA's north-eastern border, but only after its explorers, trappers, traders and priests had opened up the whole continent, teaching the native peoples such games as divide and rule, drunkenness and a desire for European goods. The British retired north of the Great Lakes, south to the Caribbean islands, or the Atlantic islands of Newfoundland, the Bahamas and Bermuda, or changed into Americans turning their back upon Europe as elsewhere would the Dutch of South Africa. Russia sold up for cash.

The **vastness** of the American continent is beyond our island imaginings. Crossing from New York to Los Angeles means crossing time zones and a score of state lines each with their own police, drinking laws and parliaments. Some execute killers, other let them rot in gaol. Some states are hot and wet as a steam room, others dry as the Sahara. Snow falls while flowers bloom. And beyond Los Angeles lies the Pacific Ocean, and far away, Hawaii, as far as if the British Isles were part of Canada's Atlantic Dominion. The vastness is not that of unmitigated sameness. Quite the contrary – the topography changes in every direction, though in the midst of the plains the eye can refute this intellectual notion, so flat it seems. The rivers are trapped in deep gorges, winding across wide plains taking hundreds of miles of lazy turns to cover merely ten, pollution ridden, full of white water tourists, or disappearing into desert wastes. So vast is the land that it covers an expanse from alligator-ridden bayous along the Gulf of Mexico to permafrost deserts along the Arctic Ocean. Hardwoods give way to farming where once was only prairie grass. Desert threatens to spread again, like the African Sahel, into the southern high plains. Along the Pacific the earth moves, a Mount St Helens spews forth a vision of hell, and sitting on the Pacific ring of fire has Angelenos awaiting the shuddering earth that may yet destroy the seventh largest economy ever known, that of California.

Early settlement

To the east are the Appalachian Mountains, long worn down to mere stumps, though high enough (Mt Mitchell is over 2,000m high!), wide enough and forested enough to thwart generations of settlers until new travel technologies opened up such gaps as existed. The Mississippi interior was opened up originally by military adventurers, explorers and finally traders. Settlers soon carved up the grasslands into some of the most fertile farms ever created. Miners carried the sweep into the Rockies of the Far West. Not one range, but a whole series of mountains and basins, these western ranges contain both the highest point in the country, outside Alaska, Mt Whitney (4,418 m) and the lowest, Death Valley (-86m).

The vast interior desert between the Rocky Mountain front ranges in Colorado and the Sierra Nevada mountains of California is so isolated that it was here the Mormons were finally able to establish their new Promised Land last century. So out of the world is the landscape that it was in these barren wastes that NASA's moonbuggy practice took place in the 1960s.

When the NASA moonbuggy training was underway a passing Navajo Indian shepherd asked what they were doing. When he heard that they were bound for the moon he asked to record a message for any Navajo already on the moon. His recorded message for the lunar Navajo was finally translated. It simply said: 'Sign nothing'.

To the south the states of the Gulf of Mexico are vast areas of fertile farmlands, once covered with forests in the east, grasslands to the west. Hot and humid for much of the year, snow and ice are a rare surprise. Once inhabited by settled, farming native Indian peoples these areas were cleared in the 1830s for European settlement. African slaves were brought in to work the expanding cotton plantations. The Indians were driven into the barren areas across the border, later to become reservations under US control. Only in the western deserts could the native peoples survive on their traditional lands; though hedged around by the US authorities.

Industrial development

As the USA expanded westwards to the Pacific the country changed economically and socially. From a once rural society of farms and small towns emerged an industrial giant of huge cities. Factories that both provided the rails and barbed wire for the western farmlands and required the increasing bounty of foodstuffs and raw materials needed more labour than the USA could provide. People poured in from all over Europe. Where once they had originally come mainly from Britain and similar northern European societies they now also flooded in first from Ireland, then from Italy, Poland and Russia, Jews and gentiles alike.

The USA today is only superficially a child of the British Isles. Rather, today's American people come from mainly continental stock, the torrent of urban and entrepreneurial peoples that flooded in before the First World War. Trade and manufacturing of an unprecedented scale developed, linking the products of the US interior with the wider world. Mostly east and southern European, these immigrants took up American English only in so far as it gave them access to political and economic power, plus social clout. They preserved the skin of America, but totally changed its core, not so much becoming Americans as changing the definition of what it was to be American.

Modern urban pluralism and rural conservatism

The 1860s Civil War population of 40 million rose to over 100 million by the First World War. By then it was too late for the older America to turn back the tide. The immigrants, and particularly their children, had created a society so buoyant, so materially prosperous that they could now simply ignore much of this older, rural America of the Midwest High Plains and the Bible Belt. The brash society of the cities had little time for and even less contact with the increasingly resentful survivors of the countryside. Sometimes the White Anglo Saxon Protestant (WASP) countryside would fight back, such as pushing through the outlawing of alcohol (prohibition) and voting to end further mass immigration. But with an ever larger proportion of consumers and voters living and working in the cities such measures were far too late. The cities were liberal, pluralist, atomistic and comparatively secular. The countryside remained WASP, small town, devout and outraged.

THE WEATHER

Where you decide to stay or to live may well depend purely upon what holiday packages or jobs are available. But the USA is so vast it helps to know what you may be letting yourself in for. The weather in the USA is not something that dominates conversation, as in Britain, but the extremes are such that the weather cannot be ignored completely except by the foolhardy.

A continental climate

The USA is continental in scale. The climate is as varied as you would find across all of Europe, from the Arctic north to the desert south. Much of western Europe is surrounded by water, whether the Atlantic or its North Sea, Baltic or Mediterranean offshoots. Though the USA is surrounded by the Atlantic, the Gulf of Mexico, the Pacific and the Great Lakes, vast areas are far from any influences from the oceans. The result is great extremes, not just in the interior but even along many coastal regions which are themselves influenced as much by the land mass behind them as by the water offshore. It can easily be 43°C (100°F) or -40°C (-40°F too!).

Summers are generally hot, and may be very humid as warm west air moves northwards from the Caribbean. Winters can be as harsh as any in the inhabited world. In between these extreme seasons hurricanes or tornadoes afflict many areas where great air masses collide. Only in Maine, the Pacific northwest and perhaps Wisconsin can anything approaching a northern European summer be experienced.

Making comparisons

The Pacific northwest alone will seem familiar to a visiting Brit in winter. The recurrent deep snows of New York City would be more familiar to a resident of Moscow than Lisbon or Rome. Los Angeles has a generally Mediterranean climate, Denver the climate of the Russian steppes, New Orleans and Washington DC a humid subtropical climate similar to that of Hong Kong (though fortunately without quite so much rain). Yuma in southwest Arizona has less rain than Alice Springs in Australia's central desert, and Miami has a tropical climate similar to that of Kisangani on the Congo River. Alaska is much like Scandinavia in both climate and topography.

Midwest warning

In **summer** the weather of the Midwest can be quite confusing. This vast expanse from the Rockies to the Great Lakes can be dull, grey and overcast, but usually it will also be very hot and humid, though the windy city of Chicago can manage at times to be as cold and uninviting as any British seaside resort in a poor summer. In **winter**, however, the Arctic air sweeping down from Canada can make the Midwest treacherous, with chill factors (temperatures plus the wind-induced extra chilling effect) being well below zero. A blue sky in winter means heat loss, and so sunburn *and* hypothermia are both possible without care. Minus 40°C is not uncommon on the Prairies where six months earlier it could have been plus 40°C. Those not adequately prepared for these extremes will, and do, perish. Appropriate hats are worn in all seasons.

Winter precautions

Winters are generally colder and longer than in Britain, with the possible exception of those areas around the Gulf of Mexico, around the southern Appalachians and along the Pacific coast. Be prepared for more snow, more ice and more chilling winds than in inland Britain. The bad winter Britain gets once every 20 years is fairly standard over much of the USA every year, even those areas of the interior so hot in summer. If you are used to crossing the Scottish Highlands on the A9 in winter you will be quite at home in an American winter, drifts and all. But in the USA, heating in homes and buildings, public and private, tends to be appropriate for the seasons, if not excessive. Be prepared to strip off into summer things if spending long in such places. Wear padded clothing if possible out of doors, even if you feel stupid looking like an explorer. Hats, gloves and boots are essential for survival, as is the ability to recognise when things are too bad to travel.

> Seeing a sprinkling of snow this intrepid writer left home an hour earlier than usual to walk to his new job which started at 8.00 am, only to find the university closed: a 'snow alert' had been called. Always listen to the radio or watch breakfast TV for such announcements.

Coping with air conditioning

Summers are generally hotter, which is okay in the dry and often high south-west, but can be very sticky elsewhere. Air conditioning in a car is not really a luxury if it means that you arrive able to work, or if it means families can survive long journeys. Sceptical hard types will say: 'Just open the window!' Fine, but don't expect to be able to breathe what comes in. And try being a backseat passenger rather than an upfront driver for a while – you will soon get air conditioning.

The only snag is that much air conditioning can be fierce. Take a pullover or sweatshirt with you to work, to the movies, even to the supermarket or art gallery. For an interesting summer experience watch a summer movie (such as *Jaws*) in the chilly air conditioning of a movie theatre. To get the full effect stay dressed for the 35°C weather outside.

When first arriving in a hot and humid summer the temptation is to spend as much time as possible wherever air conditioning can be found, loitering over the shopping, developing a passion for great works of art or the movies. Assuming this doesn't give you a summer cold, this 'cure' can make the problem worse if it means failing to come to terms in some way or another with the problem. A change of behaviour may well be called for, if only keeping out of the sun, walking in the shadow of high buildings, and taking plenty of liquids. Of course if children start to pass out waiting in the lines at Disneyworld, which happens, then you need to get them into the nearest air conditioned room. But wearing a hat, not sitting out in the sun, and lots of drinks may be necessary drills for all the family.

Air conditioning, however, has meant that lots of people from the north have been able to face moving to the sunbelt in search of work and retirement. The telephone system has helped integrate the South into the nation at large. People and businesses can now keep in touch wherever they are.

> For the **current weather** see *USA Today*'s Web page (www.usatoday. com).

WHERE TO STAY

The range is enormous, from the flea-pit to the luxury resort. Hotels are more expensive than motels, which tend to be more uniform in facilities and price.

Beware that prices quoted are before tax. In Manhattan there are city and state sales taxes plus a hotel occupancy tax, so a budget $119 double at the Manhattan (001 212 736 1600) would actually cost $144.29. Doubles at the Grand (001 965 3000) in fashionable SoHo cost from $349 plus taxes, being $423.17 in reality.

Hotels
Many US chains can be contacted directly in the UK:

- Hilton 0345 581 595 (www.Hilton.com/bounceback)
- Ritz-Carlton 0800 234000 (www.ritzcarlton.com)
- Sheraton 0800 973106 (www.sheraton.com)

US hotel discount agency **Quikbook** has opened a freephone line for UK travellers. The agency (which claims its rooms are 40–65 per cent cheaper than brochure rates) covers Atlanta, Boston, Chicago, Los Angeles, New York City, San Francisco and Washington DC. The UK free number is 0800 890011 (then ask the operator for the US toll-free number 1-800 840 6465).

Motels
Motels have two double beds, toilet and shower, plus a television as standard, often with cable TV, and a pool (although you must check there is a pool especially at the bottom end of the market). In 1998 prices at recognised chains started at about $55 per night, but prices are per

room, not per person, so for families or groups of friends this is good value. The Travelodge chain in the UK is the nearest in price and facilities to the US norm. Breakfast is traditionally not included, though as competition heats up a 'continental' breakfast snack frequently is. Chains exist for a variety of price levels with great price variety even within a particular chain (between tourist areas and less popular regions). **Best Western** and the **Holiday Inn** are more plush, and more pricey than **Super 8 Motels** or **Econolodge**, more like the UK's Travelodge chain. **Howard Johnston's** have built-in coffee shops. Most motels don't have food service, but fast food outlets and family restaurants are usually next door, often with a discount arrangement if you show your key when paying the bill. Motels are usually cheapest in the Midwest, with family motels off the freeway $15–20 cheaper than brand name motels adjacent to freeway off-ramps. The cheapest are in Las Vegas where discounted accommodation attracts gamblers. Shop around for $16 a night (and all you can eat for the same cost).

Good news

The mid-1980s saw a massive amount of motel construction leading to a series of price wars. This means that in towns with an over-abundance of motel construction, chains may reduce their prices below that charged elsewhere. Check their prices on the huge bill boards visible from the main roads, phone, or just drop in and ask.

Also, much of this new construction has been to catch trade passing along the new roads, freeways and bypasses. The older motels on the older, now bypassed, roads are often far cheaper and may well have bargains, like special mid-week prices. These can be a considerable saving (if you can avoid thinking of *Psycho*).

B & B

Bed and breakfast establishments do exist, but are traditionally only accessible through published lists rather than roadside signs. American B & Bs are generally quite expensive and must be pre-booked, though this can now often be done over the Internet. Over the border, Canadian B & Bs are more common and more reasonably priced: 'Tourist Accommodation' signs attract the casual visitor, especially in resorts such as Niagara Falls Ontario. Many US towns now have their own freephone series and Web sites. Boston B & Bs even have a free UK number (0800 895128).

For contacts:

● Home Base Holidays (0181 886 8752) for an annual B & B guide (£7.50).

- Colby International (0151 220 5848) for rates starting at $75 for a double.

- The *US Directory of B & Bs* is distributed in the UK by Verulam (£14).

- www.bbonline.com has over 2,000 categories on file, which can be searched by various categories such as state, terrain (mountain or coasts), even building types (e.g. whether on the National Registry of Historic Places). You can access individual properties with a picture of both the building and the hosts until you find something you like (and can afford).

Self-catering

Self-catering apartments are widespread in the USA. They have all the mod-cons you would expect in any motel (double beds, showers, TV and a phone) plus as standard a fully fitted kitchen with dishwasher. Some motels now seek to attract self-catering travellers, so look for kitchen facilities in motel listings. It's unlikely that any other services would be available, like room service, but a coffee shop may well be part of the complex, or merely next door or across the street. Expect to pay at least $400 a week for a two-person studio apartment, though with considerable regional and seasonal variation. The Marmara-Manhattan on the Upper East Side of New York City has 102 'extended-stay' apartments for periods of at least one month. Rates start at $3,700 per month (1998), which is comparable with a basic SoHo apartment. Call 001 212 427 3100 or Fax 001 212 427 3042 for details. If you think you have arrived anywhere at a slack period be prepared to ask for a special long-stay rate. It is usually, of course, cheaper to stay in a regular motel and eat out, but if you are based in one place for a while, say while house-hunting, and would like something a little more like a flat, self-catering may well be for you.

- *US Welcome Directory* contains a range of accommodation including apartments in New England and New York (and Eastern Canada). £10 from Stanford's (Tel: (0171) 836 1321).

- *Arthur Fromer's Budget Travel Magazine* provided quarterly suggestions for globetrotters, including US information. Subscriptions from 350 Fifth Avenue, Suite 2701, New York NY 10118 (£25 pa).

- *Essentially America* provides travel and lifestyle information six times a year for £14.70. To subscribe call (0171) 247 0537 or Fax (0171) 377 2741. Copies are also available from large newsagents.

Hostels

You can stay for as little as $8 a night in some hostels, located in lighthouses, farmhouses, ranches and private houses. But you need to be careful. Some are heavenly, others horrific. The following guides can help with your choices.

• *Hotels USA* is an unofficial and often opinionated guide by Evan Halper and Paul Karr, $15 (1997), published by Globe Pequot, offering comprehensive at-a-glance ratings for 340 hostels across the United States. Along with the usual indices such as prices and cleanliness, it takes special care to note a variety of other factors such as which hostels are located near natural settings, which have superior kitchen facilities or are particularly good for family visits. However, the unabashed low-down on every hostel is what makes this rating guide worth five stars. For example, Bell's Mountain Hostel in Tennessee is 'kind of weird for those of us who never ran off to weekend retreats with a church youth group'. Those new to hostels will find the basic information enlightening: hostels are not merely cheap hotels, being a different sort of lodging altogether. As such, hostelling isn't for everyone, but this guide is surely for everyone who hostels.

• *The Hostel Handbook* lists over 600 cheap places to sleep with information on driving cross country and on bus, airline and train services. It appears to be the most complete list in one book of hostels regardless of affiliation across North America, including Hostelling International's hostels, independent hostels and backpackers' places. Send $6 by American Express Money Order to The Hostel Handbook Dept: IGH, 722 Saint Nicholas Avenue, New York NY 10031 (e-mail: InfoHostel@aol.com).

• *California Cheap Sleeps* Rebecca Poole Foree (1995) and *Northwest Cheap Sleeps* (2nd edition), Stephanie Irving and Nancy Leson (1995), both published by Sasquatch Books, list the best hostels across the far west and north-west. *At Home in Hostel Territory: A Guide to Friendly Lodgings from Seward to Santa Cruz*, Janet Thomas, published by Alaska Northwest (1994), covers similar territory featuring hostels with a homey atmosphere from Alaska to California. For those who want to find out what the philosophy of hostelling is all about, this is it.

• *Jim's Backpacker's Bible* ($8) is a must for budget travellers with a range of general and useful ideas and information. Call 001 310 399 4018 with a credit card number ready. For those with a vehicle, try *Road Trip USA: Cross-Country Adventures on America's Two-Lane*

Highways (1st edition) by Jamie Jensen, $22.50 (1996), Moon Publications, a comprehensive guide to driving away from the interstate freeways. Jensen's guide takes the pain out of the road trip, be it across the continent or a Sunday jaunt. With directions to pit stops, scenic routes, bizarre museums and the best apple pie stands, all you have to do is drive. Simply avoiding the interstates opens up a parallel two-lane world of monuments marking the actual sites of things Americans last heard of about in high school, or souvenir stands advertised by giant dinosaurs. This is a travel book for those looking for something a bit different from McDonalds and Disney: Route 93 from Montana to Mexico, Route 2 from Washington State to Maine, and Route 66 from California to Illinois.

WHERE TO LIVE

The USA is continental in size. Prices and standards vary accordingly, especially for housing. The most expensive places are in the major cities, such as Georgetown (in Washington DC) or in fashionable suburbs (such as Montgomery County, Maryland, just outside the capital). As in Britain the cheaper areas tend to be far out in the countryside, or in the less than fashionable parts of the city, which can include some adjacent suburban areas (such as the older built-up areas of Prince George's County also just outside Washington DC). The same housing can be ten times as expensive in a booming, fashionable area as in a declining industrial town.

Even within a metropolis, such as Washington DC, you will not know where to find a good place to live without help, a lot of money, or a willingness to make awful mistakes, the latter being a 'learning experience' only single young people should undertake. The social geography of the American conurbation is also constantly changing as areas are gentrified, as racial lines of demarcation shift, and as subway lines are opened. Of course, like most Americans, you might hope a low area you buy into will rise, to your advantage, but it's a major risk even for those well tuned into the city. For a newcomer it's a lottery chance.

But a home in a certain area will not only influence your settling down as a family. It will also influence your standing with colleagues and those you meet, almost like an accent in Britain. Getting housing right is not only one of the most crucial decisions to be made but also one that needs to be sorted out quite quickly if motel fees are not to erode your savings when you first arrive.

Rental sector

This is far larger and more varied than in Britain. Though buying is seen as much the same kind of profitable investment as in Britain, many people do not wish to be tied down by being responsible for property upkeep. Many people move from job to job and prefer to rent locally, moving by rental van in an almost semi-nomadic way. Many more developers build for rent, though many have sold out to sitting tenants, in response to rent control and tenancy security legislation. The end of rent control in New York City may result in considerably higher rents than at present, even though in the long run more properties may be built for rent. Analysts expect $480 penthouse apartments to rise to $2,000 a month for new tenants. Those who seek to ape the TV characters in *Friends* may find it very tough going in the new rental market.

How to find rented accommodation
- Via college/firm's notice (bulletin) board.
- Via specialist, fee-paying agencies.
- Estate agents (*realtors*).
- Small ads in the local newspaper.
- Driving around likely areas and calling in at the rental office within each rental development.

Knowing the lingo
Before you start out on your trek you need to know the lingo which can be quite tricky:

- Flats are deemed **bachelor, studio** or **efficiency** when small and single room (plus bathroom and kitchen).
- A **walk-up** is something like a bedsitter in a block without a lift.
- **Cold-water apartments** are precisely that – you need to install your own water heater (though normally America's big city blocks have traditionally had hot water provided by the landlord rather than the tenant).

Initials abound:
- mbr = master bedroom
- wbfp = wood-burning fireplace
- fdr = formal dining-room
- .5 bath means toilet and basin, not bath.

Unless you are single or moving in with friends you will probably not want to move into the subdivided, older and larger houses in the poorer neighbourhoods, nor would you want to become involved with **urban**

homesteading unless you are already a master craftsman and could transform an abandoned property bought from the city for $1.

If you move into a post-1945 development the chances are you will have access to a couple of communal facilities:

- Laundry-room, with huge commercial wash and dry machines for renters' use only – take a pile of 25c pieces. Costs are pretty good, and the time (especially the dryers) is much lower than domestic equivalents.

- Pool, available for key-holders and guests. In heat waves this can be a great boon.

Houses may also be available for rent, much more easily than in Britain. These are often available through real estate agents for set periods.

Condominiums

During the 1970s the rental market changed quite markedly. Many developers decided to get out of the rental market, often by way of selling to other developers who wanted to redevelop blocks even though they might be full of sitting tenants. Many blocks were redeveloped at great cost, which turned out to be a back-door way of raising the rent legally. Hence such redevelopment became a way to get sitting tenants out of potentially prime sites.

City councils initially liked the improvement to the housing stock. Too late it became evident that the poor, and then the lower reaches of the middle class, were being priced out of their own flats, with the pool of accommodation they could afford declining.

This introduced a new verb into American English: **to condo**. Apartment blocks were transformed into **condominiums** (quickly shortened to **condos** which does not have a prophylactic connotation for Americans as is possible for the British!).

In effect condos are now little more than blocks of individually owned flats, the only trace elements of communal ownership being communal party rooms and sports facilities (plus the pool and laundry room).

Buying

Mortgages are more often **fixed rate** rather than flexible as in Britain. This is good news for those buying when rates are low, so protecting the purchaser from further rate rises. For those having to buy, though, when the rates are high a slump in interest rates is of no immediate benefit. Many house buyers attempt to overcome this by refinancing their loan at the new lower rate.

Unless buying a new property it may be possible to take over (assume) the existing mortgage for the amount outstanding for the remaining term, so avoiding the costs of setting up a new mortgage. If you have no US-based credit history this may be the only way to get into the housing market in middle age.

General US practice is to agree on a sale price and for the buyer and seller to respect it for 14 days, with a 1 per cent down payment. During this time the buyer completes financial arrangements and obtains a survey. If finance is not forthcoming or the property proves to be defective the buyer can withdraw and the seller can place the property back on the market or accept a waiting offer. The buyer has to move quickly in the USA, but the seller will *not* pull out once the deposit has been paid.

Savings and loan associations ('thrifts') are similar to building societies. Once upon a time they only gave mortgages to certain racial and ethnic groups, but since the 1960s civil rights campaigns this has supposedly ceased. Mortgages are supposed to be available on the basis of being able to repay the loan (plus interest) with the property as collateral.

What needs to be done?

● Buy a good local guide to property purchase and property financing. Ask at a public library for a recommendation.

● Consider using a house finding agent.

● Get good local legal advice before committing yourself to purchasing.

● Check out the viability of the 'savings and loan' (many have gone bust).

Location taxation

In the days before the British poll tax was mooted the assessment for local taxation in the two countries was very similar, though in the USA rates are called what they actually are: **property taxes**. They can be high, so check it out! If you should consider a mobile home, check as to how it will be taxed, whether as a fixed property or as a vehicle.

Housing types

Being continental in size and variety, US housing is more varied than outsiders often realise. The first surprise may well be the widespread use of **wood**. Timber-built houses (increasingly popular in Britain due to price advantages) are often called frame houses, though they often have wooden walls too, and in some areas even wooden 'tiles' called **shingles**.

Terraced houses (here called **row houses**) are less widespread in US cities. Baltimore, however, is actually famous precisely for its row houses, unfortunately often covered now with 'Baltimore stone' (pseudo-stone cladding). Many industrial towns of the Appalachian coalfields have town houses perched on hill-slopes much like in the Rhondda Valley in Britain, though wood rather than brick or stone is likely to predominate. Immigrant areas of the eastern cities had vast areas of tenements, many stories high, now often abandoned as urban decay eats out the heart of the once industrial and trading cities.

Far more than in Britain the middle-class and much of the working-class ('blue collar') housing is detached, free-standing in its own lot. In older, generally midwestern or eastern cities, houses are often more European-like, with fairly small rooms. Out west, however, rooms tend to be larger, and many lower middle-class 1940s–50s houses seem very like the farms the owners had left back on the Great Plains of the 1930s Dust Bowl days, like farmhouses without farms, all packed together, yet each on its own plot of land. As the middle classes have moved on to new property such areas have been bought by minorities so that often very poor ghettos appear, at least superficially, middle-class to European eyes.

Prices
By the mid-1990s the average price paid for a single-family house was over $100,000. The average mortgage was 7.3 per cent, with an average

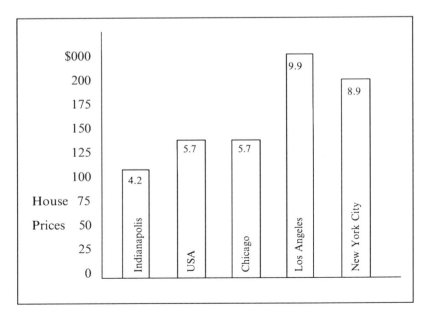

Fig. 1. Average 1994 house prices, and house prices as multiples of income in four US metropolitan areas (compared with 1990 US average).
Source: *The World Almanac*, Funk & Wagnalls, Mahwah NJ, 1994

monthly repayment of $582, which was about 19 per cent of the average US income, three per cent lower than it had been in the late 1980s. As in the UK, housing nevertheless remains a major part of people's after-tax income. To get a mortgage on an averagely priced house an annual income over $30,000 is needed, though if the rate goes back to over 10 per cent $40,000 will again be essential.

The USA is, however, so vast that national figures will mean very little to anyone seeking to buy within a particular city's housing market. Figure 1 gives an idea of average house prices in four major cities relating them to annual income in those cities. In Chicago the average house price is about the national average, almost 6 times the average local income at just under $130,000. In Indianapolis house prices are lower, about $110,000, and though wages are lower there houses only cost about 4 times the local wage. In New York City and Los Angeles, in contrast, wages are high, but houses cost even more, on average over $200,000, about 10 times an average salary. The main point is that prices and incomes vary widely across the USA from town to town (as well, of course, from neighbourhood to neighbourhood within any one town). When considering high wages it is essential to consider them in terms of what they will buy locally. A college professor with a family to support might find $50,000 okay in Indianapolis but inadequate within New York City. Nursing staff should note that large US salaries offered to encourage emigration usually involve living in very expensive parts of the country (which may be why the hospital cannot find Americans to fill the posts!).

For specific city-by-city information see David Savageau and Richard Boyer, *Places Rated Almanac*, Prentice Hall, New York 1993. This is essential reading for anyone relocating within the USA. Its vast array of statistical information is intelligently explained. A must for all outsiders.

Utilities

Utilities, especially electricity, gas and hot water, may or may not be included in any rental prices. Traditionally all utilities except the phone were included in the rental paid. As these costs rose (especially for central heating and air conditioning after the oil price rises of the early 1970s) many became separate items. If charged directly by the utility companies, bills are usually monthly, with the sanction of being cut-off if you don't pay (or your cheque bounces).

Beware: being paid every two weeks but being billed every month can get you as out of phase as being paid monthly but having quarterly bills to meet in Britain.

The telephone is worth an early mention here, if only because recent changes have complicated a system once fairly easy to use and understand for domestic users. The Bell system has been broken up into regional companies with rival long distance carriers, making long distance, especially across country, calls quite complicated and expensive. The domestic rental often includes local calls with long distance calls being separately itemised (a good idea). But even in off-peak hours long distance calls, especially those just outside the local area, are quite costly (like Washington DC to Baltimore, which though a shorter distance than Manchester to Birmingham is deemed long distance at a rate that makes the two cities seem to be in different countries). This only becomes a real problem when trying to use a call box and being asked for $5 of 25c pieces before the operator will connect you. Domestic telephone users should watch out for special deals on long distance calls that may be advertised by your companies. They often have loss-leader rates (to encourage you to get used to using them for long distance calls). For more details see pages 62–65.

For further advice
For general points to consider when moving abroad see Michael Furrell's Daily Telegraph Guide *Living and Retiring Abroad*, published in London by Kogan Page. It also has a small section on the USA, as does Roger Jones, *How to Retire Abroad*, How To Books, 1993.

More detailed considerations are raised in David Hoppitt's *Overseas Property Guide: The Do's and Don'ts of Buying a Home Abroad*, published by Telegraph Publications of London. Though the specifically US material is rather thin and only relates to Florida and California, the general issues raised are important and need to be dealt with wherever property is bought. These include when to obtain professional advice, ground rules for property purchase, time-sharing opportunities and pitfalls, with details on the legalities of purchase and the securing of the necessary financial backing. For more specific information on that most popular of British destinations see Michael Ray, *Setting Up Home in Florida,* How To Books, 1996. The chapters on mortgages are excellent and provide an overview of US procedures beside dealing with Florida specifics.

FOOD AND DRINK

Eating out
Fast-food from recognisable companies is readily available, often with extras such as gravy and mashed potatoes or a scone-like piece of bread reflecting local taste. **All-day breakfast** or **salad bars** may well be part of

the war between competing hamburger outlets. Breakfast is probably the best bargain, though all-you-can-eat meals at any time of day are good value (though to be avoided if you are on a diet).

For city restaurants you can find any style and pay any price you like, though in country areas steak may be all that is available.

What sort of weekly budget?
- Indulgent: £250 per head   But it all depends upon where you
- Average: £200 per head   are: rural hitchhikers can survive on
- Budget: £70 per head   breakfast plus roadside fruit stands.

Americans now eat about half their meals away from home, and this increasingly involves the kind of family gathering you might expect in people's homes. Budget accordingly.

Eating in

Supermarkets vary, but chains are usually excellent for price and exotic choice, including delicatessen items, alcoholic drinks (if locally permitted) and serve-yourself salad bars. Food is priced at familiar European levels, with steak generally cheaper, but with lamb more expensive (and usually frozen from New Zealand). More details on shopping, including shopping for food, are given on pages 54–59.

Incidentals

Drinking in **cafés** and **bars** can be uncomfortably expensive. A cup of coffee can easily cost a pound or two. Prices in **diners** and **coffee-shops** (especially in drug stores) can be very reasonable, often with free coffee refills (if you like it weak). **Cocktails** (where alcohol is permitted) can cost from £2 to £5, though half that in the late afternoon – early evening **happy hour**. Cigarettes may cost over £1 for 20, though prices vary greatly to reflect states' individual tax rates, and all prices are rising with regular federal tax increases ('hikes').

Tipping

The British have a usually well-earned reputation for being mean tippers, especially in the USA. Americans tend to be seen over here as over-generous. In the USA tipping is much more important than in Britain. Those in the food and drink business are usually very under-paid. In fact they usually rely upon tips to survive. Watch the US television show *Friends*! As a general rule be generous for good service.

You'll have to use your judgement over how much to leave. Taxi drivers are notorious for their contempt of those who leave less than 10 per cent. About 15 per cent is probably right for bar staff and those serving food. In bars you'll often get a bill each round, though if you become known you'll be able to run up a **tab** to make one payment when you leave. If you pay for each round and leave only the exact money you will probably get ever poorer service. Watch what others are doing. If in doubt ask your friends.

If you are paying by credit card you may notice that when the slip is presented to you, you find the total amount left blank. You are being invited to add something extra for a tip. If you've left a tip at the table make sure you don't end up paying twice.

Alcohol

The story of alcohol in the USA is the story of these United States in all their variety. Over the years America has been a refuge for those fleeing from the gin-sodden old world to a new world of freedom and temperance, and for those who arrived expecting the freedom to do, to eat, and especially to drink, whatever and whenever they liked. These two traditions have fought over and over again, and after the US Constitution had been amended (1919) to outlaw the sale, manufacture and distribution of alcohol it seemed that finally the blue meanies had won out over the boozers.

Rise of the prohibition era gangsters soon turned public opinion, and as part of Franklin D. Roosevelt's New Deal the US Constitution was re-amended in the mid-1930s to allow things to return to what they had been before. This still enabled local communities to rule whether alcohol should be available in their particular locality. College towns are often 'dry', though the first place over the county or even state line may well have bars, liquor stores and little else. In the Appalachian mountains it is possible if lost to tell whether you are in a Tennessee county (wet) or a North Carolina county (dry) by looking out for a petrol station – if they hang out a beer sign you're still in Tennessee!

No state still remains completely 'dry', though if several adjacent counties are it may start to feel that way. But even in Mormon Utah liquor stores exist, and you can drink with your meal, though you may have to bring the vodka in with you and get a 'set-up' – a Bloody Mary with everything except the vodka, which you add to taste.

As a response to the rising tide of alcohol-related road fatalities, especially involving teenagers, the general trend is to raise the age of drinking to 21, which makes drinking in a college town very inconvenient. Colleges rarely if ever allow alcohol to be sold on campus anyway (the British student union bar is unknown), *but* you'll need proof of your being over 21, hence the cry of 'you got ID?' You can be 40 and bald and still not get a drink if you haven't got an ID and the barman takes a dislike to your face (or accent).

Bars and pubs

Bars, pubs and other dives may be disappointing. They are often little more than drinking places, with perhaps picking up sexual partners as the only added attraction. Even bars which may be recommended to you may well turn out to be ill-lit, deep, narrow and uninviting. Beer on draught plus cheap drinks during the late afternoon happy hour with a chance to meet friends after work may be their only extenuating features. Fortunately US domestic beer is improving, with Sam Smith's Boston ale in draught ('draft') now available all over the country. Bars often do reasonable snacks, steak sandwiches and the like, plus Irish coffee. Have no faith in the kitchens.

Don't expect anything special from bars with the word 'Pub' written outside. They *may* have imported, even European, beers, but at best only Guinness. Other beers, though with exotic names, are usually locally neutered versions (like so much 'foreign' beer in Britain).

Places you could safely eat in, apart from the expensive bars in the equally expensive hotels, without fear for your health are likely to be dry, like the Crystal Palace in Disneyworld. Seaworld does, however, serve draught beer to those also eating.

> A favourite watering hole on Connecticut Avenue in Washington DC used to have a rat come strolling through from time to time. Several months later the place was bolted and barred: 'The public health department finally caught up with them?' 'Hell no, he didn't pay his taxes!'

Restaurants

Which leads to restaurants. Family ones rarely allow alcohol of any kind. Though this will hardly inconvenience those going in for the all-you-can-eat breakfast, at the other end of the day after a long time on the road it may come as something of a disappointment to leave your motel room for the restaurant over the way, order steaks, and then find you can order neither beer nor wine (though on your travels you could yesterday and will tomorrow).

Many communities consider that if you must have alcohol you should buy it elsewhere, and drink it only in the privacy of your own room away from God-fearing folk and their innocent children. As you watch people gorging themselves, blowing smoke everywhere as they eat, and downing Coke like there's no tomorrow, you may feel somewhat annoyed about not being able to get a glass of beer. But tomorrow night in another town the waitress will appear and ask 'Anything from the bar?' and you'll know that you've crossed an important line somewhere out back on the road.

Posher restaurants almost always serve, or permit, alcohol. Presumably such places are deemed for 'grown-ups', who are beyond redemption. Smoking, though, is increasingly frowned upon (and is now illegal in California, Maryland and New York restaurants).

If in doubt ask people you are visiting what the situation is locally. Even dry areas have people who want to drink and these people know all the dodges. They'll know where the nearest available wet jurisdiction is, and where you can take a bottle of drink with a meal without hassle. They may well stock-up themselves once a month when going into the city or over the line, and have a fridge-full ready to be shared with visitors.

If you have any doubts about the seafood, call the US Food & Drug Administration hotline on 1-202 205 4314 (almost 50 people have died in Florida from bad oysters over the last 10 years).

ENTERTAINMENT

As disposable incomes are generally high, Americans spend a lot on going out. The rich love to sponsor and to be seen at cultural events so world class **orchestras**, **opera** and **ballet** companies are found in most major cities, though tickets may be hard to come by.

Rock concerts abound, and you may well be able to see not only US groups but major British ones in those huge sports stadia that all cities and most college towns have. Bluegrass, blues, country, folk and jazz festivals abound, often outdoors in summer. They are generally excellent, and not over-expensive for the experience they provide. As gatherings dear to so many Americans they are worth visiting, if only for their colour, food and drink.

Theatre is still mostly associated with Broadway in New York City, or in the regional theatres that take travelling productions. Some cities have stock (repertory) companies which are often enthusiastically supported locally.

Tickets may generally seem expensive, especially in large cities. Bookings are conveniently made in person at *Ticketron* (see the phone book for location and details).

Cinemas are generally either for films on general release (about $10) or for old classic re-runs (about $7). New York City and Los Angeles have tomorrow's films today, to test audience reaction (at least $10). Smoking is generally banned in all cinemas, and until recently there have been no on-screen commercials. Audiences can be very raucous. In summer the air conditioning can be fierce, so take a sweater.

Museums and **galleries** are usually free, though may cost a dollar or so. As in Britain specific exhibitions can be rather expensive extras. Beware though: the onset of any federal budget cutbacks can rapidly end most evening openings of publicly funded institutions, such as Washington DC's Smithsonian Institute (including the Air and Space Museum).

Concerts and the **theatre** can cost at least $40, at least twice that and more for Broadway hits on the New York stage.

Entertainment parks vary enormously, from $20 (Dollywood in the Great Smokies of eastern Tennessee) to $38 in Disneyworld (though if part of a package holiday Disney may be much cheaper and, being prepaid, seem an almost painless cost).

DRESS SENSE

It is tempting to view the USA as a more relaxed, unfussy country as far as what to wear goes. The national costume seems to be the T-shirt, jeans and trainers. Such generalisations, however, can be confusingly misleading. There are dress codes (a phrase you may never even have heard before arriving in the US). They just aren't the same as elsewhere.

In New England, those states between New York and the Canadian Maritimes, people tend to be more formal, even stuffy, than you'll find elsewhere. Though casual wear may be okay for the garden or the beach, visiting a restaurant casually dressed would raise many an eyebrow, and in expensive restaurants service would be refused. For work most men wear suits and short neat hair. Women do not generally wear trousers ('pants'). But the suits may turn out to be yellow plaid, if not at work then at church socials or town meetings. Casual dress is more acceptable out west, especially in California, in all but the most expensive places.

However, don't be lulled into believing anything goes. Topless bathing hasn't as a rule arrived, even in areas climatically appropriate. There are militant nudists and naturist bathing areas, but nowhere is nudity as casual as, say, on a summer's day in Danish parks and beaches or around the pools in the south of France. That isn't to say there won't be a lot of exhibitionism on beaches, but the rules will be known by all, and if you cross the line you'll soon find out. Watching what others are doing remains a good rule of thumb. Beware: many public beaches as in West Florida frown upon, or even prohibit, changing on the beach. Use the changing rooms provided.

CULTURAL EXPECTATIONS

Two stories from the Washington suburbs illustrate differences between American and British cultural expectations that permeate everyday life.

Easy familiarity

A reasonably well-dressed British professor is walking through University Park near the University of Maryland, a neighbourhood of well-maintained detached homes, each with open front lawns. No fences or hedges here. Trees line the sidewalks, and though inner city problems are but a dozen miles away here all is sweetness and light. In the distance a small child is pedalling like fury towards the pedestrian. Their paths cross and the child looks up at the adult and says 'Hi' with no hesitation or affectation, an outburst of familiarity that takes the British pedestrian aback. Before he can think of anything to say the child has pedalled on and away, bound presumably for home or for a friend's.

With careful politeness and easy informality the child has both confused the visitor and at the same time confirmed a very American experience. It has obviously never occurred to the child, particularly on its own turf, to be silent, or to wait to be spoken to. On the sidewalk of life a child and a passing adult are equal. Such a democratic assumption would never have been made in the academic's own youth back in careful, deferential Britain. In a small way this tiny episode confirms what so many Europeans find so endearing about the USA. And yet that Christmas the same situation was reversed in a not dissimilar suburb not that far away.

No pedestrians here

It is getting dark, and a Scottish family have spent their sixth American Christmas opening presents, watching television and overeating, much as must be happening across the land. But though it has been a cold day there is no wind, and so the assembled revellers decide to brave the chill to walk off their turkey feast, the better to make room for home-made Christmas pudding. The air is so still and bracing no one makes a sound as they crunch their way down the path to the road and set off to walk around the block. No one speaks, it is so cold. Thinking of their forthcoming treat they hurry along wishing there were sidewalks in such residential neighbourhoods.

No provision is made for pedestrians in such new neighbourhoods: no one ever expected any. Which is what the neighbours must have thought when they looked out of their windows and saw four or five figures moving silently down the street. The quiet is only broken by the arrival of the local police, who are neither happy to be called out on such a night, nor sympathetic to the proffered explanation of a pre-Christmas pudding ramble. To the local cops the scene is so bizarre there must be something untoward going on. No one walks in such a neighbourhood, and certainly not in the dark, and most definitely not on Christmas Day.

The moral is . . .

Is there a moral to be drawn from these two incidents? Only that America too is a mass of contradictions, but ones that may only be evident to a foreigner. How you respond to such differing ideas about something as initially trivial as walking down the road can make all the difference to your stay. But it's the common language that makes us expect the Americans will be like us. When they are not we are offended, as if they have no right to behave like foreigners.

Living in the present

Americans love and ignore the past. There is an almost pathological obsession with the present and particularly the present as harbinger of the future. To say that someone is 'history' is to consign them to the ultimate waste bin. But aren't Americans obsessed with nostalgia? Yes they are, but not with the past in all its confusing and contradictory detail. Put on an exhibition at the Smithsonian in Washington DC which outlines what really happened when American moved out west and every patriotic organisation in the country accuses them of being unpatriotic, for insulting the flag, for undermining children's faith in the righteousness of the USA.

The positive side of the militant amnesia is that Americans rarely worry about where someone (or at least a white person) is from, only where they are bound. Few ask about where you went to school or college. Even fewer ask about families, unless they have already met with them. Families are in the past. It is the here and now that counts. So the past is only useful to the degree that it helps boost our entry into the future. Leaders who can capture this sense of movement can get away with almost anything else, witness John Kennedy, Ronald Reagan and even Bill Clinton. Where some may want to rake up the past, most Americans respond to appeals to look forward to the New Frontier or just Tomorrow or the Millennium. Candidates that seem to look backwards, such as Dole, are history.

Ideals and ideologies

It is traditional for Europeans to berate Americans for their failure to live up to their own high ideals. Slavery and race relations have long been used as a stick with which to beat the Americans. And yet the USA went to war with itself to retain slavery within the Union where it could be dealt with rather than allow the slave states to leave and go their own way. And though American race relations may indeed seem less than idyllic, few other countries have so publicly addressed the issue.

Despite massive economic inequalities, Americans still desperately try to provide education and employment mechanisms with which the poor can work their way out of poverty. And nowhere else have gays and lesbians been so successful in changing the nature of the debate over private and public sexuality, despite the presence of a massive and powerful religious right wing which abhors them.

In a country that seems totally secular, in that there can be no official celebration of the religious (as opposed to the pagan) dimensions of Christmas (the official White House tree has no manger), more people believe in a supreme being and regularly attend a place of worship than in any other developed country.

How such contradictions are sustained within the one country without open war breaking out is a constant source of amazement. The present unruly behaviour of various militia suggests that deep divisions are not always as well dealt with as many would like to believe. But, despite a history of lynching, gangsters, riots and chronic deaths by gunshot wounds, the United States does generally manage to hold together more than perhaps it is generally realised by pessimistic locals and snooty outsiders. Distance has something to do with it, as well as a deeply held general belief in the Constitution, one of those paradoxes when a land seemingly so lawless and focused upon the present professes such faith upon a legal document from deep in America's past.

Passion and opinions

American enthusiasms often manifest themselves in rampant over-statement, quite the opposite of British understatement. Where the beer glass is definitely half empty, for the American the same glass is half full, a far more positive, primary-colour view of the world. With a vigour and simplicity that can bewilder Europeans, Americans argue over divine creationism or Darwinian evolution, race and IQ, choice and abortion, with passion that, though it can break out into street violence, more often than not remains theatrical, like the rabid sermons and political advertisements that would be frowned upon if not prohibited in more pastel-shaded European countries, where we prefer to hedge our opinions behind notions of privacy and compromise. Perhaps Europeans have seen the face of Nazi extremism too recently to stay too near the edge. But for a visitor, naked passion American-style can be both invigorating and frightening.

Dodging the issue can seem an unacceptably dangerous form of prevarication compared to the full frontal crudity of American naiveté, which can often become evident in what appears as plain American rudeness. As a student in the 1960s I was given a fantastic present by my sister: my first hippie jeans. To celebrate my going to America she took the pair and sewed enormous triangular patches into the legs, opening them out to become hugely flared. I could see from my mother's face she was not amused, for such alterations had clearly ruined a perfectly decent pair of casual trousers. But she said not a word. Nor did anyone else as I took off to London and away.

Standing waiting for a bus in New York only a few days later, people kept commenting, unfavourably, upon my weird appearance, often to my face. My hair, short by British standards, was deemed far too long for respectable people who felt they had a duty to tell me so, and my two-tone flared pants were an obvious insult to American life that could not go unchallenged.

As the years went by such 'far out' clothes become ever more common across America, and my clothes became of ever less interest to casual passers by. But I always remembered how similar were the opinions of my mother's generation both in Britain and America, but whereas she had bottled up her opinions, Americans had felt quite at liberty to express theirs. Perhaps the British will one day silently disapprove less obviously and the Americans keep their opinions to themselves more, but I somehow doubt it.

Enjoying the differences

America can be a very exhausting experience for the newcomer. When British visitors arrive it is often very hot and humid and distances are immense. How reassuring that we share the same language and thus the same opinions, expectations and general attitudes towards the world. When Americans turn out to be so very different it can be quite wounding, as if they have somehow let us down, tricked us into thinking they were part of the family, taken us for a ride. But stay in there. The differences can be enjoyed. Some of their ways of doing things might even be better than ours. And once home we may find ourselves appreciating some of our own quirky ways just that little bit more.

SHOPPING

Shopping centres

In the late 1960s and early 1970s going from Britain to the USA was perhaps most dramatic in the contrast between how and where people shopped. The rise of huge British out-of-town shopping centres, hypermarkets and covered precincts has somewhat reduced the contrast by the 1990s.

Learn from others' mistakes: don't let your first bag of US groceries melt into a useless mass before you even get it home!

● Frozen foods must go straight home by car.

● If you must go shopping on foot do it as late as possible in the summer, and always keep out of the sun.

● Don't expect shopping to be just like home only on a bigger scale.

Today the differences for the middle classes are not so noticeable. Tesco's, Sainsbury's, Gateway and Safeway have covered Britain with stores, almost, though not quite, like US supermarkets. But whereas in Britain the out-of-town centres (such as Metro Centre in Tyne and Wear) are the exception (and still newsworthy), thousands of such suburban shopping malls exist across the USA. By the late 1980s Washington DC already had more than 15 that made a claim to be malls, half a dozen of which were modern and purpose built.

Downtown

And as such out-of-town shopping proliferated the downtown department stores dramatically declined, squeezed between suburban discounts (boxed hi-fi at cut prices but with no after-sales service) and specialist shops built into malls (on the main axis between two rival supermarkets). The expansion of jobs out in the suburbs took many commuters away from the central business district, and the impoverished inner city population couldn't support the same level of retail sales. The downtown seemed doomed.

But the 1980s saw a rejuvenation of many downtown centres (Boston and Baltimore are two of the most well known). Department stores have been revitalised, speciality shops have been reopened, and conferences, tourists and yuppies have moved in. Even so, the downtown shopping will never dominate the whole metropolis as it once did. Rather, downtown will be just one of many shopping opportunities for the well-heeled and mobile middle class.

The USA is more abroad than most Brits expect

Remember this and you'll not expect things to be quite the same as at home, and so it won't throw you off quite so much when things turn out differently from what you expected. If you are used to a range of small family businesses and shops in a town centre you may find shopping in the USA very strange. If you are already familiar with the fortnightly stock-up trips to your local hypermarket after work you'll hardly notice the difference, except for the wider range of foods.

Opening hours

Opening hours tend to be longer than even the most 'open' of British supermarkets, 24 hours a day 7 days a week being not uncommon in large cities (though rare in small towns). Shopping hours in downtown department stores are more likely to be nearer to those in Britain, closing time being about 6.00 pm, though even here a late night opening may be available. Malls tend to close about 10.00 pm, with their department stores remaining open 9.00 am to 9.00 pm. 10.00 pm is a common time for supermarkets to close.

Blue Laws

Just as Sunday opening was for so long a mess in the UK, so in the USA often complicated local options determine Sunday opening. Blue Laws are those laws restricting Sunday opening, not the selling of pornography. Generally, Sunday opening hours tend to be more limited than other days of the week, and liquor may be on the shelves, but only for sale at certain times. Sunday opening laws tend to be enforced in the USA.

Drugstores

These are more than chemists, though not so unusual for those who have watched British chemists diversify over the years. Stationery, hardware, some clothes, certain foods, perhaps liquor and usually snacks with soft drinks are generally available. Look for the green cross for the pharmacy section (or the Mercurial twisted snake symbol, also in green).

Buying clothes and shoes

The good news:
- Most clothing, especially where cotton-based, is usually cheaper than in Britain. It may not be American any more (though if it is, a 'union-made' label may tell you so, as on Oshkosh children's clothes).

- British made clothes cost less (£625 Burberry trench coat for £431 plus tax at about 9 per cent).

The bad news:
- Ignore descriptive sizes. Is 'large' used in comparison to 'small' and 'medium', or 'extra-large' and 'jumbo'? Who knows!?

- Women's sizes appear to be but aren't the same as in Britain. A UK 12 is a US 10, and 10 an 8, and so on.

- For footwear it's the other way around, a British 9 being a US 10 (or perhaps more like a 10½).

More bad news:
- Average width is often the only shoe fitting available, though these tend to be wider than in the UK.

- Expect poor standards of service in shoe shops and shoe departments of large stores. If you are used to the trained personal service of British shoe shops you are in for a disappointment. The immediate sale is what's important, not cultivating a regular clientele.

Any ways around this?
- If you like fashionable shoes and can jam your feet into average widths, shoe shopping won't be too bad.

- If you can get away with wearing work boots, these are often excellent value (and often imported from Eastern Europe!). US-made cowboy boots are magnificent and with good care can last for years, if not decades. After 20 years the author's first pair is still going back for resoling.

- Many Americans side-step the problem by using **mail order**. There are specialist firms who meet this problem by offering an excellent service, at a cost, through the post.

- Keep your eyes peeled for shoes available through factory outlets by the side of motorways. These can turn up in the most out of the way places (like firework stores in southern states).

Mail order

Sears Roebuck of Chicago produce what is probably the most well-known catalogue (nearly a million items). Since rural free delivery was introduced by the US Post Office in 1892, urban suppliers have been able to provide, if not the very latest, at least modern fashion and consumer goods to anyone anywhere. As people moved off the land and into the suburbs they kept their faith in the mail order catalogues. This means that mail order firms generally cater for a more up-market, even specialist, clientele than in Britain. Mail order firms deal directly with customers not via an agent (whose commission would either put up prices or eat away profits). Unlike in Britain mail order is not payment by instalment, but by money order (or today increasingly by charge card over the phone).

Specialised mail order is more developed than in Britain, though if you regularly use garden equipment and supplies catalogues or buy outdoor casual clothes (as from Rohan) you will already be familiar with the general standards and procedures. Specialist catalogues tend to be more exotic than in Britain, and include in many states firearms (or 'sporting goods' as they are often called) as if they were little more than fishing rods and trainers!

Shopping for food

Most urban people buy their produce from the fruit and vegetable sections of their local supermarket. The quality is debatable. Certainly fruit is huge and piled high, and is available all year independent of the passing of the seasons. Whether forced giant strawberries, though, have any flavour is hotly argued. Word has it square strawberries are being grown for ease of shipment! And when you get it all home, wash it to get the chemicals off. Some fruits even have a wax covering that needs to be removed.

The good news:

- Many cities have **roadside fruit and vegetable stalls** along the highways in the surrounding counties. Peaches, for instance, can be bought in season very cheaply from these roadside stalls, and it's very common to stop off and load up on the way back home from a weekend away.

- Many cities have **farmers' markets** downtown in a Covent Garden-like hall. Fresh food is brought in from local farms and is often excellent and reasonably priced. Food stalls at such markets can be a great treat – everything from pizzas to oysters (in Baltimore at least, with draught beer too!) Taxi drivers, government employees, policemen and visitors will all nip in for a bite to eat, so the quality tends to be fairly good, with prices reasonable. Towns such as Knoxville, Tennessee, that are trying to redevelop a decaying downtown are encouraging farmers' markets adjacent to downtown malls and theatres as a way of retaining, or attracting back, a sense of activity downtown, so quality is encouraged.

More bad news?

- The US is based upon the fruits of mutual distrust. You will often see the sign 'If you broke it you just bought it', hardly the most welcoming of approaches to a casual shopper.

- Record and book stores often will not let you take any bags into their shops, for fear of shoplifting. Don't take it too personally; they distrust everyone. Security will take the offending bag at the door, usually in exchange for a token.

- Don't forget that on return to the UK you are liable for VAT and duty for all goods over an allowance of £136 per adult, and that includes clothing, shoes, luggage and those CDs that seemed such a bargain.

Mutual distrust seems to lead naturally enough to lawyers and doctors. As a rule of thumb:

Get good insurance cover
Keep your head down
Get a good lawyer

LAWYERS AND LEGAL FEES

The USA seems to be a society held together by litigation – commerce by other means? The roots of this may well be in the written nature of the Constitution, or conversely the need to regularise relationships in those areas not adequately policed by the Constitution. This is, after all, a free trade economy operating under the rules of *laissez-faire* capitalism. The USA is overtly and militantly a property-owning democracy. A major role for contract law seems almost inevitable.

US lawyers generally work on a contingent fee basis ('**no win no fee**'). This has been illegal in Britain for historical reasons justified today on the fear that it would encourage lawyers to win at any price (else they don't get paid), with a concern not for the case *per se* but for the fee. The advantage the Americans would point out is that in the USA poor people can afford to take large corporations to law knowing that if they lose they will not be stuck with fees to pay. If they win they pay their lawyers a percentage of the awarded damages.

Unfortunately this often leads to lawyers going for vast sums, playing on widespread dislike of larger corporations, such as insurance companies, to boost their take. The result is that insurance premiums, for instance, have skyrocketed, and may now be so high that certain groups can now no longer obtain cover. Commerce by other means indeed! But 'payment by results' is deeply ingrained in the American system. Watch *LA Law* repeats for a view of what this can entail. If you do hire a lawyer on a non-contingency basis expect enormous fees.

As a tourist or medium stay visitor the only rule of thumb is probably to make sure that you carry adequate **insurance**: health, car and uninsured driver (where you insure yourself against being hit by someone you might have to sue but who hasn't any money or any cover of their own).

HEALTH CARE

US doctors are world famous. Given the amount of debt incurred to get a medical degree high fees are only to be expected. The doctors' 'plight' is helped by the fact that when we are ill everything gets focused upon getting better, so we are vulnerable in the market place – we'll pay what it takes, and doctors know that. To exacerbate the situation most medical fees are paid by the insurance company, so the sick are even less price sensitive. Add to this the doctors' fear of being sued for failure to diagnose correctly something nasty and you have a mass of tests that are deemed standard, are expensive, and anyway the insurance companies will pay up, so what the heck.

To cover themselves most doctors pay over £30,000 in malpractice and accident insurance premiums each year – and that's before any costs! So health care is expensive. Getting the prescription filled, of course, costs extra too! Expect to pay at least $300 a month for a couple for health insurance, and then you still have to pay 20 per cent of the bill.

Planning ahead

Most British visitors to the USA will enjoy a healthy, hassle-free time. Planning ahead for your health needs can ensure that whatever illnesses you encounter will not be medically or financially catastrophic.

- There are no specific health requirements for the USA, though if you intend to go backpacking or camping out in the wilds it is worthwhile considering a **tetanus** shot. If you were immunised as a child now is a good opportunity to go for a booster shot.

- If taking children whose full course of **vaccinations** have yet to be completed consult your GP.

- If you need **prescribed medicines** check you have the appropriate forms. Fortunately finding a pharmacy in the USA should be no problem. Carry a letter from your GP outlining your drug requirements to ensure passage though US and later UK customs.

- Have a **dental check up**: dental work is very costly in the USA. Any toothache can play havoc with holiday or travel plans.

Insurance

There is NO reciprocal health care agreement between the UK and the USA – so adequate health care insurance is essential. **Options** (01252 747747) has introduced a no-claim bonus on its annual policies. Two adults and up to four children (under 19) pay £85 for 60 days' worldwide cover (in any 12 months) including 10 days' winter sports cover if required.

Florida visitors should beware of 'sea-bather's eruption'. This is a large rash caused by jellyfish larvae that sting when trapped within bathing costumes. Bikinis retain fewer larvae than one-piece costumes and so produce less rash.

Further information

For more details see *Health Advice for Travellers* published by the Department of Health. Copies of this can be obtained by ringing 0800 555 777.

Try also Dr Richard Dawood, *The Traveller's Health* (Oxford University Press, 3rd edition 1991, about £7) or the Cadogan Guide *Bugs, Bites and Bowels* for about £8.

AIDS

There is no vaccine or cure for AIDS. You cannot catch the infecting virus from everyday contact, from mosquitos, insect bites or from swimming in the motel pool.

Infection comes from sexual contact with an infected person or from infected blood. To protect yourself:

- Do NOT have sex with anyone other than your usual partner.

- If you do have sex with someone else ALWAYS use a condom (US = 'rubber').

- Do not inject illegal drugs, and never share needles.

- Ensure any blood transfusion involves screened blood.

- Have enough insurance cover for first class treatment in any medical emergency.

Medical checklist

- Take a small first aid kit – adhesive dressing packet, insect repellent, antiseptic cream (kits can be bought from major chemists or the AA).

- Personal hygiene is vital – always wash your hands (US = 'wash up') before handling food, particularly if camping.

- Skin piercing (ears, tattooing, acupuncture) is unwise in unfamiliar circumstances.

- Take insect and animal bites seriously – use repellent cream, cover arms and legs in wooded areas. Ask about local poisonous plants such as poison ivy.

- Avoid hypothermia – take padded winter clothing, hats and gloves for all but most southern states in winter.

- Avoid sunstroke – hats, sunglasses and plenty of fluids anywhere in the summer.

THE US TELEPHONE SYSTEM

The popular view abroad is that the US phone system is the best in the world, being the cheapest and the most efficient. Many Americans might have agreed with you before the break-up of the Bell System. Today the system is more complex and opinions remain divided as to its efficiency and cheapness. Certainly Americans use the phone at least twice as much as the British. Economies of scale should pay dividends for both users and the phone companies. In the big cities such as Washington DC the system is generally very good for the casual user. Most phones are push-button, directory enquiries are computerised, and most phones can do tricks that have only recently appeared in Britain, such as transferring calls when you are out.

Tones
As soon as you pick up the phone you should hear a constant buzz (unless it's a payphone). The ringing tone is long with long pauses. A short bleep means the number is engaged: you got the 'busy signal'.

Numbers
All numbers fall into a standard system unlike in Britain: typically (987) 654 3210, where the numbers in brackets are the area code and the first three digits the exchange. You may be surprised to find that US phones still have letters along with numbers. Sometimes numbers are given in an appropriate word form: (800) USA-RAIL for the public railroad Amtrack. Be careful not to confuse the number 0 (zero) with the letter O which is the same as the number 6.

The other symbols and * which are still rarely used on domestic British phones are only involved if you want to programme your phone to do things like transfer calls to other numbers. The only trick you'll find useful is to push the * at the end of punching in an international number (it means: that's it, go ahead and call this number).

The main problem for travellers comes from using public phones for calling outside the immediate local area. Local calls are easy. Just dial the last 7 numbers. Unfortunately not all calls within the same area code are deemed local. Calls outside the immediate vicinity are called 'long distance' even if you don't consider the distance to be very far. **You need to place a 1 in front of the seven numbers** as in 1-654-3210. For long distance calls with a different area code (as would always be the case if calling another state, and might be the case within a large state such as

New York or California) use a 1 followed by the area code plus the seven digit number, as in 1-(987) 654 3210.

Charges

Most calls except from hotel or motel rooms are comparatively cheap, especially within the local area. Long distance calls from private phones are itemised on the next bill so you can pay back friends precisely what you owe them. Cheap rates apply from 5.00 pm to 11.00 pm Sunday through to Friday, with bargain rates from 11.00 pm to 8.00 am daily, all day Saturday and 8.00 am to 5.00 pm Sundays. Use a private phone where possible as it's considerably cheaper than pay phones.

Public telephones

You may have difficulty finding these in certain areas, such as many residential neighbourhoods. Try anywhere people congregate (launderette, gas station, 7–11 store, *etc.*). Post offices do not generally have telephones as in much of Europe.

Usually you'll need a fist if not a bag full of loose change. You have to put in the minimum fee (which varies from 25c to 35c) just to start the process. If you end up reaching an engaged number you'll get your coins back. The money gets you the dial tone and a local call, still of unlimited duration in some areas. Even to call the operator on a free number ('toll free') you'll need to start the process off with the minimum fee, which you'll get back.

If you dial a long distance number a voice will cut in to tell you how much more to put into the machine. As the largest coin is 25c you'll need lots of these handy, and your call will be for a three minute minimum whether or not you want three minutes. Where you get hold of $2.75 in quarters in the middle of nowhere at three in the morning to call ahead and warn your hosts that you've had a flat tyre is not the company's problem. They probably can't understand why you aren't calling 'collect'. You may end up having to hope your friends will accept the call. For collect calls within the USA call 1-800-COLLECT.

If you have an account with a US phone company you can use special phone boxes that take US-issued credit cards, but these are usually only available in large airports. Calls based upon price rather than time are rarely available, and again usually only from major airports. Certain UK credit card holders are eligible for AT&T's 'Calling Card'. US to UK calls can cost as little as half BT's chargecard rate. Call 0800 897801 before leaving the UK.

One gleam of light comes in the form of pre-paid phone cards by such long distance carriers as AT&T, MCI or GTI available at airports and some car rental outlets in 10, 25 or 50 units. You can use these almost anywhere by quoting a reference number. Some cards can be recharged by phone. You may have problems using a card for local calls, especially if using a rival company's card. For a UK introduction to AT&T's 'Tele Ticket' call 0800 897801. In USA call MCI on 1-800-444-4444.

Calling home

The international prefix is 011, which should be followed by the UK code (44), then the British area code minus the initial 0, followed by the number. A call home then might be 011-44-(171) 234567. To use a BT chargecard to reverse the charges call 1-800 44 55667 (which gets you through to a UK operator), then give the UK code plus local number in full. For the local US international operator punch in 00 (zero zero) or 10288 00 (if from a non-AT&T phone). But: for direct dials calls punch in 0 (zero) and check out that 'I-triple-D' is available in your area. For local operator chargecard calls ask for the AT&T International Operator Center. For international information call 1-800-874-4000, a free service (as are all 800 calls). As local operators in rural areas may not be able to help you place a call home from a public or motel phone (they may never have been asked for this service before, or if they have you may not be able to understand what they say) this number can be very useful. Telephone boxes rarely have the kind of information about making calls that is normal back home, and telephone books probably won't help either.

How much does it cost? The standard rate from New York City to Britain applies from 7.00 am to 1.00 pm local time. The discount rate is from 1.00 pm to 6.00 pm and the super discount is from 6.00 pm to 7.00 am. A one minute call dialled direct from a private phone during the cheapest period costs about $1.50, with additional minutes at half price. The minimum three minute call from a pay phone would be about $6.50.

Some useful numbers

● Local directory enquiries	411
● Non-local directory enquiries with the same area code	1-55 1212
● Directory enquiries for numbers with other area codes	1-111-555 1212
● To find an area code	411
● Operator	0
● International operator	00 (or 10288 00 if from non-AT&T phone)
● Emergency services	911
● Wrong number dialled	211
● Toll-free numbers directory	1-800-555 1212

- UK direct (for BT chargecards   1-800-44 55667 (AT&T)
  & collect calls)   1-800-80-00008 (Sprint)
      1-800-44 42162 (MCI)
- UK direct (for Cable and Wireless   1-800-500 0544 (AT&T)
  calling cards)   1-800-500 245 (MCI)
      1-800-844 4220 (CWI)

WHAT TO READ ON THE USA

There are plenty of general books on the USA. Visit your local public library and you'll find anything from a row to a room full of books on various aspects of US history, geography, politics, literature, economics and travel. But more up-to-date information for the traveller has to be sought elsewhere. The larger the bookshop the larger the choice of up-to-date guidebooks. Large city shops such as Dillons in central London or Blackwells in Oxford may well have a whole wall just on the Americas (North and South) plus as many more on general travel hints. However, since the first edition of this book, even the smallest market town bookshop seems to have acquired a selection that would have been unheard of in big cities only 20 years ago.

The vast influx of British visitors to the USA that grew when the pound was considerably higher than today stimulated a new wave of articles in papers such as the *Daily Mail, The Guardian, The Financial Times*, and *The Observer*. Keep an eye on travel pages for up-to-date information (though beware: some articles result from trips paid for by specific sponsors who may well have set a schedule to make the most of their good points). However, more reliable information can be found in *Travel Which?*, back numbers of which are available in your local public library. *The Independent's* Saturday 'Travel Update' is particularly useful.

In trying to decide which guidebook is for you, remember that:

- Practical information varies in degrees of detail. Guidebooks are most likely to be useful for background information on history, food and the popular sights. If using their practical travelling details check the date of publication as important details can vary substantially from year to year. This is particularly so for library copies, which are usually older editions than in the bookshops. Certain guides are updated each and every year, and usually make this a selling point.

- Accommodation lists can be detailed and thoroughly inspected, the personal choice of the author, or the result of users' anecdotal reports (unchecked by anyone). You have to check how and when any guidebook is compiled.

Types of guide

The degree of detail varies considerably and deliberately. There are several types of guide:

- **General travel** – may be a guide to travelling in general throughout the world, where the USA section is small, possibly superficial and only one of many country-by-country offerings, and so is inadequate for any serious traveller. On the plus side they may have information applicable everywhere including the USA if interpreted intelligently. A good example would be Ingrid Cranfield's *The Traveller's Handbook*, published by Heinemann. More specifically see Maggie and Gemma Moss, *Handbook for Women Travellers*, published by Piatkus in London 1987, or Miranda Daniel and Natasia Jansz, *Woman Travel*, Harrap Columbus, London 1990.

- **USA-at-large sightseeing guides** are useful for general essays on regions like the South, the West Coast, and so forth, plus general essays on US society, history, geography and climate. A typical example would be *Fodor's USA* guide, regularly updated (also available in parts for various regions and cities).

- **Budget guides** are geared mainly to young people on tight budgets, but their up-to-date practical hints, phone numbers, recommendations and warnings can be invaluable for all visitors. An example would be *Rough Guides*.

- **Pocket guides** are just that, but they can be very useful, especially if dealing with a specific region or city. Berlitz guides are the best example here. Beware, though, that some pocket guides assume you are six feet tall with large anorak pockets, not 5'4" with only the pocket in the back of your shorts.

Specific guidebooks

Here are some of the major guides you are likely to find readily available:

- **AA guides** are more usually associated with European countries, but are increasingly available for such US cities as San Francisco, Boston and New York. These are a revival of the definitive Baedeker nineteenth-century guides. The AA partnership is producing increasingly modern, readable and useful guides. Their layout is very attractive, with good photographs, helpful hints for seeing the sights, how to use public transport plus general history and geography of the city. Copies are paperback, but in plastic covers (with a useful pull-out city map). They are not cheap, and may be too detailed for a quick visit. Updating is not annual, so beware. Coverage of more US areas is coming through the AA's 'Essential' series (slimmer guides).

- **Berlitz Travel Guides** are cheap and cheerful; attractive to read, authoritative and carefully compiled. Some are updated each year. They are truly pocket guides, and the Florida volume in particular is good value. The colour maps are a bit garish, but nonetheless useful.

- **Fodor Guides** offer lots of practical information whether on the whole of the USA or on specific regions. They are, however, full collections of facts, though being regularly updated they offer a vital measure of assistance when arriving in a strange city on a countrywide tour. The Washington DC volume is quite useful. The *Fodor Budget Guide* to US cities is an abbreviated version of the national volume with some useful hints for budget travellers. Fodor also provide guides for adjacent areas – Canada, Latin America and the Caribbean. Newly commissioned volumes appear from time to time.

- **Michelin Green Guides** are for those with larger pockets (as in Rohan travel trousers). They cover regions and specific cities, the former for touring by car with an emphasis on historical sights, monuments and famous vistas. The city volumes are excellent, with clear maps and well-translated text (from the French originals), and they are particularly recommended for excursion suggestions, with consideration given for stays of various lengths. The New York City volume is excellent, with subway maps, bus routes and tours laid out, and includes covering material on the various neighbourhoods.

- **Rough Guides** are, as their name suggests, aimed specifically at budget travellers, particularly the young (and young at heart). They tend to be more upbeat, and give the reader the feeling that the writer has actually enjoyed visiting the place in question. Practical facts are available, as well as historical and cultural information. All visitors may enjoy their concern for off-the-tourist-trail places to visit and things to do. The New York City edition is particularly interesting. Their strong points are that they are contemporary, well researched and at a reasonable price. However, they have a distinctly budget feel about them, compared, say, to the glossy Berlitz guides, which may put off some people.

Finally there is a long-standing personal favourite:

- **Traveller's USA and Canada Survival Kit** which is specifically geared towards young people, especially students able to spend at least a long summer in North America. Compiled by Susan Griffin and Simon Calder for Vacation Work of 9 Park End Street, Oxford, it is periodically updated and costs about £10. There are sections on red tape, currency, health insurance, getting about, where to stay, living it up, and where to find the best buys with a wealth of things to do and to avoid, plus phone numbers. *Moneywise Guide to North America* (BUNAC annually) is also a great Linus blanket if you ever get into a fix. *Let's Go USA* by Harvard Student Agencies is much the same.

What's suitable?
If you are spending some considerable time in one place, like New York City, you may find it worthwhile first checking out the range of books available from libraries. The larger the library the larger (and newer) the selection. Then visit a large bookshop if at all possible and browse for as long as you can. You'll need to ask yourself:

- *How long in any one place?* If only a few days are involved, say in Florida, a pocket Berlitz will probably be enough. A week or more and a Fodor-like guidebook would be an investment.

- *Is the guide for the car, coat pocket, or for shorts?* The large Fodor volumes are heavy and are definitely for the car, whereas a Michelin can be carried comfortably even in summer.

- *How accurate and up to date must the information be for me?* If you are on a pre-paid tour by coach or even in conjunction with a particular motel chain you won't need vast amounts of budget accommodation information, so a borrowed copy giving general sights to see should be enough if you check your copy's date of publication, and make any necessary adjustment for inflation. If in doubt, ring ahead to the resort or attraction for current prices.

Longer stays
As you read such material you will come to realise that most of it refers to being on holiday, whether from a US or a UK base. People do, of course, spend up to several years on working holidays and these guides can be invaluable. But by and large these books don't cater for long-stay visitors' particular problems. *The Traveller's Survival Kit* has enough information for the long summer vacation tourist to be of some use for the long-stay resident, but for people actually living in the USA with their families a new type of guide is needed. Only gradually are such guides for living in the US appearing. You are reading one now!

For interest try also Roger W. Hicks and Frances Schultz, *Long Stays in America*, published by David & Charles, Newton Abbot, 1986. Despite an excellent cover the text's layout manages to hide a lot of excellent material. This is a book to read rather than to use as a reference source. Don't be put off by the poor quality and the irrelevance of the illustrations.

Maps
These are not generally available for the USA, except those suitable for the motorist. Town plans in guides are often of little use except in the most general sense (to show the relative locations of the sights). Fortunately most US downtowns, but not all, are on a regular grid system so sketch maps of US inner cities are of more use than equivalents for European cities. Better town plans can be obtained locally (such as the *New York Mapguide* published by Penguin) or at specialist outlets in the UK.

- The Travel Bookshop
  13 Blenheim Crescent, London W11
  Tel: (0171) 229 5260

- Daunt Books
  83 Marylebone High Street, London W1M 4DE
  Tel: (0171) 224 2295

- Stanford Map and Travel Bookshop
  12 Long Acre, London WC2 9LP
  Tel: (0171) 836 1321

- Stanfords at British Airways
  156 Regent Street, London W1R 5TA
  Tel: (0171) 434 4744

- Stanfords at Campus Travel
  52 Grosvenor Gardens, London SW1 0AG
  Tel: (0171) 730 1314

- The Map Shop
  15 High Street,
  Upton-upon-Severn
  Worcs WR8 0HJ
  Tel: (01684) 593146

- Bookland
  12 Bridge Street
  Chester
  CH1 1NQ
  Tel/Fax: (01244) 341868

The 'Let's Go' guidebook series has started to produce city maps that are pamphlet-sized and laminated for bad-weather use. *Let's Go Guide to New York City* also has 40 pages of essential information for $7.95.

For those drivers who don't want to rely upon being able to pick up highway maps at petrol stations (and gone are the days when they were both plentiful and free!) the Rand McNally *Road Atlas* is now available in UK bookshops and it covers every state and most cities. It is a wonderful book to delve into, to work out new routes, or just to reminisce. It is very widely available throughout the USA – where you will probably find a cheaper and newer edition.

For details as to how to find local maps see Victor Selwyn's *Plan Your Route* published by David & Charles of Newton Abbot. See particularly Chapter 7 on the maps of the southwestern deserts.

US equivalents to the Ordnance Survey are not widely available to the general public, except in US Parks Service bookshops within National Parks. Topographical maps by the US Geological Survey are excellent if you can find them. US college bookshops usually stock their local maps.

State by state topographical ('topo') atlases are now available in the UK from Dillons, published in the USA by DeLorme Mapping Company. Not all states are yet issued, but 14 are, with others in the pipeline (£15 each). Their AAA 'Map'n'Go' CD-Rom is excellent. Visit their Website at *www.delorme.com*, or try *www.mapquest.com* for maps for a given address or zip code.

Other viewpoints

People from overseas have visited the USA since its founding and have written many guides for explorers, travellers, visitors, emigrants or just the readers back home.

• Probably the most famous within the USA remains *The Domestic Manners of the Americans* by Mrs Frances Trollope, mother of the *Barchester Chronicles* author Anthony Trollope. Her comments from the 1830s are often unintentionally witty as she surveys the rise of the common man, slavery, utopian experiments and the new cities. Americans hated her. Mark Twain said it was because she'd hit the nail on the head. Later Charles Dickens did the grand tour, recording his impressions in *American Notes*, recently republished by Penguin in paperback. His novel *Martin Chuzzlewit* is also based upon much of this first-hand experience (and has a considerably more developed US section than appeared in the television version).

• Recent views are numerous, and many are well worth reading. Any Jonathan Raban book is worth reading: he canoed the Mississippi for his *Old Glory*, a Picador paperback. Other academics have used the novel to explore the excitement and trauma of being a Brit in the USA. Malcolm Bradbury (of *History Man* fame) wrote *Stepping Westward*, an Arena paperback which both confirms and confounds the *Dallas* glamour of the West. Later David Lodge explored the late 1960s California through the eyes of an initially staid Birmingham university teacher in *Changing Places*, a Penguin paperback. If you don't manage to read these before you visit the USA you must do so upon your return!

Americans on themselves

But what of Americans' *own* views of themselves? The list is endless. After all, most of what has ever been written in English has been written in the USA. The size and ethnic variety of the USA mean it is impossible really to read about America at large, except that many American writers were often engaged in satirising the narrowness and provincialism they sensed all about them at home.

The nineteenth century saw such great writers as **Walt Whitman**, whose *Leaves of Grass* has a freedom of line and a delight in the vernacular sounds of everyday life that exalt the promise of everything democratic while coming to terms with the reality of the Civil War slaughter. If ever visiting the battlefields read Whitman's elegies for the fallen (which of course came to include President Lincoln in 'When lilacs last in the doorway bloomed...'). **Mark Twain** too explored the quality of US society and what it was to be American (a still popular theme). His classics include the documentary *Life on the Mississippi* from which emerged his masterpiece *Huckleberry Finn* where a white child and a black slave together learn more about the ways of their world than they would wish to know, and in so doing throw into relief both America's promise and failings.

This sense that the US was finding it impossible to mature with honour recurs in **F. Scott Fitzgerald's** *The Great Gatsby* where the romantic view of American promise is shown to have been plundered by the rich, who, by the 1920s, have turned the US into little more than just another country, no worse and certainly little better than elsewhere.

The Great Depression of the 1930s confirmed this for many Americans at large. **John Steinbeck** explored the fate of many ordinary working people in those harsh times in *Of Mice and Men* (1937) and especially *The Grapes of Wrath* (1939), an epic struggle of the newly landless to survive the Dust Bowl of Oklahoma and their crushing disillusionment with the Promised Land of California. Both the book and the subsequent film (with Henry Fonda) remain classics.

This theme also affected much popular music. **Woody Guthrie's** *Dust Bowl Ballads* are still heard in the music of Bob Dylan and Ry Cooder in the 1970s and 80s.

Since the 1940s American writing has expanded beyond all bounds. Richard Wright's *Native Son* and Ralph Ellison's *Invisible Man* have opened up the black experience to an ever wider audience, though possibly the most eye-opening account remains Alex Haley's *The*

Autobiography of Malcolm X, the posthumous story of the slain radical (available in Penguin paperback). Evan Hunter's *Streets of Gold*, a Corgi paperback, explores the New York immigrant experience more realistically though perhaps less commercially successful than Mario Puzo's *Godfather*, a Pan paperback.

This leads into mention of the **movies**, for *Godfather II* (1974) is one of the most accessible explorations of New York ethnic diversity life on the big screen, though Spike Lee's *Do The Right Thing* (1989) is more contemporary.

But New York City has been seen in many lights. All offer a glimpse that can lift the visitor into a world of both imagination and concrete reality: *The French Connection* (1971), *The Taking of Pelham 123* (1974), *Marathon Man* (1976), and *Midnight Cowboy* (1969), not to mention the disturbing *Taxi Driver* (1976). Even the *Stepford Wives* (1975) explores one threatening image of the suburbs as seen by the big city enthusiast. *Three Days of the Condor* (1975) is very strong on downtown Manhattan and Washington Heights, though it is possibly television's *NYPD Blue* that best explores what many see as being the actual and threatening reality of New York City. Movie buffs can compare such television interpretations with the movies *Fort Apache the Bronx* (1981) and *Assault on Precinct 13* (1976) (though the latter is actually set in Los Angeles). Watch *Seven* (1995) if you dare. No wonder so many viewers prefer *Seinfeld* or *Friends* for their weekly view on New York's lighter side.

Learning about the USA
For those wanting a more structured and academically based introduction to the USA there are courses available both here and in the USA.

- Courses on a wide range of topics are put on by the **American Studies Resource Centre**. Enquiries can be made via:
  The American Studies Resource Centre
  Aldham Roberts Centre
  Liverpool John Moore's University
  Mount Pleasant, Liverpool L3 5U2
  website: www.americansc.org.uk
  Tel/Fax: (0151) 2331 3241.

- If you contact the **Adult and Continuing Education Centre** at your local university or college they may well have short courses on topics such as American Film, Presidential Elections or American Literature.

- The **National Federation of Women's Institutes** has put on such courses as *Mississippi: Great River of the World*; *New York City: World City*; and *The Wild West: Fact and Fiction* at its own residential college in the Oxfordshire countryside. Contact your local WI secretary for details of the college programme.

- For **courses in the USA** contact the International Study Programmes Department, Council on International Educational Exchange (CIEE) who offer a comprehensive advisory and enrolment service for summer sessions at US universities, such as Berkeley and UCLA in California. Sessions last 3–10 weeks with prices starting at £260 per week for tuition, full board, insurance, visa fee, orientation and counselling. Call (0171) 478 2000. Fax: (0171) 734 7322. E-mail: InfoUK@ciee.org

- You could go the whole hog and take a degree in **American** (meaning primarily US) **Studies**. The major teaching departments are East Anglia (Norwich), Keele (Stoke-on-Trent), Nottingham, and Sussex (Brighton) though most colleges now have some American Studies courses. A well-used option is to take American Studies not as a single honours degree but as part of a joint honours programme. At Keele, for instance, American Studies can be studied alongside: Biochemistry, Biology, Criminology, Economics, Electronic Music, English, Environmental Management, French, Geography, History, International Politics, Latin, Law, Music, Philosophy, Politics, Psychology or Russian. Keele sends 130 students to North America each year. For further details contact:

    Student Recruitment,
    Keele University, Keele,
    Staffordshire, ST5 5BG
    Tel: (01782) 584010
    (Web page: www.keele.org.uk)

- **The American College in London** has four-term MBAs (with an option to study in London or Atlanta). Tel: 0800 100 777 or (0171) 486 1772.

So what else can I read?

Books on the USA can and do fill libraries. Useful readable introductions to its history, geography and economy are less easily found at reasonable prices. A general introduction to the contemporary USA can be found in David Stuart Ryan's *America: A Guide to the Experience* (Kozmik Press, London 1986) available in some public libraries. For an hilarious read try Jane Walmsley's *Brit-Think Ameri-Think: A Transatlantic Survival Guide* (Harrap, London 1988). Did you realise that the only difference between us and the Americans is that they think death is optional?

US history books tend to be huge, heavy and expensive. Reasonably priced and recommended paperbacks include Peter N. Carroll and David W. Noble, *The Free and Unfree* (Penguin, Harmondsworth 1989) and Hugh Brogan's *The Pelican History of the United States of America* (Penguin, Harmondsworth 1990). The latter is also a bookclub selection. For a reasonably priced look at America as a place try Stephen F. Mills, *The American Landscape*, KUP, Edinburgh, 1997.

Contemporary issues are explored in a 1985-6 Macmillan paperback series by Christopher Brookeman, *American Culture and Society since the 1930s*, William Issel, *Social Change in the United States 1945-83* and Sam Rosenburg's *American Economic Development Since 1945*. For readers interested in the how and why of urban growth try Kenneth Fox's *Metropolitan America: Urban Life in the United States, 1945-1980*.

For a practical guide to places of historical interest try *The Smithsonian Guide to Historic America* (in 12 volumes) published by Stewart, Tabori and Chang, New York 1989. Each volume costs about £12, but copies are available in public libraries.

Something lighter?

But on holiday we probably seek something less serious. For those going to Florida try Carl Hiaasen's black comedy *Tourist Seasons*. If specifically bound for Disneyworld try Hiaasen's *Native Tongue*. Visitors to glotzy Miami might enjoy seeing how it used to be in Elmore Leonard's *La Brava* or Charles Willeford's *Miami Blues*. Further up the Atlantic coast but no less humid Savannah has been put on the map by John Berendt's elegant *Midnight in the Garden of Good and Evil*. For a more forensic side to southern heat try Thomas Harris's *Red Dragon, The Silence of the Lambs* or Patricia Cornwell's *The Body Farm*. John Grisham's legal thrillers such as *The Chamber* are an equally humid read. His *Pelican Brief* adds an environmental dimension, though for a more vicious eco-thriller read James Hall's *Under the Cover of Daylight*.

3
Preparations at Home

'She's leaving home, bye bye!'

Paperwork done in good time can make all the difference when going abroad. But besides everything involved in getting entry into the USA you also need to make certain arrangements at home:

- selling or leasing your home, or terminating the lease
- storing or transporting household effects
- getting yourself and your family over to the USA (see Chapter 6)
- sorting out any tax implications of changing countries (Chapter 9).

THE HOUSE

If you are leaving for a sufficiently long time, if not quite for good, you may need to consider selling your existing house. As your major capital asset you will probably need to sell in order to buy another in the USA. The Consumers' Association's self-help guide may be helpful in this.

With estate agents, solicitors and surveyors offering ever more comprehensive services, selling is not quite the hassle it once was. As you are not simultaneously a buyer you are not so deeply enmeshed in the chain of buyers and sellers that bedevils so many. This should make your property quite attractive to certain people, such as first-time buyers who are not themselves part of any chain.

Certain fundamental questions need discussing though:

Should we keep the house rather than sell?

If you intend to return to the UK it may make a lot of sense not to sell but to lease the property while away. Then there's somewhere to live upon returning.

BUT – if you need the equity tied up in your house you'll probably have to sell. If this is so, remember that when you do at last return, house prices could conceivably have risen a good deal, so you'll need to return from the USA with much more than you left with, just to stay even, never mind better off.

Should we lease the house?

If you can afford to leave your equity intact then do so, but leaving it unoccupied can be a recipe for disaster:

- Your mortgage still has to be paid.

- Your insurance is usually based on the assumption that the house is generally occupied (and by a family NOT students).

- It may become a target for thieves and vandals.

- You'll find the garden overgrown, yourself very unpopular with neighbours if you haven't made adequate arrangements for the grass to be cut, and leaves swept and so forth.

Unless you are going away for only a few months do not leave it unoccupied. Even if you are only away for the summer it is still highly vulnerable so:

- Cancel the milk, papers, coal, *etc* and get a neighbour to push mail and circulars completely through the letter box.

- Arrange for the garden to be kept neat and tidy.

- If possible arrange for a housesitter. A student relative writing a thesis might love the peace and quiet in exchange for mowing the lawn (and feeding the cat!). Or maybe friends would like to stay for a couple of weeks while you're away, using it as a holiday base?

- Join an exchange system: vetted foreign visitors use your home and car while you use theirs. Details from: INTERVAC on (01225) 892 208; Worldwide Home Exchange Club on (0171) 589 6055. On the Web try *www.nethomexchange.com* for an American perspective.

How do we lease our house?

If you are going on a staff exchange a simple house plus car swap may be possible, to everyone's advantage and convenience. Even if you aren't going on an exchange you may be able to contact someone who is coming to Britain much as you are going to the USA. Academic staff from the USA often stay at UK universities over the summer or when on a term's leave and require suitable accommodation while they pursue their research – check with the notice board of local universities' senior common room (SCR), staff house or equivalent staff room.

Ensure your building society will let you lease out your house. If you explain the situation in good time, particularly if it is for a set period, they may well be agreeable (as it's better than an empty vulnerable property).

Use a reputable agent, or rent via a reputable college. Accommodation is always needed by colleges, but you'd need to enquire as to what controls, if any, the college would exercise on its students living in your house. Contacting someone who has rented via the college may help to allay (or confirm) your fears.

Any snags in leasing out our home?

Assuming your building society raises no insurmountable objections, you need to consider:

- *Will the rent cover the mortgage plus reasonable wear and tear?* If you don't know – get out the calculator and work it out!

- *Will the tax office continue to accept that it is a principal dwelling house, and so eligible for continuing tax benefits?* Talk to your local tax office.

- *How will the rent influence our income tax liability?* Again you need to talk to your tax office.

- *What possessions to leave out and what to store?* If you are exchanging with known people you may feel it necessary only to empty wardrobes, storing what you are not taking with you in the attic in labelled boxes. If you are letting on the open market you will probably want to put into storage a lot more, such as your collection of jazz records and the hi-fi itself. It might be worth storing such items elsewhere, such as the in-laws' attic. However, the more your stuff is left in the house the more self-evidently it remains your house and home. This may be important when you return and seek repossession.

- *How will we obtain repossession upon our return? What if we return early?* A good agent may be able to help here. Getting awkward tenants out of accommodation, even furnished accommodation, can be time consuming, though if it is quite obvious that you are returning to live rather than to sell with vacant possession this can usually be managed without too much of a problem, particularly if it is explained to would-be tenants *before* they settle in. The 1988 Housing Act introduced Assured Shorthold Tenancies to ensure owners can move back in at the end of the agreed tenancy.

A few further considerations

- Don't be tempted to put everything in storage, rent as unfurnished, and then expect to move back in at a moment's notice. Rent controls and security of tenure legislation could make repossession against a tenant's wishes very difficult, expensive and troublesome. It may be possible to arrange a licence rather than a lease if you feel unfurnished is necessary. Set a definite date for your return to repossess and the licence should, if done correctly, enable you to exclude the tenancy from the terms of the Rent Act.

- Remember that you don't know your tenants as well as you might think, if you know them at all. Even family friends will now have children who may have perfected the art of wear and tear. For some families dirty shoes aren't allowed beyond the front step; for others dirty feet on the sofas go quite unnoticed!

- A general book that may nevertheless help the expatriate is Robert B. Davies's *Profitable Letting*, published by Fourmat, 1989.

- Alpha Lets publish *The Landlord's Guide to Profitable Lettings* (£10).

- For general information contact The Association of Residential Letting Agents, 18/21 Jermyn Street, London SW1 6HP.

- For blank Assured Shorthold Tenancy agreements visit the legal stationers Oyez.

Alternatives to leasing your home?
If you wish to close up your house for 10 to 12 weeks without leasing it out, you need to consider a systematic preparation of the property:

- Have neighbours check the property daily.

- Have the exterior regularly cleaned.

- Inform the police and the neighbourhood watch co-ordinator.

- Fit burglar alarms with appropriate deterrent lights, heavy bolts and five-lever mortise locks.

Home insurance brokers such as the AA can provide specific coverage for lengthy absences so long as the contents are worth less than £45,000 with few if any high value individual items. Premiums should be no higher than normal, though there may be restrictions on leaving the property empty for very long periods. For specialists in non-standard household risks contact Lloyd's broker Holman on (01277) 63345, Hanover Park (0181) 771 7772, or Andrew Copeland (0181) 656 2544.

SHIPPING POSSESSIONS TO THE USA

Travelling to the USA may turn out to be the easiest aspect of the whole saga, once the paperwork has been completed. At least you are unlikely to lose anyone *en route*. Moving your possessions can be quite another thing, and a hassle-free move will require careful preparation and a certain amount of luck. Certain questions need to be asked:

Who is paying to ship everything over?

- *Your new employers?* If so, they may have a preferred carrier. Check before committing yourself elsewhere.

- *Yourselves?* Check the rates very carefully. What minimum load is involved? If 200 kg is the minimum might it not be cheaper to prune things down to an absolute minimum and take them on the plane with you rather than involve a different carrier? And who is going to pay to bring your things back at the end of your contract, when the exchange is over, or just when you decide America's not for you?

What will it cost?

- Door-to-door rates for 5ft^3 (large size) tea chests from about £160 (1995), with discounts for sending several to same address at same time (4 chests for about £300).

- Door to (major) port rates are considerably cheaper, up to half door-to-door, but only of use to those able to reach New York City, Miami, Los Angeles or San Francisco.

- Collection within UK can add further cost so check inside/outside M25 rates. Different operators may have differing operational bases with different rate structures.

- Insurance will cost from 3½ to 5 per cent of replacement value. For operators see your local *Yellow Pages*, and the *Yellow Pages* for major airports (Heathrow, Gatwick, Manchester) available in local libraries. A typical operator active in moving British students' baggage overseas is Excess Baggage Company (0181) 965 3344 (with regional offices in Belfast, Cardiff, Edinburgh and Leeds). Try also the London Baggage Company – (0171) 828 2400 – a bucket shop for baggage.

- Airfreight is also available at £1.50 to £2.00 per kilo plus £25 handling charge (expect a 25kg minimum rate)

How bulky or how heavy?

- Check with the various carriers carefully. Bulky items in non-standard shapes may well incur penalty charges with one firm, whereas the weight may be more crucial with another.

- What's included in the price? Is insurance? Is packing? What about door-to-door service? These items cannot be too carefully checked and cross-checked. Even then you may get an inconvenient surprise once you arrive if nothing shows up.

An anecdote of warning!

A metal trunk (US = footlocker) was packed with college papers and summer clothes, sealed with the required US Customs declarations and the keys given to the shipper as instructed, some six weeks before required for the 24 August start of the new term at the University of Maryland. Six weeks later nothing had arrived at the other end, even though the agreement was door-to-door for a specific date.

On contacting the shipper it turned out that the trunk would be awaiting collection at College Park railway station. This, it turned out, no longer existed. Then the shipper said it was still on the docks at Liverpool, but should arrive for collection at the docks in Baltimore (30 miles to the north) within the month.

Six weeks later the US Customs issued a notification to collect or be charged $5 a day from Dulles International Airport in Virginia (30 miles in the other direction). The paperwork had gone astray so the trunk had to be claimed and taken through customs in person, during office hours. The loan of an estate wagon made this possible. Their invoice said the trunk came via Canada and New York by land and sea, but in fact it was stored with other items that had just been flown in from London Heathrow.

Five years later the same footlocker was booked in as excess luggage on the trip back to Heathrow, but on arrival at Heathrow it turned out still to be in Dulles awaiting the next day's flight, necessitating a further trip to the airport. Even the best laid schemes...

Excess baggage is one way to take necessary goods with you: 28 kg per person (if length + depth + breadth aren't greater than 157cm) generally goes free with the APEX fare across the North Atlantic (though this may be liable to a charge on cheaper flights to Newark). Anything over 28 kg goes at the excess rate, which can be very expensive if charged by weight rather than by piece. It may be possible to send extra baggage by cheaper freight rate if booked beforehand.

What should I leave behind?

Remember all those holidays where you came back with half the clothes unworn, half the cassettes unplayed, and half the toys unused? This time you have no room for anything that isn't absolutely necessary.

- Most British **electrical goods** are useless on the US 110V (60 Hz) supply. Even a 240/110V converter will mean the motor speed will be of no use for tape decks and record players. Whereas immigrants to Australia or New Zealand may find it worthwhile to ship out household goods like dishwashers, due to electrical compatibility and the high local prices, this is not so for the USA where goods are generally cheaper and need no adaptation for US-sized rooms.

- **Furniture** is cheap and readily available for the newcomer in the USA. Garage sales are a usual way for all sorts of people to sell off excellent furniture at rock bottom prices to avoid the shipping costs within the USA before they move. British arrivals will be amazed at what's on offer, or what may even be given to you by people glad to be able both to help out and to clear their own garage of spare beds, sofas and so forth.

    Of course shipping out **fine furniture** is another matter, whether it is antique or modern: if you can afford to ship it you'll be the envy of your colleagues. However, beware: the humidity range is quite unlike that in Britain, which may affect fine furniture considerably. Expert advice on preservation is as worthwhile as advice on shipping.

What should I take then?

During the Second World War the slogan was 'Is your journey really necessary?' Something along these lines needs to be asked, and you need to limit yourself to items that are:

    very special
    very useful, or
    very personal.

- *Personal effects:* from ornaments to books via records to jewellery. If you don't expect to return, or at least not for several years, you'll probably want your favourite Beatles EPs, your photographic albums, and your wedding souvenirs. If your stay isn't too long these could all go into storage.

- *Household goods:* though most US accommodation comes with cooker and refrigerator, buying all new kitchenware, pillowcases and duvets (even where available) can be very expensive, even if you become a great garage sale devotee. Don't bother with the garlic press you've never used, though your Edwardian parsley-cutter may be decorative enough to take along for display in your new kitchen.

- *Clothing:* a great opportunity to leave most of what fills your drawers and attic to your local Oxfam. You might like to fit yourselves out with new shoes before you go. Many Britons seem to prefer Clarks shoes to what's available over there.

Even if you leave all your furniture and concentrate upon lesser chattels it is quite likely you'll still end up with 500 kg per grown up. That's half a tonne each. If you intend to take books this figure will be easily reached.

If your library is an essential part of your professional tool kit you may need to negotiate a special arrangement with your new employer to ship them *en masse*. Fortunately the US mail permits books (as educational material) to be shipped overseas very cheaply – if sent by the mailbag load to a single address. So the return move, even if at your own expense, isn't so expensive.

What should we put into storage?

Find out how much it costs to store and insure (and who provides the packing cases and the shipment to the place of storage). If the cost of storage is greater than the replacement value you alone can decide whether or not the sentimental value is worth this extra expense. Most people returning to their stored possessions find that too much rather than too little has been retained, so storage preparation is a great opportunity for a mammoth clear-out. 'Triage' is the name of the game: three piles, one for essentials to keep, one of things to be disposed of and a third pile for the rest. The hardnosed would say store only the one pile of essentials! Get rid of the rest: chairs you know you'll never get around to repairing, flared jeans, and old school textbooks.

If your new employer offers to shift all your goods and effects rather than pay for a preset amount it might be worthwhile shipping everything over and putting the whole lot into storage over there while you look for somewhere to live. Self-storage lock-ups are now quite common in the USA. A row of miniature 'garages' will be enclosed in a compound, with a resident guard, so things should be quite secure. If you must leave valuables, such as antiques, in such a depot don't advertise or talk about the fact. Any security can be broken if the price is right!

CUSTOMS AND EXCISE

UK

Private household goods can usually be exported from Britain without too much hassle. Export licences will normally be granted for privately owned, albeit valuable, items if they are not being taken abroad for sale.

- If you have any doubts talk to your shipping agent and make enquiries from your local office of Customs and Excise (which are not based just around the coast or even just a large airport).

- For their address see the telephone book.

US

Customs will allow in bona fide household goods, clothes and personal effects. Though a container-load of micro chips will not be let in despite your hobby as a hacker, a load of obviously household and family goods will, if you can show the necessary papers to support your arriving with the kitchen sink. Do not arrive with all your worldly goods and a tourist visa (unless you can get everything into two suitcases).

- It may help US Customs and yourself if you list everything as you pack it (it helps if a box does go astray to know what to claim for). Any item could be taxed on its value, so you need to estimate some figures, though you can guess some, such as 'Sports gear $50').

- To get a sense of what is necessary ask the Customs Desk at the US Embassy for their free sample inventory list and information package Tel: (0171) 408 8027.

Remember: Meeting and dealing with incoming families and their belongings is hardly something new for US Customs, so they'll know both what they want and what they want you to do to make your arrival easy (if only for their convenience).

4
Visas and Immigration

These States are the amplest poem
Here is not merely a nation but a teeming
Nation of nations.

Walt Whitman

A SOCIETY OF IMMIGRANTS

The USA is not like the Old World, a place of relative permanence and
continuity, adapting only so far as it preserves what has been. The USA
continually reinvents itself, turning 'them' into 'us'. It is a nation that
does not grow from affinity with the soil or even with one language
whose origins are lost in time. Instead the USA is polyglot, an
ingathering of all the races, peoples and religions of the earth. It has
always relied upon attracting peoples from elsewhere. Even the native
peoples (mistakenly taken for 'Indians') came from Siberia in the dim
and distant past.

Recent newcomers
Europeans came initially to dominate the modern influx, but just as the
British came by the turn of this century to be outnumbered by peoples
from eastern and southern Europe, so too this once novel combination
has recently been overtaken by a continuing influx from Latin America,
south-east Asia, and even from Africa. The dominant black and white
mix has recently given way to browns and yellows.

Thirty years ago most immigrants came from Europe or from
Canada. By the early 1990s most are Mexicans, Filipinos, Vietnamese,
Koreans, Indians, Chinese and West Indians. They arrive on jumbo jets;
they walk across the border; they are washed ashore on the Florida Keys.

Fears and suspicions
A flickering fear says aliens are overrunning the country. If the USA is a
lifeboat in a world of trouble maybe it is in danger of being swamped.
Racism re-emerges, fuelled by fears of recession-led competition for

jobs. The long-standing mutual fears and suspicions of blacks and whites give way to mutual apprehension that those browns and yellows recently let in will throw open the gates to one and all, levelling down, with English but one of many possible tongues.

But this has always been the fear. Benjamin Franklin feared that the Pennsylvania of the 1750s would be overrun by Germans. In the 1840s the Irish seemed about to swamp the towns and, while digging the canals, the countryside too. Later Jews, fleeing Czarist hostility, brought their Yiddish language, their Hebrew writing, and their Saturday Sabbath into the growing cities which many Americans feared were being turned into foreign countries. Working for the good of their children, immigrants stood together when necessary and plunged into the mainstream when possible, learning English, voting, investing their lives in almost any job that would keep the family intact.

Beginning life anew
John F. Kennedy, son of an Irish family made good in the USA, saw his country as 'a society of immigrants, each of whom has begun life anew, on an equal footing'. For him America's secret was that it was 'a nation of people with the fresh memory of old traditions who dared to explore new frontiers'. It was in his memory that the USA abandoned the old 1920s quota system which, if too late to keep the USA White Anglo-Saxon and Protestant (WASP), at least had kept it predominantly European. Since 1965 new waves of immigration have brought newcomers not just from Europe but increasingly from the Third World. Of over 600,000 legal immigrants each year the largest number came from Mexico (about 100,000) the Caribbean (100,000), the Philippines (50,000) and Vietnam (35,000), about the same as Britain and Ireland combined.

Recognising the changes
For British settlers (or even visitors) recognition of this change is essential. The British have a very ambivalent attitude towards the USA. The temptation is to see it as a richer, larger version of the south of England with more snow and more sun, but still recognisably British (if not quite English). If this were ever true the mass influx from southern and eastern Europe of Italians, Yugoslavs, Jews and Poles last century has long since swept over this British heritage. The countryside is full of people originally from Scandinavia and Germany, as the place-names of the Midwest tell us (see Harrison Keillor's *Lake Wobegone Days*, Penguin 1986, for a loving but caustic look at such people in Minnesota).

Today's Third World influx is changing the very language and landscape of America. Where once there were small ethnic enclaves like San Francisco's Chinatown, now there are vast Spanish-speaking neighbourhoods in most cities. The Governor of New York City may be from an Italian background, but city mayors are likely to have been born in the Philippines or in Cuba. Each year the Immigration and Naturalization Service (INS) catches over a million illegal immigrants. The US Census Bureau reckons they missed between two and three times more. Most are from Mexico, crossing the land border in a dash from the conditions of Bangladesh to those of Switzerland in one night.

No wonder that the INS requires visitors to provide proof they intend to leave. A cynic might say that the less the INS can control the 2,000 mile land border to the south the more it needs to demonstrate its authority where it can with those coming openly into the USA at airports.

BEING AN IMMIGRANT: SETTLING IN

Travelling into the unknown
The USA has always offered immigrants a prize: land, a job, or freedom of expression. But it has rarely been an easy bargain. The streets have never been paved with gold. Those who expect gold have been severely disappointed. Just being alive is a risk. We are all immigrants in the sense that we are all travelling into an unknown. To go to the USA is to compound that. You are going into someone else's future, which you must make your own. The familiarities of home, relatives, bank holidays, the passage of the seasons, cup finals, TV programmes, *The Archers* or *Desert Island Discs* will all vanish to be replaced by the occasional long-distance telephone call, harsher seasons (or no seasons at all), cable-TV with 36 channels spouting religions and languages you don't recognise, not to mention more advertisements that you thought possible. From all this novelty you'll have to carve out a new routine, a new set of familiar surroundings which you'll have to be prepared to jettison at a moment's notice when promotion means leaving Portland, Maine, for Portland, Oregon. And you may see the children even less than before.

Coping with further changes
Arriving in the USA it may be tempting to see yourself as remaining essentially who you have always been, though with more money as befits being within a wealthier economy. Feeling like this many immigrants have been very bewildered when they were asked to change their lives again and again. The company may be taken over and all existing staff fired. The department of history may be closed as a university cost-cutting device. The union may call you out on strike, and you lose.

Such traumas are of course increasingly likely back home. Indeed changes such as these may be what encouraged you to leave for the USA! But the price of that extra pay, the extra promotion prospects, the better funded library or laboratory may be the greater risk. If your company gains a military contract you will have to go along with that or leave with no other job in sight. Being offered promotion may be on the 'up or out' principle (take it or leave the company) which may leave you in a part of the USA you'd never intended to visit never mind settle in.

Being flexible

Great courage and flexibility will be needed in this kind of situation. If you really do want to stay in the city where you've started to settle down, greater flexibility in job selection than you've ever had before may be necessary. Teachers drive cabs, act as tour guides, write freelance, and even work for political candidates in the hope that their election will lead to a job in their office.

As there is less of a safety net in the USA, networks of friends and family take on ever more importance, and hard work and commitment are essential, with an enthusiastic endorsement of the US's 'can do' attitude, rather than the more pessimistic 'what if it doesn't work out?' US attitudes to success and failure, while rewarding success more, also encourage risk and so don't take failure to be a mortal sin. It is not a sin to be knocked down. It is only a sin to stay down. By having taken the leap of faith necessary to become an immigrant you are already making a stake in becoming American, and may find flexibility more appealing and less threatening.

Moving on

All members of the family should have talked the options and implications over though. If after staying for a year in one place a move seems imminent it will again need to be talked through, and if all were aware early on that this might happen the house can be treated like a long-lease summer cottage and all the further packing, saying goodbye, changing schools and so on can be seen as a further adventure so that the family can stay together rather than a rude awakening.

GETTING A VISA

There is a bewildering variety of visas, and the appropriate regulations can and do change at any time without notice (though any major change would get considerable publicity). For up-to-date visa information phone the US Embassy on 0891 200 290 (you will be charged for this call). Visas are broadly:

- **non-immigrant** for those intending to return home at some date, and
- **immigrant** for those wishing to settle permanently.

In practice, however, there are intermediate statuses, some of which can be changed, and some which cannot. So it's essential to know what status you want, and what the limits and potentials are of the status with which you enter the USA.

How do I know which visa I need?
The non-immigrant or immigrant distinction seems pretty straightforward. Unfortunately it isn't always quite so simple:

- *Going for a look around prior to applying for a job?* You'd probably do best to go in as a tourist (see next section). But if you tell the welcoming Immigration officer that you are on a job-hunting exercise you may well be refused entry. Enter and leave as a tourist. Then apply for an appropriate visa to re-enter later.

- *Not wanting to commit yourself to settling down but wanting to enter the job market free to change jobs at will?* An immigrant visa is necessary. Visas given for those with specific job contracts stipulate that you must leave if you end your contract with the sponsoring employer. However, once legally inside the US it may well be possible to change your status (say, for instance, if you've married or have had children while living and working in the USA).

NON-IMMIGRANT VISAS

There are twelve types of non-immigrant visas (each with a different letter prefix). All applications must satisfy certain conditions. Applicants must be sound in body and mind, have no drug or dependency problems, with no criminal record (which includes advocating polygamy!), must not be nor have been a communist (or Nazi collaborator!). And of course applicants must be not entering the USA to 'overthrow, by force or violence or other unconstitutional means, the Government of the United States or of all forms of law'. Or as the US guidelines sum up:

> 'In short, aliens who do not measure up to the moral, mental, physical and other standards fixed by law are, with very few exceptions, excludable from admission even if they have the necessary documents.'

Important point: A US visa is *not* permission to enter the USA. It is merely a statement by the US authorities abroad that they know of no reason why the bearer shouldn't be permitted to enter. Admission is actually granted by an Immigration and Naturalization Service Officer at the port of entry. Arriving on a valid tourist visa with all your worldly possessions and all the family (including grandma and the dog) would suggest to the most hardpressed INS officer that you might be entering the USA for more than just a few days at Disneyworld.

If you fail to declare a reason why the US authorities might want to exclude you (such as a prior conviction) you can be removed from the USA without a court hearing, and be excluded permanently.

The conditions which applicants must satisfy are set out in some detail in the official booklet *United States Immigration Laws: General Information* issued by the INS and available from the US consular authorities (ask for booklet M-50).

Visa types

There are twelve basic types. When applying it is essential you know which category is appropriate or your application will get rejected, which can add to the already lengthy process time that you can ill afford to lose:

A diplomats and consular staff with authorised families
B visitors for business or pleasure (but see visa-free proviso later)
C transit visas
D ship and aircrews due to leave soon
E businessmen or investors
F students to 'pursue a full course of study at an established institute of learning'
G diplomatic visas for international organisations
H temporary worker, defined as an alien who is to perform a prearranged professional or highly skilled job for a temporary period, or to fill a temporary position for which there is a shortage of US workers; the employment must be approved in advance by the Immigration and Naturalization Service in the USA on the basis of an application filed by the prospective employer
I bona fide media people
J student, academic or nanny to join a recognised programme
K fiancé(e) entrance, valid for 90 days only prior to marriage and change to permanent resident status

L   intracompany transfer

Q   international cultural exchange participants who will be employed but whose primary purpose in the US is to share their cultural tradition with Americans; this might involve folk musicians working in a museum in a programme approved in advance by the US authorities.

Most visa types permit spouse (and children under 21) to go with the applicant, though care needs to be taken as to whether or not they can then work. For instance, the spouse or children of a student (F) visa may not work or even apply for permission to work. Intracompany transfer spouses and children may only work if they've successfully applied for work visas in their own right.

Documents needed to support an application depend upon the visa type sought, and whether or not the issuing official suspects fraud. Proof of intent to return home is necessary. But how can anyone prove intent? Well of course you can't but you can provide evidence that returning home is more important than staying on in the USA:

● The need to return to complete a degree or to further a career:
  – a statement from your college saying you must be back by a specific date or forfeit your place
  – a statement from your company setting a date by which you must return or forfeit promotion.

● A return ticket (rather than just money or a credit card) suggests an intent to return home by a specific date (say 12 months for an APEX ticket).

The more footloose and fancy-free you appear to be to the US authorities the more necessary it is to show you have a compelling reason to return home.

Someone with a mortgage, children in school, an established career and a return ticket plus a package tour to Disneyworld is less likely to be asked for further proof of intent to return than a recently graduated single male with no return ticket, or a single female with child care qualifications and a single ticket to a wealthy suburb (who would appear to the suspicious INS as a potential and illegal nanny).

Visa-free travel
Citizens of the United Kingdom no longer need visas to visit the USA. Requirements for visa-free travel are that the individual must be:

(a) a UK citizen travelling on an unexpired national (or EU) passport

(b) travelling for business, pleasure or transit, and

(c) staying in the USA for 90 days or less

plus if entering by sea or air

(d) holding a return or onward ticket

(e) entering the USA aboard a sea or air carrier that has agreed to participate in the programme, and

(f) in possession of a completed form (I-94W) obtained from the shipping or airline company

or if entering the USA by land from Canada or Mexico

(g) in possession of a completed form (I-94W), issued by the immigration authorities at the port of entry.

Inspass

A new system allows regular (mostly business) travellers to register with the INS. An electronic hand print is encoded on a plastic card which is presented at the border post for entrance without further checks.

Restricted visas

Some travellers are NOT eligible by law to enter the USA: people with certain contagious illnesses, criminal records, previous deportations from the USA or similar problems. Such travellers should apply to the Embassy of the United States of America, Visa Branch, 5 Upper Grosvenor Street, London W1A 2JB for special restricted visas. They may not use the no-visa plan. If such people attempt to travel visa-free they will be refused entry on arrival in the USA.

More than 90 days?

Visa-free travel does not include those who plan to study, work or remain more than 90 days. Such travellers do need visas. Beware: if the US Immigration and Naturalization Service officer at the port of entry believes that the visa-free traveller intends to study, work or stay longer than 90 days entry will be refused and you will have to return to the UK.

Please note: citizens of the **Irish Republic** DO require tourist visas and should apply to their nearest US embassy or consulate for the appropriate forms, in plenty of time before their intended date of departure. If possible, obtain a visa well before the early summer rush.

Organising the paperwork

For immigrant visas (see next section) there is a lengthy procedure.

Applicants for A, G, H-2, H-3, most I, and L visas will be handled by someone else, usually an employer (or would-be employer). K applicants, of course, will have a fiancé(e) to help them with the necessary papers. E and I visas are special cases, dealt with as such, and F and J visas involve the appropriate college providing evidence of status.

If a visa petition has been submitted to the INS in the USA to establish a preferential status, say for an immediate relative, the paperwork comes from the overseas applicant's US contacts to the INS for approval. If successful the INS forwards the paperwork directly to the consular office dealing with the applicant overseas. For certain employment visas (H-2, H-3 or L categories) the 'intending employment party' must file, whereas professional or 'exceptional ability' status applicants file with the INS themselves via the local US embassy.

From October 1994 it has been necessary to write to (NOT visit) the US Embassy to get a visa application and payment slip. Expect to pay up to £30 depending upon the visa type (in cash at a Barclays branch) for a stamped payment slip to send with your visa application. If in a hurry ask your travel agent to recommend a visa handling agency, or ring The Visa Service (0171 833 2709), Trailfinders Visa Service (0171 938 3848) or Worldwide Visas (0171 379 0419). Agencies charge fees over and beyond any fees payable for the visa, but know the ropes and use courier services.

IMMIGRANT VISAS

The great age of mass immigration came to an end in the 1920s following the arrival of an unprecedented number of people from eastern, central and southern Europe. A system was then introduced with high quotas for the countries of northwest Europe, and low quotas elsewhere. In the 1960s this was recognised to be a system inappropriate for a nation attempting to rid itself of the legacy of a deeply racist history. Instead, immigration was ended for everyone, except for those able to present themselves as legitimate exceptions. The guiding principles for being allowed to enter became:

• refugee
• family reunion
• to help the USA (skills, investments, *etc*).

In theory at least there are no special preferences beyond these necessary for the ordinary conduct of business, commerce, trade, tourism, certain humanitarian concerns and the needs of the US economy. In practice, though, reality is a little more complicated. To start the process call 0898 200 290 and request immigration visa details (this is a charged call to the visa section of the US Embassy).

Refugees
These have an automatic right of entry. In practice anti-communist refugees (such as the first wave of Vietnamese boat-people) have been welcome (if they had some US link), whereas those from right-wing regimes are not (hence Cuban refugees are welcome but not those from Haiti). Economic refugees are most definitely NOT welcome these days.

Family reunions
There is a complex preference system to allow in about half a million immediate relatives of US citizens (children, spouse and parents). Children must be unmarried and under 21.

The preference system was reorganised in 1990, and complicated transitional arrangements are in place. Even so the US Congress can and will change precise numbers and quotas. There are strong immigrant lobby groups, such as the Cubans and the Irish, who can and do exert pressure for rule changes as important elections approach. So the preference systems outlined below are presented only in their barest formats, to suggest how complicated the rules have become, and why so many people use a specialist lawyer. For further details see Richard Fleischer *Applying for a United States Visa*, How To Books/ International Venture Handbooks 1993.

To help the US economy
Applicants whose arrival within the USA would substantially benefit the US economy have specific quotas. About a quarter of a million skilled and professional workers, plus investors, can be recruited overseas, though usually to fill specific job and investment shortages. There is also a complex preference system.

Family preference system
- *1st preference:* US citizens' unmarried adult children.

- *2nd preference:* spouses and umarried children of 'lawfully perm-anent residents', that is, families of immigrants who have yet to become citizens.

- *3rd preference:* married children of US citizens.

- *4th preference:* siblings of adult US citizens.

These applicants are often called 'family-sponsored immigrants'.

Employment preference system
- *1st preference*: priority workers, which means senior managers of US

and multinational corporations, or persons of extraordinary ability in the sciences, arts, education, business or athletics. Such people would usually be well-known personalities.

- *2nd preference*: professional of exceptional ability holding higher degrees in science, arts and business.

- *3rd preference*: skilled workers with US Department of Labor certification and at least two years' experience to fill shortage areas. If there were critical shortages of off-shore oil workers then US corporations would be permitted to recruit overseas.

- *4th preference*: 'special immigrants', such as ministers of religion, certain international organisation employees, or specially deserving current or former employees of the US government.

- *5th preference*: investors with substantial amounts, usually in excess of $1,000,000.

These applicants are usually referred to as 'employment-based immigrants' by the US authorities.

A leaflet is available from:

Visa Branch   Visa Branch
5 Upper Grosvenor St   Queen's House
London W1A 2JB   Belfast BT1 6EQ

For recorded information: 0891   200 290

For a human voice: (0171)   499 6846

For an appointment: (0171)   205 7090

The US Government has various Web sites. Try the US Information Agency International Home page (on *www.usia.gov*) or the US State Department (on *www.state.gov*).

The lottery

If the preference applications have been filled and there are still some spare places others from designated countries may be invited to apply on a first come first served basis. No job is necessary at the time of initial application, but must be on offer in writing with appropriate 'Labor Certification' as per the preference system applicant if the visa comes to be issued. You may well have heard the INS have 40,000 visas to distribute each year by lottery. You may even have read advertisements offering professional help obtaining just such a lottery visa, at a price. But:

- lotteries are not held every year

- UK citizens (except those born in Northern Ireland) are not usually eligible (eligibility is country specific and reflects ethnic group lobbying on Capitol Hill)

- initial applications do not require professional help with the form

- costly 'professional advice' usually means merely copies of forms available for free from the US Embassy.

If another lottery is announced contact the US authorities direct on 0891 200 900 *and* hunt for a job offer immediately. Expect a $25 + application fee.

Using your visa

Once an immigrant visa has been issued you need to use it within four months if you wish to establish 'permanent residence'. This status doesn't mean you can never leave the USA, but that if you do so without first having taken out US citizenship you may lose your right of re-entry if you stay abroad too long.

OVERSTAYING

If you overstay for a few weeks don't expect to find the FBI after you, but if you should be unlucky enough to get caught you may find it goes against you should you ever try to return. If you leave by way of Canada there'll be no one to collect your US Immigration form (you'll probably just get waved through on the US side of the border). If you have overstayed on the US side the Canadian authorities will want to know that you are leaving straightaway: they don't want to be lumbered with you as the US won't take you back. You may, however (if you keep mum), be waved on into Canada and so be able to leave for Britain without trouble (few western countries are interested if you are on the way out).

If you want to stay legally you will need to contact the INS (see the phone book to check their location and times of opening). As they will assume you are trying to stay to work you should take necessary papers with you. The best thing to do if possible is to take a US relative or friend along to vouch that you are staying on for family reasons, have a place to stay, and intend to return home. You'll need to complete the INS form *Application for Issuance or Extension of Permit to Re-enter the USA*. Written proof that you have to be back home to start a job, enter college, or some such would be very useful (as would a return ticket).

If you want to change your status you will need a lawyer. Initially, though, you need to know what a lawyer can and cannot do for you. Read Richard Fleischer's *Applying for a United States Visa*, How To Books/ International Venture Handbooks 1993. This has copies of all the forms you'll ever be likely to need to know about, with categories of both immigrant and non-immigrant visas comprehensively explained.

ALIEN REGISTRATION

Every alien 18 years or over is required to carry a Certificate of Alien Registration or Alien Registration Receipt Card. Being more scared of losing this than of being found without it, I kept mine safely at home, carrying only a driving licence locally, and licence plus passport if going further afield. Changes of address must be filed within 10 days, and every year aliens must report their address whether it's changed or not.

All of this is very complicated, seems very organised, but ignores the fact that most illegals enter the US over the Mexican border not on 747s from Europe. But those who wish to be in the system as soon as they arrive had better get used to the idea that the paperwork needs to be done, and done right. Of course if the paperwork is done for you by family, college or employer in the USA it's a very simple system, with perhaps only a single trip to the consulate necessary.

Go to it!

EXPECTATIONS – YOURS AND THEIRS

Despite a tradition of immigration a 1985 poll found that only 27 per cent of Americans agreed with the idea that 'America should keep its doors open to people who wished to immigrate to the US because that is what our heritage is all about.' Some 67 per cent agreed that 'this philosophy is no longer reasonable, and we should strictly limit the number.' Some 56 per cent said legal immigration is now too high, though 66 per cent still approved of offering sanctuary to those oppressed overseas.

If Americans are uncertain as to how they should respond to continuing immigration how should would-be immigrants respond to the USA? In the past British emigrants have been able to disappear into the White Anglo-Saxon Protestant mainstream. Many adults lose their British accents almost as quickly as they pick up US words and phrases. Children make the transition in weeks. But what if the USA turns out to be something like *NYPD Blue* rather than *Dallas*? Actually even then the difficulties are not too harsh.

Slotting into place

The very rules that require immigrants to be skilled, educated and going to a specific job or family reunion mean that most British people will slot right into workplace and neighbourhood with little more difficulty than if they had merely moved to somewhere at the other end of the UK. In fact, moving to another EU country might well be more confusing with language and legal systems so different from the US-UK traditions. Some people, however, find a move within Europe less traumatic than one to the USA. Continental countries are so obviously different and foreign, whereas the differences within the USA may only creep up, as when there's an illness, or there's a sudden need for assistance and you turn out to be the only person in the car park who can speak English. Of course if you treat the USA as a foreign country, which it is, such problems may seem less bizarre and unexpected when they do occur.

Responding to US expectations

British immigrants will be caught in a cross-fire of US expectations. A British accent means you are stuffy but sophisticated, swinging but old-fashioned, staid but cosmopolitan, and so forth. You'll be expected to play darts, golf and soccer, drink only warm beer, stout or G and Ts, and eat only fish'n'chips and roast beef. And of course you'll be pressed to drink tea even if you'd prefer coffee or even a beer! Enjoy it or ignore it. Just don't complain that the water wasn't hot enough in the tea (or that the coffee is very thin by European standards).

As an immigrant you may have to be prepared to be more serious about life than those settled back home can be. But this can make the adrenalin flow, that most American of juices.

For British arrivals, though, experience suggests that the more highly skilled, the more firmly middle class, the greater the chances both of making good in the USA, and of becoming American. For the USA the immigrants' greatest value is as a leavening agent, yeast to reinvigorate society and the economy. Economically immigrants generate more than they themselves consume. Socially they add variety for which the US is famous, acting as an antidote to the blandness otherwise enveloping much of the USA.

Straddling two cultures

Ironically, most immigrants, or at least their children, seek to merge with the mainstream. And the British arriving as part of the brain drain have not gone into exile in the same way as the Vietnamese, the Cubans or the Soviet Jews. The exiles didn't so much abandon their countries as feel their countries abandoned them. The brain drain scientist can always go home for visits, for funerals and wakes, or even to return. The exile cannot.

Both groups, however, straddle two cultures. They leave behind a train that continues on its way regardless. The Britain they leave will not spin its wheels awaiting their return. Yet the emigrant/immigrant can never become a true American, for that requires more than even citizenship or allegiance to a set of ideas. It requires the experience of growing up in a country, the sense of 'my home town'.

ENCOUNTERING THE HISPANIC AMERICAN SOUTHWEST

Many British immigrants are in for a big surprise. They often have some sense of the rich and poor divide and its racial dimensions, but the high profile of the African American middle class, especially in government or education, can be a surprise. But it is reasonably easy to adapt to the realisation that certain people are more rather than less like yourself. It is quite another thing to find so many people who are neither black nor white and who rightly consider themselves American.

Whereas the large numbers of Russian-speakers merely seem like a hangover from the last century rather than something totally unexpected, in the southwest things are quite different. **Spanish** is the coming language. The immigrants are mostly from across the border, not from across an ocean. Mexican Americans are living in what was their country until the USA took it from them, but unlike the American Indians they have as their homeland one of the poorest, fastest growing, urbanised countries in the world across an undefended land border. Maintaining their links back across the border Mexican Americans are gradually outnumbering (and so outvoting) white residents who seem to have forgotten that they have only held this land for about 150 years.

To Hispanic Americans recently arrived British immigrants seem like bizarre outsiders, people who should adapt to the changing cultural politics of the southwest or go some place else. British immigrants can be disorientated particularly where the very notion is decaying that public life is always in English. Where once public notices would be only in English now they are more likely to be in Spanish. The English-speaker can feel very out of things in shops and offices where Spanish is the norm rather than the exception.

5
Getting to the USA

BY SEA

It used to be fairly straightforward to travel to the USA by sea. This was often cheaper, avoided flying for those who still feared this method of tempting fate, and enabled large amounts of baggage to be taken along at reasonable rates. Containerisation has undermined traditional freight services that provided such passenger accommodation. However, some travel by **freight vessels** is still possible. Fortunately there is a Cadogan Guide *Travel by Cargo Ship* (£10) which deals with 120 itineraries to 300 destinations worldwide, with details of companies and fares. Call Cargo Ship Voyages on (01473) 736265 for details of worldwide routes.

Only if you want a cruise en route and they offer you a good baggage rate (so you can take all your boxes in the hold) should you consider going over by **transatlantic** liner. Some cruise liners bound for the Caribbean do go over to New York City first of all (to pick up the bulk of their passengers) so you might be able to find a place. Certain student families returning home from New York City to Britain have returned on vessels such as the liner *France* just for the baggage allowance (with a glimpse of the high-life thrown in). Call Cunard on (01703) 634166 or (0171) 491 3930 for the Transatlantic Timetable, which contains arrangements for independent travellers. There is a Berlitz Guide *Cruising and Cruise Ships* for about £14 covering worldwide information and advice.

Strand Travel on (0171) 836 6363 can arrange places on **cargo boats** sailing from Thamesport to Montreal, leaving several times each month. The trip takes 10 days and costs £985 per person. Leisurerail on (01733) 33559 can arrange **trains** onward to US destinations.

BY AIR

The North Atlantic is the most heavily used long-distance route anywhere. So the good news is that there's plenty of flights. The bad news is that the fare structures are very confusing (even for travel agents!).

No summary can hope to do justice to the complex web of prices. Try looking at page 200 on Teletext for a sense of the range of travel possibilities and varied prices.

The main variations are:

- ordinary full price
- advance excursion booking (APEX)
- charter fares
- last minute deals
- economy airlines
- consolidator fares
- courier flights
- package tours
- round the world via USA.

> **Note**: Since October 1997 there has been a new US airport tax.

Ordinary full-price tickets

These provide great flexibility as any ticket is almost as good as money, being exchangeable with and between airlines. Tickets can be cancelled without penalty, and there's a generous baggage allowance with good service. If your employer will pay for this, then well and good.

Who buys ordinary tickets? Those for whom money is no object and where flexibility is essential.

Advance excursion (APEX)

These tickets are the most popular form of advance booking as they have a significant price advantage over full-price fares. Tickets must be bought some three weeks in advance (though sometimes this period is changed to meet market demand). Once into the three weeks period, though, no change of departure or return date is permissible (except at deliberately prohibitive cost). Single tickets (costing half the return price) are usually available, which is useful if you wish to return from somewhere else or at an unfixed future date on an 'open jaw' ticket. These tickets are increasingly sold as part of a fly-drive package, where a hired car (but no accommodation) is included.

Who buys APEX? Those needing to trade off price for flexibility, and staying no longer than a year (maximum validity). If you know your dates APEX may well be for you.

Seasonal variations can be extreme. A September fare to Boston is £648, by October £482, down to £450 just before Christmas puts prices up again.

Charter fares

These are supposed to be for interest groups booking together, though travel agents have been known to cobble together passengers of no common interest except that of a cheap ticket. There's always the danger of being stranded if your firm goes broke (or hasn't paid its bills). Increasingly though chartering firms are airline subsidiaries or package holiday firms.

Airtours on (01706) 260000 do Las Vegas from Manchester for £240 including a week's mid-winter accommodation (about £150 cheaper than by scheduled equivalent fare only deal).

Who's for a charter? Those who can't resist the chance of a bargain, and who will not be too inconvenienced if things go wrong, such as single people. You need to be young enough to sleep on airport floors if things go wrong, which seldom happens in transatlantic travel (thanks to US regulation of carriers).

Last minute deals

Companies have ways of filling seats still unsold at the time of take-off. At certain times of the year deals may be readily available, but at other times you may have to hang around for days, hardly possible with a schedule to keep to, or with young children involved.

Who's for such deals? Single, young people with flexibility at both ends of the journey. But first check out the Web site *www.bargainholidays.com* for late availability of flights and holidays. For flights only try *www.A2Btravel.com* for reputable last minute deals.

Economy airlines

These have been instrumental in forcing the larger companies to increase their flexibility, helping make economy fares a normal feature of air travel. Though People's Express and Laker have disappeared, Virgin Atlantic still provides scheduled serves with and without frills. Their low price reputation may mean that they are booked up long in advance for the holiday season, though at other times you may be able just to book on the day. Though once associated with second rank travel, Gatwick and Newark rather than the more popular Heathrow and JFK, such days are gone and all the airports have been substantially upgraded in facilities and flight connections. Don't forget to try airlines that are no so well known in the UK as Atlantic carriers, such as Air India (01753 684828, El Al (0171 957 4100) or Air Kuwait (0171 412 0007) via agents such as Bridge of the World (0171 911 0900).

Consolidators

These specialist agents (once known as 'bucket shops') handle the airline companies' spare seats which are regularly available at certain times of the year to specific destinations. Discounts are up to 50 per cent, the tickets are legal and valid, and the system is supported (if somewhat surreptitiously) by the airline companies. Target 1998 price is £250 off season. Try Trailfinders (0171 937 5400), Bridge of the World (0171 911 0900), the Post Office (0171 930 1193), Flightbookers (0171 757 2000), Airline Network (01772 727757) STA Travel (0171 465 0484) or Major (0171 487 3361). Don't forget that no one can reduce the flat rate taxes that you now have to pay on top of any discounted fare.

Who could make use of them? If you are too late for APEX tickets and can't face hanging around airports for last minute deals, then consolidators may be able to help, especially for off-season travel.

See the travel sections of the Sunday papers for the wide array of companies seeking your custom, many specialising in North America. Of course if you only want to see a fleeting glimpse of at most a couple of large US cities there is one further option: as part of a grand tour deluxe.

Courier flights

This is the cheapest way to fly. Firms want packages hand delivered by the next plane and need responsible and reasonably presentable couriers. Phone at least two months before you want to travel, and be prepared to be on call until the appropriate delivery turns up. The flight might cost about £100 and you may be restricted as to how long you can stay (7 or 14 days).

BA Travel Shop	(0181) 564 7009
Courier Travel Services	(0181) 844 2626
Polo Express	(0181) 759 5383
Bridges Worldwide	(0195) 465065

Unfortunately this option seems to have become more difficult since the travel pages of most newspapers started advertising the existence of courier services.

Package tours

Virgin Holidays (01293 744261) can provide 3-day packages starting at £479. But if you have the money, specialist tours can provide more than this standard fly-drive plus motels route around the main tourist circuits. **American Adventures** (01892 511894) organise active camping tours ranging from 7 days along the west coast to 42 days across country, with exotic routes such as the Yukon and Alaska, or trail walking the Rockies. Other similar groups advertise in the YHA members' magazine and the growing array of walkers' magazines available in large newsagents. Try **Trek America** on (01869) 338777. For self-drive itineraries call **Drive America** 0645 213145, **Cosmos** (0161) 480 5799 or **Globebusters** (01444) 458611. For more upmarket packages try **Premier Holidays** (01223) 516688, **Bon Voyage** (01703) 330322, **Hamilton Travel** (0171) 344 3399 or **Travelpack** 0990 747101.

The Round the World option (RTW)

Most airlines restrict stopovers to six locations, usually flying in one direction only. Target prices are about £850. But **Air New Zealand** (0181 741 2299) allows unlimited stops, backtracking if necessary, so long as the overall mileage is below 29,000 miles. Top-up mileage rates are available. Unfortunately this £933 fare only links into Los Angeles in the USA. **Trailfinders** has a BA/Qantas RTW package for £869 plus taxes with stopovers in Singapore, Sydney and Hawaii (add £50 for a further Los Angeles stopover). Other RTW specialists include **Bridge of the World** (0171 911 0900), **Flight Bookers** (0171 757 2000), **Quest World Wide** (0181 546 6000) **Travel Bug** (0161 721 4000) and **Campus Travel** (0171 730 3402) which at 52 Grosvenor Gardens, London SW1 (near Victoria Station) also has a branch of Stanford's, a specialist travel shop with a wide variety of materials for the would-be RTW traveller. Also worth contacting are the travel club **Wexas** (0171 589 3315).

If you do want to fit the US into an around the world trip the best start may well be with Katie Wood and George MacDonald, *The Round the World Air Guide* (Fontana paperback) which provides information on all international airports, with advice on route planning, tickets, stopovers and possible hassles. Try also Frank Barrett's *A Consumer's Guide to Air Travel* (a reasonably priced Telegraph Publication paperback), or Thomas Cook's *World Travel Pass Guide*.

INFORMATION UPDATE: INFORMATION OVERLOAD

A caveat to all travel information is necessary: it is now impossible to give concise, accurate and up-to-date information on flights to North America that will not be out of date by the time the information reaches the reader. It is vital to be aware of the range of fares, carriers and packages. The details presented here are merely to suggest the complex range of fare structures that present themselves these days.

Fares change so rapidly it is essential to keep an eye on those newspapers that will bring you up to date. *The Independent*, for example, has a 'Travel Update' section in its Saturday editions, which regularly includes US information. The same paper's weekend section often deals with regions of the USA (such as the Rockies or Texas) including details on travel operators, hints for independent travel, target prices and any new regulations, taxes, *etc*. An hour spent reading back copies (in large

city or university libraries) may well pay substantial dividends in up-to-
date information. *Holiday Which?* also has similar updates, but less
frequently deals with the USA, so that relevant articles may well be out
of date on prices by the time you come across them.

It also pays to phone around these numbers:

American Airlines	0345	222111
British Airways	0345	222111
Northwest Airlines	(01293)	561000
Jetsave	(01342)	312033
Virgin Atlantic	(01293)	747747
Delta	0800	414 767 (a free call)
Continental	(01293)	776464
Trailfinders	(0171)	937 5400
United	08458	444777
Icelandic	(0171)	388 5599

WHAT ARE YOUR NEEDS?

Consider your family status: are you really willing to take the same risks
with others as you did when you were a student? Or as a student do you
really want the frills when a day or so camping out at the airport could
leave you with enough money to hitch out to the west coast? Be honest
with yourself as to your real needs, discuss it with others, and then make
a coolly reasoned decision. How critical would things be if it turned out
you had made the wrong decision!

DESTINATIONS

Most Europeans bound for the USA fly into eastern airports, though
those bound for the west coast can fly direct into Los Angeles, for an
overcrowded and unpleasant experience, or San Francisco. Travellers
from the Far East or Australasia will pass through customs and
immigration in Hawaii (an attempt to take the pressure off Los Angeles
International).

Flying 'direct'
United 08458 444777 fly 'direct' to Las Vegas. Pay your money and a 14
hour scheduled flight awaits you. But don't expect to fly straight to Las
Vegas. Rather prepare to fly to San Francisco (for immigration control)
and then fly east to Las Vegas. Direct does not equal straight through.
Flying to Las Vegas on British Airways is even more confusing as it goes
via Los Angeles where flight BA 7309 is actually not on a BA plane at all
– you have to change onto USAir. Direct to Hawaii will mean via Los

Angeles, with an enforced stopover possible. BA to Washington DC actually means BA to Kennedy Airport in New York and then on USAir's 'Eagle' (almost a crop-duster) for a spectacular low-level flight down over the Chesapeake to Dulles International Airport. 'Direct' does *not* mean Heathrow non-stop to National Airport. With children such changes can add considerably to anticipated angst. Northwestern from Manchester to Orlando actually goes via Amsterdam, an exhausting finale on the long journey home. And as UK airlines change their US partners such interchanges can only get more confusing.

UK connections
Don't forget you may have to fly first to a London airport. Some companies provide free regional airport connections, though usually not during high season. If you have to use a regional airport consider by-passing London all together. Fly to Amsterdam for KLM-North-western flights direct to Orlando rather than fly to London, then New York or Atlanta only to have to change for Orlando.

TRAVEL PROTECTION

The bonding situation is complex and potentially bewildering. Keep up to date by watching and listening to travel programmes and by reading the travel pages of the press. The most accessible explanation of the situation is given in *Holiday Which?* (available in most public libraries or by subscription from 2 Marylebone Road, London NW1 4DX) which has warned that not all scheduled flights are covered by existing bonding arrangements (though if you pay by credit card you may be able to claim against the card issuing bank). If in doubt book with an IATA airline through an IATA-appointed agent, ringing the airline to confirm that your booking has been accepted. Don't rely upon ATOL or ABTA bonding as these cover only tours or package holidays. For a free booklet on the ATOL system ring (0171) 832 6353.

Travel insurance
About a third of Brits going overseas have inadequate insurance. In the USA you need full coverage, and then some. And don't delay seeking insurance until you arrive. CDs may be cheaper in the USA, but insurance certainly isn't. And buying your insurance package in the UK means that travel insurance will be included, covering cancellation and loss of luggage, besides health and accident liability once in the USA. You will also be acquiring reasonably priced insurance as an ordinary traveller, whereas once in the US already you will have become an exotic,

and therefore risky and hence expensive, outsider.

If you feel that exam failure may force a cancellation, Campus Travel (0171 730 3402) have a cancellation clause for you. With other policies check what is and isn't covered. Death of a spouse is almost certainly covered: change of mind won't be. Older travellers may dislike increased premiums and higher excess limits. Policies vary though. Perry Gamble (0181 879 1255) age loadings only apply to those 70 and over, and then only on long-haul journeys over two weeks. Age Concern (0181 679 8000) has no age loading on long haul journeys.

It pays to shop around, particularly if you are intent on dangerous diversions. British Activity Holiday Insurance Services (01892 534411) are specialists for those intending active holidays. To include winter sports try Inter Assurance (01251 717766) or WorldCover Direct (0800 365121). Cheaper coverage is available for non-skiers without offspring through Columbus (0171 375 0011). Don't rely upon being covered by promises of 'free travel insurance' given by credit and debit card companies, though gold card customers may be offered some useful cover. And you don't have to buy the insurance package offered by the travel agent from whom you bought the fly-drive package. Insurance mark-ups are high, and you may well obtain a better deal from going to a specialist such as Endsleigh (*www.endsleigh.co.uk* for details of your nearest shop).

The recent success story of travel insurance is the annual policy, which has become increasingly competitive. Try Wexas Travel Club (0171 589 3315) for a competitive price on policies that allow any number of trips of up to three weeks a time. A year-long policy will also cover baggage and money within the UK, particularly worthwhile if you take holidays at home as well as abroad.

SINGLE PARENT FAMILY TRIPS

In the US families with only one child have traditionally had to pay adult fares, or only slight less, for the first child. If there were bulk buying on behalf of single parent families, prices would surely come down. One Parent Family Holidays (OPFH) negotiates discounts across the USA. A brochure can be obtained from OPFH at Kildonan Courtyard, Barhill, Girvan, Ayrshire KA26 0PS. Telephone (01776) 889500 between 9.30am and 5.30pm (Tuesdays to Saturdays) or (01465) 821288 evenings. Using motel accommodation in areas like Orlando, two-week holidays cost from £600 to £650 per adult, children under 12 costing £400–425 (1997 prices). A £50 supplement will still apply where only two people are sharing.

NEW YORK CITY

London to New York City must be the world's most competitive international route. All major airlines want to run scheduled services between **London-Heathrow** and **John F. Kennedy**, the major terminal on Long Island, or failing that between **London-Gatwick** and **Newark-New Jersey** (just across the Hudson River from Manhattan). Previous restrictions on which airlines used which airport have been eased recently, making guidelines for travellers that much more difficult.

Kennedy Airport is easier to navigate these days as immigration, baggage reclaim and customs have been modernised. Changing money and getting into town are easy: 24 hour banking and Carey Coaches into Manhattan. Beware of unlicensed (and hence uninsured) cabs. On returning for a UK-bound flight don't expect much of small, disappointing duty-free shops, quite unlike Heathrow.

Things should improve for the Millennium as the operators of Amsterdam's Schipol Airport, one of the world's finest, have recently taken over the running of JFK and the first new terminal for 27 years has just opened with the east coast's largest duty-free shop, a spa and a microbrewery! It has fully automated security systems that can detect explosives, screen baggage and match passengers to their luggage by computer.

Fare structures are complicated and confusing, but (March 1995) range from £180 midwinter Gatwick to Boston via a consolidator such as **Flight Bookers**, Tel: (0171) 387 9100, to over £3,000 on Concorde. If you have time to wait around some airlines offer standby tickets to fill seats left empty at the last minute, but check out the current situation before setting off! For those with schedules planned well in advance there are APEX returns round about £500 (with low season and midweek special offers to those who enquire).

Specialist travel agencies worth contacting include:

Airline Ticket Network	0800 727747
Trailfinders	(0171) 937 5400
United Vacations	(0171) 313 0999

But still the best way to keep abreast of new deals is to see the weekend newspapers.

Gatwick (very accessible via Victoria Station, through-trains from the Midlands and North via Kensington-Olympia, or the M25) may be a better source of cheap fares than Heathrow. Don't forget regional airports such as **Manchester**, **Glasgow** and now **Birmingham**.

Weekend breaks

- Virgin Atlantic – (01293) 747747 – periodically offers a package of return flight, two or three nights' hotel accommodation plus a ticket for a Broadway show at eye-catching prices. Other firms offer similar packages from time to time. Try **Time Off** (0345 336622) or **Travelscene** (0181 427 4445).

- For return flights and accommodation in a three star hotel, try **Crystal** (0181 241 5040).

- BA's Concorde trips to New York are not for the frugally minded, but worth considering for a special occasion.

- A useful Web site is provided by the city's tourist board (*www.nycvisit.com*).

WASHINGTON DC AND BALTIMORE MD

BA flies direct in Dulles International Airport, which though in northern Virginia is only twenty miles by purpose-built expressway from the White House and Interstate 95, the major north-south motorway along the east coast. Fly-drive packages are available from about £450 for two weeks unlimited mileage, with pre-paid accommodation vouchers from about £40 a night available from most agencies.

Beware: you may well need to book ahead for motel accommodation in the DC area due to the number of American visitors to the national capital area.

The alternative is to fly into Baltimore-Washington International which lies on the freeway linking Baltimore Maryland and Washington DC. It is actually very little further from central DC than is Dulles, and for those visitors for the capital's northern (that is Maryland) suburbs a deal more convenient.

SOME OTHER GATEWAY CITIES

- **Atlanta**. Delta flies from Manchester and Gatwick to Atlanta connecting to Nashville and much of the south east. Atlanta is a major travel hub for road and rail connections onward.

- **Boston**. Virgin Atlantic, BA, American and Northwestern all have direct flights from the UK to this city that is considerably nearer Europe than even New York. Take the subway into the city centre from this conveniently off-shore airport, or try the $9 water shuttle if only for the view.

- **Chicago** is the great hub of the interior Great Lakes area. Try American Airlines.

- **Dallas** is served by BA, for links to much of the Great Plains and the Rockies, particularly ski resorts such as Aspen.

- **Los Angeles** has the famously overcrowded LEX to which you can fly directly over the Pole avoiding the even longer flight to the east coast and across the continent. If you come via Asia or Australia you may find you go through Customs and Immigration in Hawaii, relieving the pressure on LEX.

- **Miami and Orlando** are increasingly major entry points for Europeans and South Americans, though Miami is a day's long drive from Disneyworld.

FLY-DRIVE PACKAGE OR INDEPENDENT TRAVEL?

The easiest and cheapest way to explore the Rockies would be to fly to Denver, then tour by a hired car waiting for you at the airport. Such a fly-drive package costs about £500 per person if two travel together. But the Denver APEX flight on Continental can be as high as £697 (though as low as £465 via a consolidator, and there's still the car-hire to arrange). Fly-drive packages often make pre-paid motel vouchers available, further enhancing the package option.

TIPS FOR THE JOURNEY

If you've never flown before here are a few essential points to bear in mind:

- It's the safest way to travel (and possibly the most boring).

- Drink only water, juices and soft drinks. Flying such long distances produces dehydration, which alcohol only makes worse. So save the free little bottles of wine and spirits for later – in some motel late at night when you've just pulled off the freeway you'll really enjoy a well-earned shot of your favourite tipple.

- If you order vegetarian meals say so (with seat number) as soon as you board the plane, or take your own food.

- The number of airlines permitting smoking over the Atlantic is declining rapidly as US law forbids smoking on domestic flights. If you disregard the ban you can be refused a return flight. As with on board disturbances, carriers can land and charge the extra landing fees to the offender. Don't be tempted to smoke extra cigarettes before boarding to compensate for a nicotine-free flight – the drop in nicotine levels will be that more intense and the withdrawal symptoms worse.

Getting to the airport
The flight will be stressful enough. Go easy on getting to the airport. Major motorway black-spots such as the M4/M25 near the Heathrow airport access road and the M6 southbound through the West Midlands should be avoided if possible. Birmingham, Manchester and Heathrow now all have purpose-built mainline railway connections. The newly opened Paddington to Heathrow service runs four times per hour and costs £10 each way, though for passengers coming from the North it may still be quicker to take the airport bus or the underground.

Immigration control
Have your passport ready on the plane (not in your luggage in the hold) for filling in the various official US forms. The immigration form asks for your address (a relic of the view that new arrivals are coming to settle down rather than to travel around as tourists). Give a friend's address, or a motel address (make one up if necessary, for example the Holiday Inn, Orlando, Florida).

After the immigration official has checked your form it'll be stapled into your passport above your visa. Keep it like that until you are leaving (when an airline representative will take it and return it to the authorities).

Customs
There may not always be a red/green choice, so every arrival may meet an officer face to face. Keep your passport ready – if only because customs officials seem less understanding for returning US citizens. Be prepared to open *all* your cases as they check for drugs, weapons and fruit.

You may be required to identify your baggage immediately you clear immigration, but it may then disappear for collection elsewhere. Presumably dogs and X-ray equipment have access to the baggage. The process is particularly evident in large airports, and those with substantial links with Latin America (such as Orlando International Airport next to Disneyworld).

Insurance: property and health

It is necessary to buy cover before leaving the UK. It is unlikely to be available in the USA (until you become resident, but that's another matter). Check with your credit or charge card company as to whether or not 'free' cover is available for those using their card for booking the flight and accommodation. If you have an 'all risks' household insurance package you may already have 60 days' world-wide cover. Check your policy's small print, and double-check with the agent (and even they may have to check with authorities higher up). Beware of the amount you have to pay before the insurer pays up (the 'excess'). You may need further cover for portable computer equipment or musical instruments (try Lambert Fenchurch on (0171) 560 3398 for such specialist quotations). For the USA you do need $2 million worth of health cover. Will the policy fly you home if you are seriously injured? Will it fly your relatives out if you are too ill to move? Over 65 years old? Expect double premiums. What's the cancellation/curtailment cover for your trip of a lifetime? Are certain activities such as white water rafting excluded? Can they be included? If you intend to visit the USA frequently consider yearly cover rather than per trip. It may well be cheaper to obtain single cover for health and baggage. Quiz your agent.

Returning home

Always phone to confirm your return flight at least a couple of days beforehand. Schedules may be changed for all sorts of reasons – air-traffic controllers elsewhere may be on strike, or bad weather may have trapped planes half a world way. Check in in good time, especially if you have lots of luggage and a family. Early check-in is available for Virgin flights out of Orlando at Disneyworld itself. Just get to the airport in time for the final flight call later that day. Getting on board in a relaxed frame of mind is always a good idea, especially when planes are likely to be full. Families will want to sit together, and a good seat for the film may save a lot of on-board aggravation from disgruntled offspring for the shattered father or harassed mother. And remember: you can only bring £136 worth of goods back into the UK per adult before VAT and duty become payable.

Luggage claims

Insure your baggage, but keep hold of it at airports. Thefts at New York's JFK continue to increase, mainly when travellers accept assistance only to see their bags take off. Heavy suitcases may be safe on baggage trolleys, but holdalls have been known to be snatched, particularly at kiosks. At Heathrow solo parents and pregnant women can now call for a porter, free of charge, via a Help Point in car parks, terminals and baggage reclaim halls. British trolleys remain free. At many US airports (such as Dulles) you need US coins or low denomination bills (save these from a previous visit). Kennedy and Newark airports have introduced self-service luggage carts available free of charge at international arrival terminals.

Being 'Bumped'

Scheduled flights are regularly overbooked by 15 per cent to take account of those who don't turn up ('no shows'). Computers predict no show levels, but can get it wrong. Then airlines ask for volunteers to take a later flight (plus £240 compensation if your long-haul flight started in the European Union). If you don't reconfirm your flight you may not get on your flight if it is overbooked, especially if you arrive last. Reconfirm and arrive in good time.

Jet lag

Tired? Nauseous? Just flown across more than four time zones? Feelings of disorientation are not just due to sleep deprivation, or even the thin air (less pressure inside trans-Atlantic crossings is about the same as being at 8,000 feet) but may well have something to do with melatonin, a hormone produced by the brain to set the body clock. Whether synthetic melatonin, available from health food shops and pharmacies in the USA, can eliminate jet lag is still debated. But what is generally agreed is that long journeys should start with a good night's sleep (how many of us stay up late packing only to get up very early to reach the airport just in time thinking we'll catch up on our sleep on the plane!). If you can afford to stay at a hotel near the airport so much the better.

But what else can be done on the journey?

- Reset your watch to the time at the point of arrival on take off.

- Sleep with eyeshades.

- Use earplugs to minimise the effect of pressure changes. Boots sell an upmarket version with a ceramic filter to allow air to seep in while protecting the inner ear.

- Eat lightly.

- Drink plenty of water before and during the flight.

- Avoid excessive alcohol.

- Get a good night's sleep on arrival. This can be difficult if welcoming hosts insist on celebrating your arrival, but from my experience this is the most effective part of any strategy.

If you are going just for a weekend break you can either stay on UK time, getting up and going to bed early even by American standards, or go straight to US time catching up on your sleep once back home – easier on those returning on a morning flight rather than the traditional overnight 'red eye'.

You may have had a big party before coming back home, but don't turn up at the check-in inebriated, or you might be refused a seat. The UK Civil Aviation Authority can seek fines of up to £5,000 or even two years in prison for abusive in-flight behaviour, and airlines would rather avoid problems by leaving people behind.

Check-in

Most flights to North America involve very early starts. Many passengers find it easier to stay overnight at an airport hotel. Ask your agent if they have any special deals available (which may include free parking while you are away). If possible check-in your luggage the night before. American Airlines (0345 222111) have a 'moonlight check-in' facility 6.00 pm–10.00 pm for passengers flying next day to the USA.

SUMMARY

- Going to the USA is now far easier than for previous generations but paradoxically the very large numbers of ways of getting to the USA, particularly the ever growing number of flights, fly-drive packages and all-in holidays means that any prospective visitor can suffer from information overload.

- This chapter has suggested some of the main ways of travelling to the USA, but which is best can still be difficult to work out. Try coming at the choice from two different directions: what's affordable and what's the realistically minimal convenience needed. If you have these two sorted out, most options fade away to leave a considerably smaller field from which to choose.

- Don't overestimate what you can do as you get older, or with children, or with changing financial circumstances. It is all too easy to become locked into a way of approaching travel that reflects previous, perhaps fitter, single or more flexible days.

- And equally don't underestimate the cost of moving around the USA once you get there. The image remains of cheap travel whether by bus, car or plane. Per mile it may be cheap, but those miles just go on adding up. Take every advantage possible of cheap deals negotiated *before* leaving the UK, whether bus passes, multiple stop-over plane trips, or merely a good deal on car hire through a transatlantic airline.

AMERICA AT THE CLICK OF A MOUSE

When this book was in its infancy there were hardly any books for US-bound travellers, with the sole exception of the BUNAC student guide. Now even the smallest bookshop in the most unfashionable town has both a travel section and at the very least a shelf of guides, not just to the USA but to specific areas and even individual cities. But just as the guidebooks seem to have cornered the market in providing advice everything may be about to change.

Browsing the Web

Today there is the Internet, or as it is more popularly though not quite correctly called, the Web. Not only have guidebook publishers started to provide information via the Web, so has almost everyone else. Summer camps, transit authorities, the US Immigration and Naturalization Service, motel chains, B & Bs, states, unions, chambers of commerce, all have their Web pages. And better still, there are ways of finding their Web addresses that don't require you to already have the very information you are actually looking for, as happens all too frequently when using printed sources like directories.

Go to a Web browser ('**search engine**') and type in a phrase such as 'US rental accommodation' and you will find that a whole page of people offering accommodation may appear. Scrolling down, it may immediately become apparent that there are just too many people listed, so you have to learn how to give the browser enough but not too much detail. And then you'll realise you are in the wrong category as everyone seems to be offering unfurnished apartments and houses for long-term rent.

If you want holidays lettings in Virginia near the beach try 'vacation rental accommodation Virginia' and only those interested in holiday lets will be displayed. Beware: if you type in 'holiday rentals' you will only find details of rental arrangements for US public holidays such as 4 July. Two weeks off in August is a vacation, not a holiday. You need to adjust to local usage quickly!

But with each refinement the search narrows. Indeed many pages start with a nationwide map, where you just click the state you are interested in, and so on downwards. Sometimes your search will end with a particularly property with associated directions and a map. If you were looking for Bed & Breakfasts you might well end up looking at photographs of the resident owners.

Getting the details

This ability to obtain great detail can be very useful. If you want to stay at motels while in the Washington DC area, type in the name of a motel chain. You will be offered a list of states, or perhaps a US map. With a few further clicks you can be looking at an array of motels in the District of Columbia area, each with their own street map and directions off the interstate, with details about reaching the main tourist sites. Without a single phone call you can find that there is indeed an Econolodge within easy reach of Mount Vernon (George Washington's home) and that there is also a Travelodge on Columbia Pike along which buses bound for the nearest Metro station pass every few minutes, for those visitors wanting an easy access to the downtown sites without having to worry about downtown parking. Some sites may even have photographs of the accommodation, and each motel will be listed with its own map which you can download and take with you, a great help if you travel using merely a highways map where urban detail is only provided for a few downtown blocks around the downtown.

Making enquiries

Many Web sites, such as those for B & B, will come with not just a traditional address, but also an e-mail address. Send off an enquiry, and when you log onto your mail the next morning there may well be several replies already. It's a lot quicker than the postal service, and you don't have to have a fax machine for an instantaneous connection. If you do send a fax (and most desktop computers with Microsoft Windows of whatever version usually have a basic fax facility) don't forget to leave your machine on overnight for the reply (unless you gave the recipient the number of a dedicated fax machine or one of the new generation of external modems that can take messages even while the PC is itself switched off). You may not read what you had hoped: all the places you can afford may well be full when you want to stay. But at least you know now and not in two weeks' time, and can quickly act accordingly.

Becoming your own travel agent

What the Web now allows the PC owner to do is to compile detailed information beyond the capabilities of even the most specialist travel agent. You can become your own travel agent and book not just your stateside accommodation but also your translantic flight, car rental and insurance. If in doubt where to start, go to *www.yahoo.co.uk* and click the 'Recreation and Sport' category. Then do the same for 'Travel', refining your search until you type in an airline name. Yahoo will then find the correct address for that company, and away you go. But others may have done this already, as on *www.4airlines.com/* where you can find live connections to more US and foreign airlines than you have ever heard of. For a comprehensive cyber travel agent try *www.flifo.com/*

where all manner of services can be ordered there and then. With Flifo, you can book flights, look up US domestic and international flights, secure a fare, look up information about hotels, and rent a car. You can even check if a US flight is on time.

You can still enquire via the Web and book through travel agents, but you may well feel by now that that it is bit too much like having a dog and barking yourself. Of course, an agent can still be useful if local as they can provide tickets almost immediately, but late arrangements can usually be made to collect tickets at airline desks at the point of departure. Airlines increasingly recognise the need to do business direct with the customer. That way they won't have to pay agents' fees for your business.

But beware: if you are trying to find information about services, such as flights or insurance, you are buying over here, make sure you are using a 'UK and Ireland' specific search engine. Yahoo will often default back to its US parent unless you make sure you hit the 'UK and Ireland' button before a search. When seeking US contacts you can, of course, go straight to the US version of Yahoo and its rivals, (of which my favourite remains *dogpile.com*.).

Making payments

It is possible to e-mail credit card numbers, though you might reasonably feel less than enthusiastic about this. Who knows where the numbers might end up? But money can be wired from banks. Money orders can be sent. Of course, for UK services you just put a cheque in the post. And though Web access is not for free (besides the PC you have to have a modem, the right software, and an account with an Internet Service Supplier), once you have the technology in place an e-mail to America costs the same as one to your neighbour, and an hour or so downloading Web pages shouldn't cost more than a pound or so if done outside peak hours, particularly if you have a 56k modem, the fastest available in the high street and the standard modem in new PCs. And once abroad you can seek out local cybercafés where you can access further Web information.

Useful Web sites

Before you leave:

Airports   http://www.hotelstravel.com/airports.html
Airlines   http://www.princeton.edu (click on weather,
                        travel, air travel)

American Airlines	http://www,americanair.com
British Airways	http://www.british-airways.com
Continental Airlines	http://www.flycontinental.com
Delta Airlines	http://www.delta-air.com
TWA	http://www.twa.com
United Airlines	http://www.ual.com
Virgin Atlantic	http://www.fly.virgin.com
Health advice	http://www.swiftcall.co.uk/medical
Travel health	http://www.cdc.gov/travel/travelmap.html
Distance calculator	http://www.indo.com/distance
Online maps	http://www.uniglobe-gem.com
Embassies	http://www.worldculture.com/
Embassies	http://www.embpage.org/
General tourism	http://www.thebiz.co.uk

Accommodation in the USA and across the world

http://www.accomodata.co.uk

http://www.gdserve.com.80/hps/bb/index.html

http://www.greathotels.com

http://www.hotelnet.co.uk (Internet hotel finder)

http://www.travelweb.com (online reservations)

http://www.oitc.com/Disney (Disney reservations)

http://www.doubletreehotels.com

http://www.fshr.com (Four Seasons and Regency Hotels)

http://www.holiday-inn.com (Holiday Inn)

http://www.radisson.com (Radisson Hotels world-wide)

http://www.westin.com (Westin Hotels and Resorts)

http://www.holiday-rentals.co.uk (cottages to castles)

http://cyberrentals.com/homepage.html (US rentals)

http://10kvacationrentals.com/ (more US rentals)

Youth hostels	http://www.taponline.com/tap/travel/hostels/pages/facts.htm
	http://www.yha-england-wales.org.uk:80/docs/world.html
	http://bgislesvisitorsb.com

Getting to the airport	http://www.travelcity.com
	http://www.ukonline.co/uk/ukonline/travel
	http://www.rail.co.uk/
	http://www.railtrack.co/uk/travel/
	http://www.nationalexpress.co.uk/
	http://www.herb.algonet.se:80/~sirius/anders travel/htm
	http://www.cpoint.co.uk/tw/uk/rail.html (London tube)
Home exchange	http://www.homexchange.com/index.html
Federal Express	http://www.fedex.com
Travel books	http://www.gorp.com/
	http://www.excite.com.reviews.regional/travel
Travel guide	http://www.cnn.com/travel
Travel magazine	http://www.traveler.net/

Any listing is out of date the moment printed, Web addresses frustratingly so. A quarter of the above are probably defunct by the time you read this, but the listing does suggest the range of materials that a good Web browser will find.

6
Travelling About

WHY TRAVEL?

The USA is continental in scale. Not to experience this is to miss an essential ingredient of the country (almost like Americans visiting Europe and seeing nothing of its historical traditions). *But*, being so vast, the distances can eat up much of your precious time, whether you are a visitor or a resident. Hence the attraction of flying.

Do not try to see too much, especially in your first trip. Vary your schedule so that though some days may involve 400 miles of freeway, others will involve taking detours to visit historical sights (Civil War battlefields or colonial settlements are excellent, and usually inexpensive). Driving the country roads can be very interesting and a great change of pace. Driving from Atlanta to Washington DC? Try US15 across Virginia, or even the Blue Ridge Parkway, both of which run parallel to major freeways.

Don't expect to visit four national parks in four days. Even if you can manage the driving you will probably get scenic overload (as in 'Oh no! Not more mountains' felt towards the end of six weeks' criss-crossing of the Rocky Mountains). Would you want to 'do' Snowdonia in one day, the Lake District the next, and then the Highlands before Edinburgh *en route* for London-Heathrow?

A useful video is now available:

- New York and the Poconos from Travel Television of Hindhead, Surrey. Tel: (01428) 607213. Besides being a guide to a specific tourist area it provides advice on all aspects of being a traveller in the USA.

TRAVELLING BY CAR

For anything but a coach tour a car really is essential for everyone visiting the USA. Even a one-resort holiday can be greatly improved by a few days visiting nearby sights, theme parks, or just experiencing the open road.

The USA is larger, and the distances between cities greater, so the time needed to explore is that much greater than in the UK. Costs per mile are low compared to Europe, but the distances so great the overall costs can still be quite a surprise. There *are* positive aspects though:

- Local car hire is very reasonably priced.

- Petrol is very cheap by European standards.

- Motoring means wide roads and lots of places to park.

- For most of the freeway network driving is actually relaxing due to the legal 65/70 mph speed limits. (Around cities, though, freeways are like bad sections of the M1.)

So a holiday based, for instance, near central Florida's Disneyworld can be both wide-ranging (Florida Keys to the south, Fort Augustine in the northeast, and Panama City to the northwest) *and* very reasonably priced, especially if car hire is booked as part of the flight and accommodation package, or just pre-booked from the UK. Such special rates usually involve collecting and returning the car from the same airport, and may require you to stay within the one state (which may be larger than the UK!).

- A useful overview is provided in *Driving in the USA* from Columbus Press, 28 Charles Square, London N1 6HT. Tel: (0171) 417 0700.

- A video is also available: *Driving in the USA* from Travel Television Ltd, of Hindhead, Surrey. Tel: (01428) 607213. £12.45 including postage and packing.

- For general information contact:
  The American Automobile Association (AAA)
  8111 Gateway Road
  Falls Church, Virginia 22047
  Tel: 001 703 222 6000.
  http://www.aaamidatlantic.com/

The 'Triple A' publish a useful *Handicapped Driver's Mobility Guide*.

CAR HIRE (US = rental)

A few numbers to try in the UK before booking:

- Alamo: 0800 272200
- Avis: (0181) 848 8733
- Budget: 0800 181181
- Thrifty: (01494) 442110
- Hertz: (0181) 679 1799
- Dollar 0800 252897

One of the best sources for rental information is Breezenet's Guide to Airport Rental Cars (at *www.brim.com*) where for each US city best deals are listed, with online booking instructions.

Questions to ask

What's the **collision damage waiver** (CDW) and the **passenger accident insurance** (PAI) situation? US booking clerks will assume you know what these terms (or even initials) mean, and may never have had to explain them before. Ensure that *you* know what they mean!

Without CDW you are liable for collision damage (up to something like $3,000). For peace of mind CDW is probably essential, though costly (an extra that can be up to 30 per cent on top of the quoted or pre-paid costs).

PAI is more modest, but may be unnecessary if you have already bought adequate health insurance for your trip before leaving the UK. Check your policy's small print for whether you need extra PAI. Don't rely on advice from the sales clerks: they won't know.

Remember: your UK car insurance will not cover your trip to the USA so you will need a complete coverage. US clerks are used to dealing with American customers who already have their car rental insurance needs covered by their domestic policies. And complete insurance is expensive if bought in the USA: buy it at home.

Don't rely on the £3 million cover in your general travel insurance – its personal liability section covers everything except driving. So in case you are sued by a third party (someone you hit) you do need extra cover. And don't think the free travel insurance you got by paying with a credit card will give you third party cover – it doesn't.

- Is the car hire restricted to the one state? What about a trip from a Florida base over into Georgia? Is this permitted? Is suitable insurance cover available? At what extra cost?

- Can the booking be done via the airline company at the time you buy the airline tickets?

- What's the minimum age for hiring or driving a hired car? Premiums may be required for under-25 drivers. Under 21 is usually prohibited.

- What size of car would be suitable? A family driving any distance (Miami to Orlando is a 6-hour drive on the freeways!) should avoid sub-compacts (Metro equivalents) and go for at least a mid-range 4- or 5-door saloon (or at least a Ford Tempo) which will have adequate luggage space, a good air conditioning unit, and plenty of inside room. Travelling 55–65 mph on the US highways may be smooth, but it may also be very boring, so comfort, room to stretch, and a suitably powered engine (less noisy if nothing else) are essential.

Remember: Travelling just around Florida is like travelling up and down the length of Britain in terms of distances. Travelling around the USA is *continental* travel. Would you drive the family from London to Athens in a Fiat Uno or a VW Beetle? If you can, fly. If not, use as large a car as you can afford.

- Can a trip **start** and **end** at **different** places? If so what are the drop-off charges? These can be very steep: sometimes equal to the initial hire charge. But having driven from Miami to New York City who wants to drive back down I95 to avoid a couple of hundred dollars drop-off charge? It may be worth paying the charge to be able to stay and enjoy New York City rather than to end a family holiday with four days driving flat-out on the freeway (plus motel charges that would probably equal the drop-off charge alone).

- Can **all payments** (except petrol of course) be made **before leaving** for the USA? Or will there be extras, such as state tax or deposits on the vehicle? Taking a 'fly-drive' package from a major UK or US airline may mean low or no deposit, minimum hassle, and priority booking (at an advantageous price). Will there be a fuel charge? This may involve an additional service charge but means no need to refuel before returning the car.

- If your **credit card** is used for ID (identification) will it also be used to **block-off** a line of credit as a **deposit**? This question needs some explaining. Even though you may have pre-paid for your care hire (perhaps as part of a 'fly-drive' package) most hire companies will still require Mastercard, VISA or American Express as ID.

    So far so good. But beware: they may well use your card to block-off a credit line of several hundred dollars as a deposit. This is not a credit from your account into theirs, to be recredited upon your returning the car intact. Rather it is blocking off a part of your unused credit line.

    For instance, if you have £1,500 as your limit with £500 of outstanding debt, then you have a credit line of £1,000 left. If the car hire company were then to block off £200 for the duration of your hiring their car you would only have £800, not the £1,000 you might have thought you still had.

This only becomes a problem if you have only, say, £200 left of your credit line (surely enough for an occasional extra on a pre-paid holiday given all the travellers' cheques you are carrying). All your £200 may well be blocked off, without your being made aware of this. Upon arriving at a motel cash desk you present your card, only to have the central computer in New York say that you have no credit left, not even the £200 you expected. At the end of a three-week stay you may well have spent more than you expected, relying upon that £200 for the last couple of days.

Such inconvenience might even continue after you have returned the car intact – it takes time to unblock a blocked line of credit.

Ask exactly how much of a credit line is being blocked, and if possible, before leaving home pay off as much of the credit card debt as you can to enlarge your line of credit. And do this in enough time for the central computer to have the new state of your account before you use your card in the USA.

For summer 1998 hire firms quoted £100–200 per week for even the smallest car (including CDW) plus tax and personal accident insurance per day. Budget on $10–15 per day for petrol on long distance trips.

Rentals: any alternatives?

- **Part holiday hire.** Here you pick up your car only when you intend to travel away from your arrival area. If staying a week at Disneyworld-Epcot before touring it might be worth your while to take a bus or taxi from the airport on your arrival, picking up the car only when you actually need it a week later. You'll hardly need a car at the self-sufficient Disney complex.

  Similarly if you intend to spend a final week in central New York City it might be wise to return ('check in') the hired car as soon as you arrive (after perhaps a circuit of the main highway and bridges), travelling by subway or even by taxi to avoid car parking costs (astronomical). *But*, if you want to explore central Florida or New York's Long Island keeping the car will be essential. Don't rely upon being able to borrow friends' cars – they'll probably need them just to function normally.

- **Delivery driving.** Drive a car for someone flying long distances. Specialist companies, listed in *Yellow Pages*, will link you up with people seeking to avoid long-distance driving. Be prepared to be fingerprinted, photographed and charged a $250 deposit that will be returned when the car is produced safe and on time. The general route will be set out for you, with 300 to 400 miles per day expected. In

Miami cars may well be available for New York City using I95, with small detours allowed for accommodation. For a couple with luggage this can be a godsend.

An Aussie leaving Norfolk, Virginia, bound for Sydney by way of Los Angeles got to drive a rock-star's British registered Daimler right across country, complete with peaked cap for driver. His wife rode behind in style!

- **Motor homes.** These huge motorised caravans (also called **campers** or **RVs/recreational vehicles)** give plenty of space for a family of four, though are probably no cheaper than a car plus motel accommodation unless pre-booked as part of a bargain package. All mod-cons are standard – toilet, shower, mains-voltage generator and hook-up facilities for organised stopping sites.

  Unlike cars they usually have to be returned to the place of hire (no one-way rentals), and they only give about 10 mpg. But they can allow you to explore the main highway: US parks are plentiful, well kept and often have hook-up facilities, though parks such as Yosemite in California are now so popular entry has to be pre-booked very early in the year for school holiday periods.

  More importantly, staying in such parks allows you to meet ordinary middle-Americans (the famous 'Silent Majority') in fairly relaxed surroundings. Unlike the situation in impersonal motels people do mix in park camp sites, children soon find playmates, and barbecues sound to the music of the banjo and guitar. Officially alcohol is usually banned, but if no one gets silly beer (and ice!) usually appear from the huge coolers people take with them everywhere.

- **Borrowing from family or friends.** This is not usually a good idea, unless as part of a house swap. The easiest way to outstay your welcome is to have your host's car when their work, shopping and kids' routines all depend upon them having two cars. Having said that, though, Americans are amazingly generous with offering the use of their cars, albeit the second one. However, it's probably only a good idea for an odd day here and there.

  If you need one every day you should hire one, or re-think your visit to concentrate upon those attractions with easy car-less access, as with the museums of central Washington DC, well served by the new Metro (but even so only from certain suburbs).

TAKING THE CAR TO THE USA

In a word: DON'T. At least don't unless it is an exceptional, rare or vintage (low octane) vehicle. The shipping costs are only the start:

- If you normally use 4 star (96-8 octane) you can't buy it in the USA (US 'premium' grade is about 93 octane). Even if you have a 2 or 3 star car the use of 'premium' is expensive (by US standards).

- If you are staying more than temporarily you will have to meet very strict federal emission regulations (or worse, California's even stricter rules). The only exceptions are for pre-1956 cars (almost vintage in US terms!) for which no modifications are required or for pre-1966 cars for which only minor modifications to the crankcase are needed.

- Horror stories abound of cars failing to meet US standards being destroyed at the port of entry.

Words of warning:
- Even importing US-specification cars will require at least a new catalytic converter if the car has used leaded petrol in Europe.

- Though a European-bought car may get into the USA, such a private import will have no US warranty, which can make repairs expensive.

As a general rule buying or hiring a car is going to be a better bet, cheaper and more convenient. If you still want to ship your car (or motorbike) call a specialist firm such as Excess Baggage Company on (0181) 965 3344. Don't forget: if you need to ask the cost you can't afford it. Still want to know what it costs? Cunard charge £1,775 for cars not over 5,500lbs (plus £65 port tax plus an unspecified steam cleaning of the underside charge). And you cannot leave any baggage in the car.

BUYING A CAR IN THE USA

This may be a very good idea if you are staying for any length of time. Foreign cars have swamped the market, are available at good prices, and spares are readily available. For Europeans such smaller cars are probably easier to handle, especially around town. The only snag may be some residual anti-foreigner feeling, though unless you are going to do business with a US car company or supplier, such feelings are unlikely to affect you. In fact as Americans become more used to foreign cars it is quite likely that names such as Nissan will become as 'American' as Volkswagen!

British volume cars are not available in the USA, but Range Rovers,

Jaguars and Rolls-Royces are, and driving one of these will stimulate much favourable admiration. If you are using your Britishness as a selling point driving a British car may be a positive advantage. Patriotic Americans expect others to be equally patriotic. And a £56,000 Jaguar XK8 convertible only costs £42,000 in many US states (final prices reflect local taxes).

What's good value for money?

- **Air conditioning** may seem like a luxury to those who think 21°C (70°F) is a heat wave. But in a hot and muggy 33°C (90°F), air conditioning can make the difference between being able to carry on or not.

> **Beware:** Relying on moving the heat control from hot to cold will not do the job. All that happens is that hot outside air will be blown through the car without being first further heated by the engine.

There are a few snags with air conditioning:
1. It can easily put a mile per gallon onto your fuel consumption, but at US prices this is hardly worth considering (power-steering also adds a further loss).
2. In under-powered cars such as the old Ford Tempo, putting on the air conditioning produced a noticeable loss of power. By the 1990s this problem seemed to be overcome though.
3. Again, in under-powered cars the radiator may boil if the air conditioning is left on while taking the car up long mountain passes. Overloading an under-powered car to go uphill is never a good idea.

- **Size** should not be despised. Though the days of the 'gas-guzzler' may well be over, US cars are still by and large bigger than their UK equivalents. If you intend to go across country, especially with family, you will all welcome the space. If you drive a Mondeo in Britain do you really want to drive the equivalent of London to St Petersburg in something no larger than a Metro?

  On holiday you may find that it is worthwhile to get a larger car than usual. After all, do you normally spend most of the day in the car with most of the family? A trip over to Salt Lake City from Atlanta is not a dash down the M1 to see family in Nottingham.

- **Cruise controls** are only recently becoming available in Europe. Put simply, the control is pre-set to a particular speed, say the legal 65 mph maximum. You press the button, and that's the speed you keep to up hill and down dale, come what may. To pass you can still accelerate. Braking, or moving into a lower gear, will cancel the control, to be resumed at the touch of a button.

So why bother?

1. It does wonders for your mpg on long trips.
2. It avoids the problem familiar to long-distance drivers of gradually speeding up as the miles pass by, leading to a speeding ticket. And this does happen!
3. It makes long, smooth freeway drives less tiring, especially out west.

Buying new

Good news: As with most consumer goods cars in the USA are generally cheaper than abroad. The vastness and wealth of the market mean the economies of scale can be enacted for basic features, and a wide variety of options can be available.

Bad news: The US 'sticker price' is even more misleading than in the UK. The price that caught your eye may be for the most basic model. The car actually available in the showroom already comes equipped with 'optional' extras, and these mount up. This practice is taking quite a hammering from the Japanese whose cars tend to be fully equipped as standard. *Always* check item by item that what you see is actually included in the asking price, even for foreign cars, then 'dicker' (haggle).

Buying second-hand

Many bargains can be obtained in the USA as a result of the far more widespread desire to have the newest model, come what may. *But* beware:

- Americans by and large maintain their cars far less well than comparable Europeans (ignore that well-cared-for look).

- Used-car warranties are usually for about a month, and compared to Europe almost worthless, even when from reputable dealers.

- The statutory protection now available in the UK is not generally available in the USA.

- Cars in the snowbelt can suffer from killer corrosion due to the vast amounts of salt put down on the roads.
  (*Good news:* Where there is no snow, like southern California, corrosion can be negligible.)

- Spares may be hard to come by for certain foreign cars, impossible in certain areas. Though Jaguar parts may be easy to obtain in New York City, in Manhattan, Kansas, they may be next to impossible (and so have to be sent from New York City!).

- In certain states sales tax is payable on private sales. So if you buy a second-hand car from a colleague for $5,000 you will have to pay $250 tax (if the rate is 5 per cent). Don't think you can conveniently 'forget' to pay this: when you go to re-register the car you'll be asked for the receipt and the 5 per cent will be required there and then.

- The AAA 'New Car Service' is available for *all* car purchases for AAA members.

- *Guide to Used Cars*, Consumers Union of USA, Inc, 110 East 42nd St, New York, NY 10017, identifies models with poor reliability or repair records.

REPAIRS AND MAINTENANCE

Getting your car serviced can be very expensive. As elsewhere many businesses in this field are run by 'cowboys'. To avoid this trap many people resort to using the authorised dealer, though their rates may be so high as to force you back to the 'cowboys'. As a student I tried to keep my VW Beetle on the road using the local VW dealer, but eventually had to resort to the local cut-price cowboys just to be able to pay the bills (and going overdrawn on a US account simply produces cheques that bounce).

A tune up is often the only maintenance that US cars ever get, not counting the car wash. Tune-up chains will, in theory, check the points and the timing, changing the oil and the plugs for you. But as these chains make their money by rapid turnover and the use of cheap and therefore unskilled labour, you may get better value for money learning to do these jobs yourself, or even getting the neighbour's car-mad teenager to do them for you. Otherwise it's just a case of asking friends and colleagues for their recommendations, and once you have found someone reliable, stick to them. Regular customers generally get the more reliable service. The AAA can provide a list of approved auto-repair facilities in any particular area (for members).

If you are just visiting the USA, car hire will take most of the strain. If the fanbelt breaks on the freeway a reputable company will come and collect you (and allow extra time at the end of the hire period to make up for lost time).

PETROL

Petrol is very cheap compared to Europe. Prices are those last seen at home over 10 years ago. Though many economists think US prices are too low, given higher world prices, for the visitor this is wonderful.

Unless you drive at 90 mph over hundreds of miles daily, your fuel bill will be the least of your worries. Credit cards, cash and usually dollar travellers' cheques (such as Bank America's VISA cheques) are all readily acceptable.

Most gas stations are now self-service. The days of the personal service are generally over, though facilities are still usually good. But you need to turn the pump on when you've taken the nozzle out of the cradle, unlike in the UK. Most gas stations are more than that (as is becoming the case in the UK). In certain states, such as Virginia, gas stations even sell beer and wine.

Petrol is **regular** or **super**, approximately 2 or 3 star and lead free. Follow your car hire recommendations.

A word of caution: most interstate freeways do not have motorway service areas as such (though there are exceptions as along parts of the New York Thruway and Florida Turnpike) so you must leave the freeway to get petrol – hence the enormous company logos looming up in the distance as you approach an exit ramp.

• Petrol is available everywhere *but* beware of being caught short in certain areas such as national parks, especially scenic drives such as the Blue Ridge Parkway in North Carolina and Virginia. Some petrol stations do exist on such limited access tourist roads, but they are not well advertised, and you may have to leave the parkway to find petrol. Do *not* leave by the unmarked local access points or you will get hopelessly lost. Wait for the fully signposted exits (such as 'US220 to Roanoke').

• Likewise out west distances can be so vast between places large enough to have a gas station that you must be careful not to run too low, so fill up before long desert or mountain crossings. Check water and oil too. Do not leave the main road looking for services. If there were any they would be alongside the roadway, or clearly signposted. Put up your bonnet (US hood), tie a handkerchief to the aerial and wait for assistance. Sections where tourists regularly break down or run out of petrol are well known, and usually state patrol cars will turn up (eventually). Traffic going the other way may well use CB (Citizens' Band) radio to alert 'Smokey the Bear' (police) that you need assistance. Many an empty car has been found by rescue services, but with no sign of the driver, who is later found dead at some distance from the highway.

CAR INSURANCE

This is certainly essential, and mostly required these days. Rental companies will generally offer **collision** and **accident insurance** when you pick up the car. If staying for longer or buying your own car you really must obtain *adequate* cover. But be careful. Read *all* the small print, and ensure that you have bought the cover that you need, and that you have bought what you *think* you have bought.

> I found that my policy didn't cover the theft of the car engine on one occasion, nor on another occasion the theft of the car, presumably by 'joy-riders', with several hundreds of dollars' worth of damage on its return.

Check the arithmetic on your bill. If you have failed to pay the last dollar for whatever reason the company may well refuse to pay, and lawyers cost money to put the pressure on.

Insurance is very expensive, and it may be very tempting to obtain the minimum legal cover. Resist this temptation if at all possible.

Uninsured-driver liability insurance may seem a luxury against a very slight and unlikely risk, but given the number of uninsured drivers it isn't. In many states where insurance is required failure to have it still only produces a derisory fine, and may only be put into effect if the driver has committed a moving violation. Premiums are usually three times higher than in the UK. Even for those with a clean driving record and 10 years behind the wheel comprehensive cover is very expensive. And if uninsured drivers are really poor you won't be able to sue them, so you do need to be insured against the uninsured.

LICENCES

Is a British driving licence valid?

Driving is a state responsibility, so the regulations change from place to place. A full British licence is valid for a year in most states, though if you take up residence you may be required to take a state test before that, say after three or six months. Usually there's a highway code test (sometimes automated, often multiple choice). Whether you then have to take a road test depends on the particular state. My Maryland test required the car merely to be parked neatly alongside the kerb, with little else beyond the highway code test and the fee!

Generally northern states have stricter requirements, the southern States more relaxed ones though most are now quite sophisticated compared to 25 years ago. You'll probably be asked to surrender your old British licence. If you do so you will have to tangle with the Swansea DVLC on your return. Avoid this inconvenience by saying you haven't got one to hand in.

What about the International Driving Licence?

This has a confirmation that your licence is in fact a licence, with a dozen translations, one being in Russian. As a British licence is in English it is usually okay on its own. Don't rely just upon the international one – all traffic cops and most rental clerks don't know what it is and don't intend to find out.

Date of birth

The snag with an old-style British licence was its lack of an obvious date of birth. All US licences have a date of birth (hence their use as ID to buy alcohol). Use your passport if you have to rather than explain about the expiry date being your 70th birthday (which amazes most Americans as their licences are only good for a few years usually). New Euro-pink licences have a date of birth clearly visible (available from DVLC in Swansea).

Moving state

If you move home from one state to another you'll need to reapply for a licence. Cars have to be re-registered too. If you settle down you may still have to renew both from time to time. Sometimes this is automatic, sometimes upon application (plus fee, re-test of the eyes and the highway code).

Passing through

If you are just passing through your licence is valid if valid where issued even if, for instance, you are too young to get a licence in the state you are driving through. Reciprocity exists between not just adjacent states but cross the USA (but your behaviour still has to conform to local requirements even if you are passing through).

Passing the test

The good news is that getting a test is very easy. It may be necessary to book a test, or you may be able just to turn up on spec. Fees are nominal too. Most people pass. If you can't drive in the USA you are looked upon as eccentric at best, suspicious at worst.

Other ID

Certain jurisdictions issue 'This is not a driver's permit' pieces of identification just so that people who don't drive for whatever reason can carry ID with their full date of birth and full name in a government issued format.

WORDS OF WARNING

Driving in the USA can be a relaxing activity in a large air-conditioned car along the interstate highway out in the countryside. But in cities, especially at rush hour, it can be a nightmare. The width of roads and parking spaces, the use of power steering, and the cheapness of the petrol can all make driving part of the holiday *but* in heavy traffic many US drivers are far from competent. It can also be quite intimidating to follow cars with guns on the back shelf and a bumper sticker proclaiming 'Jesus said it. I believe it. That settles it.' Just pull back slowly and continue on carefully towards the Magic Kingdom.

Cars crowd together even more than in Britain, driving far too close to the car ahead in rush hour traffic. Overtaking takes place on all sides, which can be very alarming even to drivers used to heavy London traffic or the M6 through the West Midlands (Europe's heaviest traffic at rush hour). Drivers of large trucks often drive right up behind cars and intimidate them right out of the way.

After two weeks' leisurely driving across the South arriving in the Washington DC area can be a nightmare at almost any time of day: the traffic is likely to seem aggressive, fast and far too close together. The use of the metro (the underground railway) suddenly becomes very appealing.

And *always* drive defensively.

TRAFFIC REGULATIONS AND ROAD SAFETY

Generally these are the same as those you are familiar with at home, though with some tricky variations to keep you on your toes. **Roundabouts** hardly exist, except in a few larger cities, and then only at the junction of large boulevards. If they are called anything it will be **rotaries** or **traffic circles**. Of course, traffic goes anticlockwise, often confusing to those of us who normally drive on the left and are used to giving directions clockwise.

Traffic lights are usually called **stop lights**. Their location can take some getting used to as they are generally on the far side of the intersection to which they refer. Draw up to them at your peril: you will soon find that your rear end is stuck blocking the intersection behind you. There are also a number of interesting complications:

- **Flashing red or orange** – beware! This means a four-way stop (see below) but with someone having the right of way. At night a main city avenue may well have flashing amber at every intersection. Go through with the right of way, but beware of crossing traffic. Flashing red means that someone else has the flashing orange right of way.

Stop. Cross or turn only when safe to do so. Fortunately this system only operates when traffic is sparse, such as in the early hours of the morning.

- **No turn on red** means that when there is a red light traffic may not turn right. Though this may seem blindingly self-evident to a newly arrived visitor, it actually tells drivers that the normal rule is for traffic to turn right when there is a red light so long as they have come to a full halt and it is clear to do so. Most, but not all the states, have this rule. Beware of cities that have spread over state lines. Different rules may apply on either side of the state line.

- **Right lane must turn** is a delightful invitation to turn at right angles to the direction you have been going, and it is compulsory. If you have stayed in such a lane too long and try to go straight on you will find you get a ticket, at best, or a punch-up with irate drivers you block in when you find that by going straight ahead you've come up against no available lane. Even when the lane you want is blocked by roadworks you must obey the signs for your particular lane, or risk the consequences. I was once physically assaulted in just such a case.

- **Four-way stops** require *all* traffic to stop, but the driver there first *from whatever direction* has the right of way. In case of a dead heat give way to traffic coming from the right. See the opening sequence of *LA Story* for what can happen if you don't. Numerous local variations exist, which can be quite a trial for the outsider. For a **two-way stop** one road has the right of way, and on a **three-way stop** only one direction has the right of way, all others must come to a halt. The signs all look superficially much the same, and may not be placed in the most obvious position. Usually, though, these arrangements are only found in residential neighbourhoods away from the main roads.

Road signs
As with so many directions in the USA, literacy is assumed. Only reluctantly have pictograms (such as are used in international signs) been introduced, even in tourist or immigrant areas.

State of the roads
Since the New Deal of the late 1930s paved roads have been built even in the most out of the way areas. Nevertheless vast areas of the West still have gravel or even dirt roads. Through-travellers will probably see little of this though. Motorways are generally well maintained, and at a far better standard than found in many cities.

The winter snows sweep much further south (occasionally even to the Gulf of Mexico) that you might expect. Traffic in the northern states usually adjusts fairly smoothly, but where snow is a novelty traffic can be crazy, with people driving either too fast or far too slowly. Snow-tyres are required in many states, both to avoid a ticket from the highway patrol, and simply to get about. Snow-chains may be essential in out of the way areas and in ski-resorts.

Speeding

Officially speed limits are set by each state, not the federal government. However, the federal government can withhold federal highway grants from states not agreeing to enforce federal standards on interstate highways (almost all of the motorway standard dual-carriageway). The 60 or increasingly 70 mph speed limit has thus become a national limit, but one rarely observed within metropolitan areas or in the vast distances out west. Buried traffic monitors record the proportion of traffic obeying the speed limit, and states lose highway grants if more than half of passing traffic is over the limit. Paying state patrolmen to slow the traffic down can become fiscally necessary given the expense of highway maintenance. So a guerilla war rumbles on between CB radio-equipped truckers and state patrol cars ('Smokey the Bear'). Western states periodically attempt to have the limits changed, or threaten to ignore the limit and take the consequences.

In towns limits are usually 35–40 mph, but watch for local variations, often set to catch the unwary outsider who can then be required to pay a fine or post bail on the spot (which amounts to much the same). Obey all limits, at least until you have been in an area long enough to get a feel for how the traffic locally responds to them. At corners there are often advisory limits (on a yellow background). In the mountains limits tend to be both realistically set and observed (drivers who don't observe them don't survive).

Traffic into cities such as Washington or Boston travels much faster in certain designated **High-Occupancy Vehicle** lanes. Signs indicate **HOV-2** for a minimum of 2 people, though **HOV-3** is more usual. Otherwise avoid this car pool/bus lane or collect a ticket.

Parking

Parking downtown can be as bad as in central London. Fortunately, though, many downtown banks and stores have their own free or subsidised parking lots. Parking meters are often available, and feeding the meter is permitted if you dash out in time. Regular parking, though, can be very expensive, and is increasingly only available for all-day commuters using high-occupancy vehicles (HOVs). You can see cars being parked by attendants in the reverse order their owners can be expected to come and collect them at the end of the day.

Certain areas have surprisingly large parking areas available. Washington DC's central Mall, around which many sights and most of the museums cluster, has parking areas just for visitors, though in high season these will fill early on, and using the metro may well be a better idea.

Safety tips
- If you think you are being followed, drive to the nearest 24 hour convenience stores, hospital or police station.

- If you are hit from behind in a minor collision, drive to a well-lit service station before stopping.

- At a red light leave enough space to pull out quickly if someone approaches you.

- Keep doors locked and windows shut.

- Keep your petrol tank at least half-full to avoid searching for petrol, a vulnerable state to be in.

- Keep car keys separate from house keys.

- At rental pick-up ask for a map to reach main highways safely.

Driving in deserts
The western deserts stretch south from the interior of Washington and Oregon all the way to Mexico, becoming wider and more extreme the nearer the border you are. Beloved of generations of movie-goers is a series of quintessentially American landscapes (though many spaghetti westerns were filmed in Spain!). Explore and enjoy, but take care. These landscapes can be both beautiful and deadly. And if entering the native American reservations please obey the posted regulations (such as not leaving the main transit roads).

An excellent series of guides are now available in the UK: Moon Handbooks. These exist for Arizona, Colorado, Nevada, Texas, Utah and Washington (which though wet around Seattle is very dry to the East) – from specialist shops such as Stanfords Map and Travel Bookshop, 12–14 Long Acre, Covent Garden, London WC2E 9LP. Tel: (0171) 836 1321; Stanfords at British Airways, 156 Regent St, London W1R 5TA. Tel: (0171) 434 4744; Stanfords at Campus Travel, 52 Grosvenor Gardens, London SW1W 0AG (near Victoria Station) Tel: (0171) 730 1314.

Points to ensure an embarrassment doesn't become a disaster:

- Tell someone where and when you are going (and stick to it).

- Check out the hire car's facilities *before* setting out.

- Keep out of Death Valley (May–October).

- If you must drive – keep to main roads
                    – travel outside afternoon heat.

- If you must go away from roads ('off-road')
                    – minimum groups of two
                    – keep to 4-wheel drive vehicles.

- Take lots of water, soft drinks, but NO alcohol.

- Take a first aid kit.

- Wear appropriate clothing (long sleeves, hat).

- Always stay close to your vehicle in case of breakdown.

- Light a fire (but beware of starting uncontrolled fires).

If you drive out into the desert to **hike**, heat stroke can soon be a real problem. The body's normal cooling mechanisms easily fail to cope, evident in an inability to sweat, high body temperatures and growing confusion. Not enough water is the usual problem, which can be complicated by a lack of salt (to replace that lost by sweating). Strenuous activity in the heat of the day can soon produce problems. Adults generally need two to three litres a day, but in strenuous conditions 10 litres may well be necessary, which means people have to drink far beyond the quenching of any immediate thirst. In fact just like camels travellers need to suck up and store vast quantities of water, while avoiding alcohol, which only dehydrates the body. Just as important, though, is the need to wear loose-fitting, preferably white cotton, clothing and a wide-brimmed hat. As a desert hitch-hiker I used to use an umbrella when stuck by the roadside, more for the sun than for the sudden storms of rain. And who could drive on by an Englishman under an umbrella 'out in the midday sun'?

Maps

It is now possible to buy up-to-date city and state maps in the UK. Stanfords (0171 836 1321) stock Rand McNally's folding maps. Don't expect free maps from gas stations these days (though state welcome centres still provide them). Prepare in the UK for long journeys with Rand McNally's *Road Atlas and Vacation Guide* (£14), or *Hildebrand Road Atlas: the West* (£10) from large bookshops.

ALTERNATIVES TO DRIVING

Do visitors have to drive everywhere? Fortunately not, for alternatives do exist:

- buses, both long distance and local
- underground systems
- taxis
- cycling
- walking
- flying
- trains.

The most exotic of these is undoubtedly walking. *Time* (the US news magazine) had an article in September 1987 on how the British *of all ages* still actually do it for fun! Is there no end to British eccentricity?

Long distance buses

The most well-known network is **Greyhound**. Unfortunately the number of towns served has declined substantially over the last few years as cross-route subsidies have been phased out, leaving the major cities well served, but unfashionable areas not served by either train or bus, though some local services do exist.

Though the 99 days for $99 are long since gone, fares are generally quite low, though the vast distances may disguise this. Bus stations are usually in the older parts of the town, so long bus trips can be a salutary reminder of the underside of US life. Rest stops may be at peculiar times of the day or night, often in out of the way fast food strips in the middle of nowhere, a plot to make the British traveller suddenly start to appreciate motorway cafés back home!

Advantages:

- See a slice of the USA you might not otherwise come across, which includes a motley collection of passengers. Remember the opening and closing scenes in *Midnight Cowboy*?

- Comparatively cheap, especially if you bought the ticket overseas (or in the US with passport)
  7 day pass $179
  10 day pass $229
  15 day pass $269
  30 day pass $369
  45 day pass $399
  60 day pass $539.

- Efficient, clean and tidy, with on-board WC.

- Good luggage facilities (far more than by plane, which may make the trip worthwhile by itself).

- APEX tickets available if you can book a week or a month beforehand.

Disadvantages:
- Slow (comparatively).

- Can be very boring for cross-country travel.

- Bus stations have seen better days (and may be intimidating for women and children).

Contact:
- Greyhound @crystalholidays.co.uk or *www.greyhound.com*

- Greyhound International, Sussex House, London Road, East Grinstead, West Sussex RH19 1LD. Tel: (01342) 317317. Fax: (01342) 328519. Request Ameripass brochure.

- Or any ABTA travel agent, or once in the USA contact direct on 800-231-2222.

Local buses
These exist in most large towns, but tend to focus on the downtown serving the rush-hour commuter traffic. Los Angeles has DASH (Downtown Area Short Hop) that serves the downtown and the main landmarks, with dedicated fast services to Beverly Hills, Hollywood and Pacific Palisades. New York City has a complex system including a reasonable frequently night-time service. A ride costs $1.50. In the daytime the subway is probably a better bet (out of the extremes of weather).

Underground trains (subways)
These exist in only a minority of US cities, and those that do exist vary enormously:

- Bay Area Rapid Transit System (BART) is clean, reasonably priced, and an efficient way to cross the **San Francisco Bay** to cities such as Oakland and to certain suburbs, though many places are only linked in with feeder bus services.

- **Los Angeles** has a new, highly contentious, subway that being in its infancy you can easily miss, though if you are already downtown it may be worth a ride. Grandiose plans to link the Hollywood Hills with Long Beach are just that.

• Washington Metro serves **Washington DC** with the surrounding suburban communities in northern Virginia and Maryland. Despite the rapid expansion of the suburban economy over the last 20 years this brand new system focuses upon the governmental city centre, and its radial routes serve only certain select communities, so cross-town travel remains difficult and certain parts of the city, and of the metropolis at large, remain inaccessible. Beware of the network maps which show the system as it may one day be, not as it is now. But for all that it is cheap, very efficient, crime, garbage and smoke free, and certainly on a par with Europe's better systems. Only the new Kiev system is supposedly better.

• **New York City's** subway system is cheap ($1.50 any distance with free transfers), vast, quite scary at times, can be very dirty, and is an amazingly efficient way of travelling around to avoid the congested streets above. Four million people use it every day. The 230 miles of track are the amalgamation of once separate systems, which can lead to quite complex interchange stations, especially between express and local trains. For travelling around Manhattan it is excellent as the buses get bogged down in the traffic. For Long Island the service is not so good, though there is an express route using modern trains to and from the station nearest to John F. Kennedy airport, with buses from the station to the terminal. The Michelin Guide has route maps designed to help visitors navigate the system. An interesting alternative is provided by the new water taxis on the Hudson and East rivers between W46th Street and the Fulton Ferry Landing under the Brooklyn Bridge. Round trip is $15. Details on 001 212 681 8111.

Some systems are not underground at all, but as in **Boston** and **Chicago** elevated (as was the case in much of the New York network originally). The 'El' helped blight large areas around the downtown. To get some idea of what it must have been like having to live near such overhead systems, watch the John Belushi and Don Akroyd 1980 movie *Blues Brothers* set in modern Chicago.

At some suburban stations you may see 'Kiss and Ride' signs, pull-in bays for drivers to let off commuting spouses. Park and ride facilities are also available at certain suburban stations.

Taxis

These are more likely to be of use in the more European cities of the east than in the more American cities of the west. In **New York City** it may be actually quicker to walk 10 or even 15 blocks given the traffic, though a cab ride will ensure that you don't arrive wet through. Summers are long and very sticky. Winters are often very snowy. Taxis are metered, but don't expect cab drivers to be able to change large denomination notes. Many drivers may not speak English and may have little if any knowledge of anywhere outside the major destinations. In certain cities only certain cabs are allowed to drive over the city boundary, so check before the meter starts. In the national capital (**Washington DC**) a drive to most suburban communities involves crossing over into the next state, foreign territory to many inner city drivers.

Long distance taxi rides are possible, but very expensive. It would usually be cheaper to hire a car and drive yourself. But in a domestic airline strike, for instance, such long distance rides to another international airport that is open may turn out to be essential. Get a price *before* the trip starts, though.

Remember: Many cities are as large as London, and taxi rides across Los Angeles or New York City can be very expensive indeed.

Orlando International Airport is on the south side of the metropolitan area, with easy accessibility across to the hotels and timeshare villas of International Drive near Disneyworld. BUT Sanford airport, often used by tour operators, is far to the north-east of the city, a $100 cab ride to the tourist area to the south side: an unpleasant financial surprise after a long flight.

You can arrange to take a vehicle that is half way between a cab and a bus – a limousine. These long huge cars may take half a dozen travellers plus baggage from out-of-town communities to the airport for bus-like fares for a taxi-like service. Check *Yellow Pages*, and book in advance.

Cycling

Cycling as a sport is increasingly popular, but commuting is only viable for a very few in places like college towns. States such as Florida are waymarking cycle routes, but they tend to be minor roads rather than traffic-free routes. Resorts have cycle hire. Each state is covered by a County Road guide outlining round trip one-day routes and longer tours – from Whitehorse Press, 154 West Brookline Street, Boston MA 02118.

Walking

This is an art, one that has all but been given up except by a hardy few.

Suburban neighbourhoods may well lack sidewalks altogether. Paths lead only from the house to the kerb! Certain neighbourhoods may be suspicious of any strangers, especially those on foot.

Some downtowns now encourage shoppers to use the shoppers' bus between the main shopping intersections. This encourages less walking per person, but probably helps raise the number of people walking along the streets. In hot and humid cities learn to walk down that side of the street giving some shade. Whatever the season work on the general assumption that car drivers cannot see you. Never assume a right of way, even at marked crossing areas (British style zebra or pelican crossings don't exist). But walking across as and where you will may result in a ticket for jay-walking (even in the deserted downtown on a Sunday morning if your luck has run out).

Overall walking is okay for young people, especially when combined with buses and subway trains. But it is not feasible for most families, if only for the extremes of heat and cold. Downtowns can be less than safe, and distances great. The central mall of Washington DC is deceptively laid out. Distances from monument to monument can be enormous, and with children impossible. The DC police patrols have been known to use bull horns to warn twilight pedestrians to leave the open spaces immediately for their own safety! And darkness comes much more swiftly than in northern countries such as Britain.

Flying

Flying is cheap per mile by European standards, but as distances are vast prices can still seem very expensive. Standby tickets are available, though around public holidays all seats will have been long since booked up. But given the sheer size of the USA flying is often the only way to travel any distance within the time available.

Traditionally the USA has had a network of international, regional and local companies, nested together to provide a service to most places within the USA. The cost of the overly cosy arrangement was seen as a lack of competition, higher than necessary prices, and an over-extended network necessarily subsidised by higher than desirable fares on the most popular routes.

Deregulation of routes has caused a major change in air travel. Popular routes attracted new services at lower fares, so forcing large companies to follow. Conversely many smaller places have lost their services altogether. Even large companies have gone bankrupt, been taken over, or have merged. The situation is still, and may well remain, in flux.

The implication for visitors is that whereas it has become cheaper and generally more convenient to fly into and out of large metropolitan areas (where, after all, most people live) it may be difficult to fly on to specific, smaller destinations. Relatives who could once have met you at Cullowhee airport North Carolina (a small college town in the Great Smoky Mountains) may now have to go to Ashville some 40 miles away across the mountains, though as a freeway has just opened on this route this is now no real hardship. They may even prefer to drive some hundreds of miles south to Atlanta for the novelty of meeting you at the international airport. Few Americans get any opportunity to meet arriving foreigners, so may be eager to travel to meet you.

Book from the UK whenever possible to take advantage of special rates not available once you are within the USA. These are often available via your transatlantic carrier (or its affiliated airlines within the USA). Various packages are periodically on offer, with a series of vouchers or an 'airpass' being purchased that can be exchanged for tickets, though if you know your schedule an inflexible series of flights can be booked from the UK. Transatlantic carriers often offer special internal flights to attract custom, and specific places can be visited by means of stopovers before an eventual destination.

- **Bon Voyage** can book airpasses or help plan a series of stopovers. Tel: (01703) 330332.

Fly-drive

With an 'open-jaw' ticket this enables you to fly into one city, drive to another, and fly home without having to drive all the way back: great for cross-country trips. Two weeks across country from New York City to Los Angeles, with a week in each place as well can be an ideal introduction to the USA. The extra drop-off charge at least means you don't have to dash back to New York City, and can instead spend a leisurely week in California before flying home.

Air-travel seasons

These are rooted as much in the calendar as in the weather. For travel purposes three unfamiliar seasons appear:

- low – off peak, especially term time
- high – summer holidays
- shoulder – late November (Thanksgiving).

Summer is set by convention having almost the power of law. It opens with Memorial Day in late May and lasts until Labor Day in early September. To get, for instance, student rates after Labor Day may necessitate having convincing ID (identification papers) as all US students will then be back in school (or college).

Trains

Trains do travel the length and breadth of the USA, but services are less frequent and serve fewer places since motorways and flying have taken most of the long distance passengers. Despite the poor state of repair of much of the remaining network, using the train has certain major advantages over flying or driving:

• You will be seeing the country from an increasingly unfamiliar perspective that cannot possibly be provided by high altitude flying.

• It is relaxing not having to do the driving.

• It is useful for travellers going from one downtown to another, such as tourists or certain business people.

Unfortunately only a railway enthusiast would want to do the whole cross-country journey, if only because of the timetable implications, not to mention the length of time involved. For details see John Pitt *US by Rail*, a Brandt guide with details of passes and 28 long distance routes (includes steam railways and museums). For an enthusiast's view see *The Great Trans American Train Ride*, a video produced by Haysbridge Video (0990 110 156).

It is still worthwhile taking one of the more popular sections of the network, which is now run by **Amtrak**. This semi-nationalised passenger network tries to keep the passenger services going, but is restricted to using other companies' track, which is maintained to a variety of standards. Trains may have to crawl through certain areas to avoid track collapse, only to speed effortlessly away once back onto a commercially maintained freight network. Compared to the European system, the Amtrak network is very rudimentary. Only in the northeast's Boston to Washington DC corridor does it have anything like an Inter-City feel about it.

Useful **links** connect the **New York City** based corridor north to **Canada** (which has its own full system quite unlike the US) and south to **Florida**. With careful planning it is still possible to go over to **Chicago** or down to **New Orleans**. Changing trains and spending four days en route can enable the hardy traveller to reach the **West Coast** at a leisurely 40 mph. Once in Los Angeles there is a well-used service south to **San Diego**.

For travellers on the Atlantic seaboard bound for the **Pacific Northwest** it is probably better to go north to Montreal in Canada, take the trans-Canada system west to Vancouver, and then go south again into the USA. The service is good (though not so elegant as it once was) and the scenery is spectacular.

Amtrak's **Southwest Chief** runs from Chicago to Los Angeles (and back again). Speeds rarely reach 70 mph, but this enables riders to relax as the scenery rolls gently by. This route is something of a flagship for Amtrak's long-distance routes, with quite a high level of service, which includes films, leaflets on points of interest, and even speakers to talk about the areas being crossed. **On-board facilities** are appropriate for people used to travelling long distance by Greyhound, if not quite up to airline standards. Coaches are on two levels. The lower level has several airline-type toilets, changing rooms, luggage storage, and seating areas for those who find it difficult to negotiate the stairs to the upper deck. There is also a formal dining-car and a cafeteria, though as with captive markets everywhere prices are not cheap. One of the advantages of this particular journey is that a stopover at Flagstaff, Arizona, can be made. Take a hired car (or even hitch as I did) north to the nearby **Grand Canyon**, truly one of the wonders of the world.

Unfortunately this level of service is not yet provided on all other long-distance services. For the 30 plus hours from **Seattle to Santa Barbara** a basic service is provided (2 berth sleepers available on the Coast Starlight). Watching the landscape change and talking to fellow passengers is usually enough to while away the hours. Some places that you might expect to be on the system aren't, such as San Francisco, but the trains do call at Oakland across the Bay, with connecting buses available.

The new trains on California's **Metrolink** (intercity) system should ease the well-used sections. Call **Trailfinders** on (0171) 937 5400 for up-to-date details.

If you would like to get the feel of what it is like to arrive in a small western town by train, to step down onto the side of the tracks only to watch the train leave you standing in the middle of nowhere, read Malcolm Bradbury's novel *Stepping Westward* published in 1965, now an Arena paperback.

Practical train information

A complicated discount structure exists for foreign passport holders in the USA:

1998 USA Rail Pass fares

US-wide	15 day	off peak/$285	peak/$425
	30 day	off peak/$375	peak/$535
Northeast Region	15 day	off peak/$175	peak/$195
	30 day	off peak/$215	peak/$230
East Region	15 day	off peak/$205	peak/$250
	30 day	off peak/$255	peak/$310

West Region	15 day	off peak/$195	peak/$315
	30 day	off peak/$260	peak/$395
Far West Region	15 day	off peak/$185	peak/$240
	30 day	off peak/$240	peak/$310
East or West Coast	30 day	off peak/$225	peak/$275

Off-peak period = January to May and 8 September to the end of December. Peak period = June to 7 September.

Schedule information: *www.amtrak.com/amtrak/schedule/*
Reservations may be made: *http://reservations.amtrak.com/*

Reservations and/or ticketing for the USA Rail Pass and International Gateway fares (travel between Washington DC and Boston, and intermediate stops) must be handled at any Amtrak station in the USA or may be processed at a travel agent. A valid passport is necessary to purchase the USA Rail Pass, to receive tickets to travel, and for identification while onboard. Unlike the situation in the UK, most long distance journeys require advanced reservations and payment at all times. People do not generally just turn up and expect to travel (as they do on the long distance buses). To make matters more complicated, Amtrak will not quote schedules or fares via e-mail. When the reservation site is down, information can be obtained by called 1-800-872-7245.

Specimen fares for the late 1990s

New York City to Miami	$160
Seattle to San Francisco	$160 (including bus connection across the bay)
Los Angeles to Las Vegas	$75
New York City to Montreal	$80

For more detailed information contact:

● **American Express Travel** (0171) 924 2889
● **Compass Travel** (01733) 335599
● **Great Rail Journeys** (01904) 679969

For Web details:

www.viarail.ca
www.amtrak.com
www.amtrakwest.com
www.coaststarlight.com
www.amtrakintercity.com
www.microserve.net/~amtrakpa/

- For **disabled passenger information**, see 'Access Amtrak' available free from Amtrak Department, Western Folder Distribution Company, 1549 West Glenlake Avenue, Itasca, Illinois 60143.

- Call **Amtrak** in the USA on 1-800 872 7245. In the UK call (0171) 253 9009.

Unfortunately the daily *Palmetto* from New York City to Tampa via Washington DC and Charleston has recently been discontinued. The daily *Crescent* from New York City to New Orleans via Washington DC and Atlanta now only runs three days each week on the final Atlanta–New Orleans leg. Chicago and Seattle is daily only as far as St Paul–Minneapolis; further west it's only 4 days a week. The Chicago–Salt Lake–Los Angeles train runs only 3 days a week.

Camping tours
For independent travellers who don't want the hassle of travelling alone, try organised camping tours, all kit, driver and van included. This is only for those who don't mind sharing! From £450 for a west coast two weeks tour up to £1,500 for a two-months' US-wide tour (all prices are plus food, and airfare to and from the USA).

- **American Adventure** Tel: (01892) 511894
- **AmeriCan** (01892) 512700.

Packs
There are two main types: a conventional rucksack with an internal frame for serious hiking; and the travel model that transforms itself into a suitcase-like holdall. The convertible pack, in hiding its frame and fastenings, can be handled like a case in both airports and hotels where it may be advantageous to appear less the hippie and more the business traveller. Available from Cotswold – the Outdoor People (01285 860612) or YHA Adventure Shops (0171 836 8541). Expect to pay from £75 for 60 litres to £190 for 85 litre capacity.

TIME ZONES

North America stretches over eight-and-a-half time zones. When it's noon in Alaska it's 7.30pm in Newfoundland. As you travel west you 'gain' time. If you drive from Pittsburg to Denver you may well leave at 10.00 am one day and arrive at 10.00 am the next, driving straight through. But the journey will have taken 26 hours. If you go from west to east you 'lose', so if you left Denver at 10.00 am and arrived at Pittsburg the following day at 10.00 am it would have taken you 22 hours (maybe you missed the traffic driving in this direction and saved a few hours!)

Most Americans, however, live with a four-zone world, from Atlantic to Pacific. Eastern Standard Time is five hours behind Greenwich, Central six hours, Mountain seven, and Pacific eight. So midday in London is 7.00 am in New York City, 6.00 am in Chicago, 5.00 am in Denver, and 4.00 am in Los Angeles. This is complicated by:

- **Daylight Saving Time** which operates much the same as Summer Time in the UK. However, certain states refuse to use it, so watch out in Arizona, Hawaii and parts of Indiana. The switch-over is on the last Sunday in April, which is not usually the date(s) used in Europe.

A further complication is the refusal to use the 24-hour clock (except perhaps in the military). Timetables will only use the 12-hour clock, with bold type for times after noon. This has confused many overseas arrivals who think there are no trains, planes, buses in the afternoon on the very route they want to make! It makes you realise how even the 24-hour clock, like metric temperature, gradually catches up with even the most dyed in the wool Brit.

TRAVELLING WITH THE KIDS

The USA is a wonderful place for families. From the moment you arrive you'll realise that it's still a more child-oriented society:

- Most hire cars have rear seat-belts fitted as standard, and major agencies can provide safety seats for young children.

- Most motels let children share their parents' room without extra charge (and most rooms have double-beds anyway as standard).

- Restaurants keep high-chairs or booster-seats ready, and children's menus are common. Colouring books may emerge from folded children's menus too!

Don't despair! Children's food is not compulsory for adults. All-you-can-eat meals (a speciality in certain chains) have everything from sugar-puffs to spicy sausages at breakfast, via scrambled eggs, muffins and juices. Breakfasts are good value and usually provide something for everyone to feast upon.

Theme parks, whether Disneyworld and Seaworld in central Florida, or Dollywood in east Tennessee's Smoky Mountains, are for children of all ages; young children aren't ignored; and parents needn't feel like social outcasts for turning up with their offspring. Even more 'serious' places such as the science museums of Washington DC encourage children to touch, watch puppet shows, and generally behave like children. National Parks, such as the Rocky Mountains and Mesa Verde

Parks in Colorado, have talks and activities especially for children. For family attractions close to cross-country motorways refer to the *Guide to Crossing America* by the National Geographic Society (£16).

Snags

It would be foolish to suggest travelling with children turns up no problems:

- Summer heat can be so overwhelming that the car may become the only haven of air conditioning (and thus sanity) for all the family. But distances on cross-country trips can be extremely demoralising. A sufficiently large car is essential for all concerned.

- Motels rarely have anywhere for children to play, nor are playmates available as would be possible staying with friends or in a country hotel.

Good news

Overall most visitors would say the good outweighs the bad:

- At least there's television (morning cartoons are everywhere, not just for a few minutes as in the UK). Most motels have a pool (check *before* booking to avoid disappointment). After being cooped up for long periods in the car a pool is usually very welcome by everyone.

- Standards of hygiene are high throughout the USA; bathrooms with showers are standard in all motel rooms; disposable nappies (diapers) are at every drugstore; and the locals by and large speak English (for when the fan belt breaks late at night as you are crossing the South).

- Toys are excellent. Well, the range and price of toys is very good. In fact the range (and volume) of toys is as likely to startle you as the viciousness of the war toys. If you haven't seen a large toy shop in the UK for 30 years you'd probably get a shock! Use the local *Yellow Pages* to find the nearby 'Toys R Us', part of a vast chain of toys-only supermarkets giving both good value and great variety.

- Children do enjoy the USA. Even young children will both cope with and enjoy it (though maybe no more or less than anywhere in Europe). Swimming together at the end of each day's travelling or exertions remains a fond memory for years after. Even surviving the ferocious summer heat becomes a well-earned battle scar. Also, for adults taking children can provide an open sesame to people and places you'd never otherwise visit.

Even if you do intend to take your family for an extended stay and wish first to try out living together in the USA it might be worth considering house-swapping rather than a touring holiday.

Tick those items you'd think would provide you good experience of what it would be like to live (rather than holiday) in the USA:	
touring holiday	house-swapping
on the move	stay in one place
motels	house with garden
eating out	eating both out and in
always together	more flexibility
strangers	neighbours
always something new	return to base each day

Books of advice

As there are more and more parents taking more and more children abroad there are ever more how-to-do-it guides. Those worth looking at include the following:

- David Haslam, *Travelling with Children: A Survival Guide for Parents*, published by Macdonald, London, 1987, has readable and authoritative sections on planning, safe car and air travel, strategies for journeys, eating and drinking, burns, bites and bugs. It's a useful introduction for anyone considering going abroad with children, for however long.

- A similar paperback is Pamela Hyde's *Holidays with Kids*, Piatkus, London, 1987, which is very general, but has useful and reassuring sections on keeping children entertained, fed and healthy, besides sections on choosing which type of holiday is appropriate for particular families, a vital consideration for such long-haul visits as to the USA. There is little specifically geared to US travel as such, but its general approach is useful. An alternative would be: Anne-Louise Norton, *Baby Travel*, published by St John's Wood Press, London, 1987.

- *Family Travel Handbook* was published by Bloomsbury in 1992, covering similar ground.

DISABLED VISITORS TO THE USA

The USA may well be the best country to visit if you are physically disabled and well able to afford such a distant trip. Though medical costs are very high and specialist medical cover is recommended, the action of 'physically challenged' groups in the USA has opened up most public buildings, the Washington DC subway system, and most if not all places of public accommodation (if they don't want to be picketed).

For up-to-date information contact the following:

- Florida Department of Commerce (Division of Tourism), 1st Floor, 18/24 Westbourne Grove, London W2 5RH, Tel: (0171) 792 0087 for information on how to obtain their leaflet *Information/Referral Numbers for Physically Challenged Visitors*, also available via travel agents.

- Society for the Advancement of Travel for the Handicapped, 26 Court Street, Brooklyn, New York 11242 (Tel: 001 718 858 5483). Please send an International Postal Coupon for their advice.

- **Mobility International/USA**, PO Box 10767, Eugene, OR 97440 offers advice on low-cost options for travellers with disabilities (and information on living exchanges, internships and work camps).

- *Smooth Ride Guide* (FT Publishing, £10) gives details of hotels with appropriate facilities and accessible attractions for wheelchair users. There are now specifically US and Canadian editions. Call (0181) 340 6654 for further details.

Call trans-Atlantic carriers for contact numbers for enquiries from disabled customers.

7
Finding Work

There are two major reasons for going to any foreign country:

- interest
- job or career

Of course you can make a holiday of a student summer camp job, and you may have taken up a job just to follow up your interest in the USA. But though all reasons are in some ways interconnected it helps to establish what your priorities are if you sort out in your own mind what the main reason is. If it is a relaxing holiday then don't undermine that perfectly reasonable aim by being on the telephone all the time trying to set up useful business links!

Short-term options for young people will be dealt with later in Chapter 9. Let's look now at the various possibilities for those who don't have to be back for next term or for a purely UK job.

STAYING IN THE USA FOR FUN

Many people find going abroad is something for the young, with few ties, between college and going to work. But consider the alternatives:

Staying in Britain	Going to the USA
Getting into a career	Getting experience of life
Getting into the housing market	Not being tied down by a mortgage
Having a family while fit and young	Being more flexible and able to take risks
Getting a job while one is still available	Expanding your horizons
Building up seniority in a firm	Gaining useful confidence
Becoming a sober, hard-working citizen	Changing job tracks

Now add your own counter arguments in the spaces provided! Once you've done that, choose which options are for you. If most are in the left-hand column:

- you could work hard at home but holiday in the USA
- you could try for some US-based experience with your firm
- you could house-swap for three or four weeks one year.

If most are in the right-hand column:

- consider taking a degree in the USA
- take a long trip with casual work
- consider what foreign experience would interest an employer when you got back.

Career advantages of a stint in the USA

The universities and colleges pour out new graduates each and every year, each waving their newly minted degrees. Three hundred applications for a single job is not an unusual situation. How can you stand out from the crowd?

Everyone wants someone with experience, but if no one will give you that initial chance it can all seem futile. But take heart: a new employer's interest may be raised by an applicant who has travelled, not aimlessly, but in relation to their field of interest. Political science students who've spent a term at a college in Washington DC have something no amount of pulling pints in the students' union bar over the vacation can provide.

A three month stint working in the USA offers an employer someone with just a suggestion of adaptability, initiative and a willingness to try something different, unafraid of trying something new. A stint in the USA may be the only thing separating you from the pack when a short-list is drawn up. And being a year or so older than the rest of the pack when you return may also be in your favour – you are just that bit more mature, that bit more self-reliant, and so should need just that bit less supervision. And employers like that.

Of course you may be looking to the USA for a more long-term job rather than a stint overseas to help you once back in Britain. Many British people do exceptionally well in the USA, from butlers to athletes, but don't expect the USA to provide increased career prospects, a better material standard of living, or just a good time by virtue of your arrival with a British accent. If you don't like hard work, long hours and a lot of knocks, the USA isn't going to do much for you except see your time and money slip away.

Working for fun

If you want to be able to return to the USA you need to be legal. See

Chapter 4 on visas for how this can be done. But the best laid schemes come adrift and you may find yourself out of money far from friends or the airport. Summer harvesting, working in bars, helping friends move or decorate, acting as a nanny: all can pay well, but the longer you remain within the black economy the more risky it'll become. If you do it only for a few weeks before moving on little risk will exist, but it's still illegal, and though it's possible to get the ever necessary ID (identification) via driving licences (US 'driver's license'), social security number and bank account it's an increasingly risky business.

The degree of paranoia this lifestyle can produce can be gauged by a certain non-event in New York City. The Immigration and Naturalization Service (INS) estimated that there are some 70,000 illegal Irish residents within this one city alone. An amnesty was declared: 'Make yourself known and you'll be allowed to "regularize" your status.' Two (yes, that's 2) people turned up at the INS. The source of this story has been checked with RTE (Irish Radio, 7 May 1987, Gay Byrne morning show).

Beware: if you think that the worst that can happen is for the INS to catch you and deport you, remember:

- The Internal Revenue Service (IRS) will first want their back tax before they'll let you leave the USA.

- If you want to return to the USA you need a statement on your exit papers that you are not a tax delinquent, even if the IRS and INS will let you go this time.

Remember: It was not the FBI that got Al Capone. It was the IRS who put him away for non-payment of taxes!

THE BUSINESS CULTURE IN THE USA

It is a sad fact of life that many people who go to work abroad, either on secondment to an overseas branch or subsidiary of a UK employer or on contract to a truly overseas company, give less thought to their circumstances than they would if they were simply to be going abroad on holiday for a few weeks.

(Harry Brown in *Working Abroad?*, 1986)

Join another company, go to another school, or just change jobs and we're likely to find that many more things have changed besides our physical surroundings. Even if our job description remains much the same the way things work around us may change, sometimes so subtly that at first we don't notice what's going on. But soon we find people interpret rules slightly differently, a pleasant surprise when it's in our favour, but a bit of a shock when we seem to lose out. Expectations may be a bit different. How we bend the rules changes. In fact it's a little bit like being in another country. Those who study businesses say that each business has its own culture. How much more potentially confusing when the change of job is compounded with a change of country! Two cultures, one large, one small, change both at once, and we're expected to adjust without missing a step.

So it's easy to see why staying with the same company if you are moving countries can be a great advantage, particularly if the style of management remains the same. If you have been 'Americanised' during your time already with the company then moving to the USA will not be such a jump into the complete unknown.

If American companies pay well they do so because they expect quite a lot. This is a capitalist dog-eat-dog economy, which though not averse to protectionist barriers and government handouts still has a more raw edge to its business dealings than in Britain.

> **A word of warning**: Don't be taken in by those firms that have a laid-back, casual air about them. These mainly new firms, especially in software and the media, can be just as efficient and hardnosed when they want to be, and if your presence turns out to be a waste of space they'll 'let you go' (fire you!). Read Crichton's novel *Disclosure*.

Being British means having certain immediate assumptions made about you. Your accent (whether Geordie, Liverpuddlian or Sloane, it matters not) will be seen as very formal, which will confirm their expectation of you as dour, a bit stand-offish, especially out west (where I have been taken for a Boston, Massachusetts, native, the distinction between England and New England being a little too subtle for certain laid-back West Coast residents!). Unless you really are pompous, colleagues are quite likely to tell you, say in the bar round the corner during Friday's happy hour, that you're not as stuffily formal as they'd expected. This will be a personal point, and will in no way change their belief that everyone else back in Britain is a stuffed shirt.

The greatest shock for most Britons starting work in the USA comes from the long hours and short holidays. The business culture demands it (and thinks it essential to continued prosperity even though those Germans in work tend to have five or six weeks' holidays and are at least as prosperous!)

Long hours

The minimum working week in the USA is often still 40 hours (not the 38 so popular in the UK), the 8 hours per day meaning just that, with people expected to be at their seats working away bang on 9.00 am, and not leaving until precisely 5.00 pm. There's no five minutes grace, and certainly no couple of hours off for the dentist, unless sick-leave is first agreed.

This may be how your UK office was run, so it wouldn't be quite the surprise it is to some. What may be a surprise is that many people start earlier, at 8.00 am. Colleges usually schedule their first classes at 8 am, and having to discuss the finer points of a course so early can be quite a shock to the British visitor. Colleges too may schedule classes to start as late as 7.00 pm, so for some academics it can be a long day.

Holidays

The real surprise comes over holidays. In the first year employees may receive no holidays except for the six public holidays required by law, a week if they are lucky, two weeks if very lucky indeed. Each year of employment raises the entitlement by a day, but it may take some years to gain a three week break. Academics expecting an Easter vacation will find there isn't one, and the long summer vacation is often unpaid, so it's necessary and expected that you'll teach summer school, intensive courses for people either in a hurry to graduate, trying to catch up or having to repeat a failed course.

Bad news time

US public holidays are not necessarily 'long weekends'. Only Memorial Day (the last Monday in May) and Labor Day (the first Monday in September) are always part of a weekend, and as the first and last days of the summer season these weekends are good days to avoid freeways, airports and resorts. Christmas Day, New Year's Day and Independence Day (4 July) obviously fall on any day of the week, and the days to the nearest weekend are not necessarily holidays. (Boxing Day is unheard of so expect to work the day after Christmas Day!) Service and retail employees will probably have to work most holidays (except Christmas and New Year's Day), albeit on overtime rates.

Sick leave

This is usually only gained after a probationary period with the firm, say three months. You'll be lucky to get five days a year for long service. When changing companies negotiate to keep your sick leave entitlement if at all possible. Remember too that sick leave involves any time off for medical reasons, not just being on your death bed.

The contract

The USA is a country where litigation is endemic. If things don't turn out how you expected it will be very difficult to play the litigation game to your advantage without the protection of a carefully prepared contract. If you came expecting full medical cover for yourself and for your family, plus a company car, first make certain it's all in the contract, and legally watertight. Fine words butter no parsnips, or as Sam Goldwyn (of MGM fame) warned: 'A verbal contract ain't worth the paper it's written on.'

Compassionate leave

Try to keep the length of your stay under your own control. If your family, particularly ageing relatives, are still in the UK you need to be able to leave your job and the USA for pressing reasons. If you are under contract with an over-the-odds salary you may not be allowed compassionate leave short of quitting and taking the consequences. Longstanding employees are more likely to be able to obtain emergency leave. Read your contract carefully. If a US company pays you over the odds (salary plus a moving allowance) they aren't going to be too happy about your leaving for any reason, especially for an open-ended period.

Smoking

Despite resistance from civil liberties groups and tobacco-growing states, about one-third of all US employers have already barred workplace smoking, and for fear of costly health insurance and increased days lost through illness are trying to discourage out-of-hours smoking. Don't assume your smoking will be treated as a private matter.

WORK PROSPECTS IN THE US ECONOMY

Whether going to the United States for temporary or long-term work it is useful, if not essential, to know something about the US economy, particularly which skills the job market requires and, equally as vital, where these jobs can be found. The US economy is so large and the country so vast that without even the most rudimentary awareness of what is going on you will be like someone blindfold in a china shop.

The traditional view of the US economy saw a great industrial heartland from Boston south to Baltimore and west over the Appalachians to Chicago. Here lived most Americans once the US had been settled from coast to coast. After the Second World War the west coast, particularly California, became a major rival to the northeast, given its entertainment industries, defence industries and increasingly its aerospace industries. The south was seen as poor, rural and hostile to black people, Roman Catholics, and in fact most outsiders. The industrial midwest merged into the prairie and thinly settled mountains. Alaska far to the northwest remained a barren, frozen waste, and Hawaii a tropical paradise somewhere in mid-Pacific.

The effects of oil

Gradually this picture has changed as the global role of oil changed. As OPEC pushed up oil prices domestic suppliers in Texas, Oklahoma and Louisiana became very wealthy, able to invest in the further industrialisation of what came to be called the Sunbelt. Prosperity moved west to link up with southern California, and eastwards into Florida where tourism, aerospace and retirement developments forged a major rival to the once dominant northeast.

The oil crisis that boosted the Sunbelt exposed the old decaying industrial bases of what came to be known as the Rustbelt, or Snowbelt: cars, shipbuilding, machine tools all collapsed as foreign competition took vast slices of the US market. Unemployment rose to levels unknown since the dark days of the Great Depression of the 1930s. This view of a prosperous southern rim and a decaying northeast is still widely held. But beware: just as it takes its place in the public's 'mental map' of the US economy the map changes.

Bankruptcy for some

The 1980s and 1990s have seen the farmers of the Mississippi valley plagued with over-production and falling prices. Like the heavy industrial cities of Appalachia and the Great Lakes before them they have hit bankruptcy, dispossession and decay. In contrast California still retains its prosperity, at least from Silicon Valley just south of San Francisco to Los Angeles, though even here Orange County faces bankruptcy. The oil price decline of the mid-1980s has undermined the once assured prosperity of Alaska, Oklahoma, Texas and Louisiana, where unemployment has risen dramatically above average levels, and is especially high for those in exploration and drilling concerns.

The US government policies that produced the economic boom of the early 1980s left a huge $200 billion national debt, slowing growth in certain areas to a barely perceptible level before the perilous mid-90s boom. Along the Atlantic coast growth persists, especially in the suburbs, but California lost 100,000 jobs as military contracts were cut back after the Cold War ended. For the impact upon men who thought they had a job for life see *Falling Down*.

The midwest, whether rural or once industrial, has for the first time replaced the south as the region with the lowest incomes. Agriculture, oil and declining heavy industry ('smokestack' industries in US journalism) have all lost ground, pulling the great Mississippi-Great Lakes heartland down. High-technology and service industries such as banking, insurance and advertising have enabled the coastal states to pull ahead.

Job-seekers need to move

The importance of this for would-be job seekers can be gauged in the growing migration of many Americans away from places such as Texas. Don't expect jobs to be available for the asking in Dallas, whatever memories the TV series would suggest. Don't even assume that investment in these areas will automatically hit pay dirt. Retrenchment of people's incomes puts often fatal pressure on small entrepreneurs.

Regional diversity

Awareness of regional diversity is essential. Central Florida may well have peaked – by 1994 Disney had started to lay off workers (though only 100 out of a total workforce of 38,000). Las Vegas, however, boasts three new casinos marketed towards families rather than singles. Central Florida is more prone to shifts in foreigners' confidence. Ten foreign visitors were killed in Florida during 1992: the following year visitors from Germany fell 37 per cent, from Italy 17 per cent. No wonder Florida is trying to ensure visitor safety.

Skills in demand

It is often recurrent fluctuations in demands for certain skills that explains the US Immigration Service's rules requiring emigrants to have a specific job prior to the granting of immigrant status. A skill by itself might well not be sufficient, and might threaten the jobs of existing workers in a dwindling job market. With 40 per cent of all college teachers on part-time contracts (up from 20 per cent in the 1970s) foreign applicants for full-time posts would need to prove they were not . taking a job from an existing resident.

Finding out about the US economy

On the next page are some magazines and newspapers (often available in public and university libraries) that regularly carry articles on the US economy. How many of them do you read?

Look at the pattern of your answers. Do you think it would be useful to read the business section of more newspapers and news magazines?

What other sources are there for more detailed information on specific sectors of the US economy or even for individual corporations? You should be prepared to investigate:

- trade magazines

- magazines of professional associations
- specific interest magazines.

To do this you need to explore not just the racks of magazines at the biggest W H Smith you can find, but also to seek out your local big city library, the reference room of your local college, and the periodicals section of your nearest university library. The range of professional and trade journals is almost limitless. You will be amazed to see computer journals from Australia, ceramic association newsletters from the USA, even Russian journals in translations.

		Often	Seldom	Never
The 'quality' press	*The Guardian* *The Times* *The Daily Telegraph* *The Independent*			
US papers available in Europe	*The Herald Tribune* *Christian Science Monitor* *US Today*			
US-based news magazines available in Europe	*Times Magazine* *Newsweek* *US News & World Report*			

For a standard textbook view try Sam Rosenberg's *American Economic Development Since 1945*, Macmillan, Basingstoke, 1985. And for an excellent, speculative and highly personal look at the prospects for the post-industrial economic order by a Clinton adviser see Robert B. Reich, *The Next American Frontier: A Provocative Program for Economic Renewal*, Penguin, Harmondsworth, 1984.

WORK: PRELIMINARY CONSIDERATIONS

The whole complex issue of US entry visas has been dealt with in Chapter 4, but jobs and visas do need to be considered together. So here are a few facts to be going along with.

Which foreigners ('aliens') can take a US job?

Only those allowed to live in the USA for compassionate reasons, whether to reunite families or to obtain asylum, are generally speaking allowed to take whatever job they can.

Everyone else must satisfy the US authorities that their reason for entering the USA is *not* to take a job. Only then will an entry visa be issued. Tourists, diplomats and transit travellers will have legitimate business within the country, but may not work within the US job market. If you aren't entering the USA on compassionate grounds and you intend to work then you need to provide proof that you should be considered an exception to the general rule, as provided for by the Immigration and Naturalization Act, Section 212(a)(14). Don't despair! Exceptions are many and are provided for. You just have to prove that you fit the criteria.

Making your case

Aliens (that's officialese for 'foreigners' not people from outer space) seeking permission to enter the USA to take up skilled (or unskilled) jobs need first to obtain a verification from the Department of Labor that there aren't sufficient US citizens (or permanent residents whom the US regards as trainee citizens) who are able, willing, qualified and available to do the work the alien proposes to do, and that if an alien takes such a job it won't adversely affect the working conditions of persons similarly employed within the USA already (that is, you're not there to break a legal strike or to force down contract rates of pay).

As you can imagine no single applicant can possibly do such a thing. However, companies actively recruiting overseas can make such a case to the US authorities on behalf of someone they want. If companies have made a conscientious effort to hire within the USA to no avail, then looking for someone overseas is not taking a job from an American, and may positively influence the job market by enabling other Americans to operate more effectively as vacancies are filled.

Now this all seems straightforward. However, if a US college, for instance, is trying to attract a specific person from overseas the job description might be so tightly drawn, tailor-made in fact, to fit no possible US applicant (*eg* 'must have engaged in at least 10 years full-time field work within the British Isles, speak and read English and Welsh, and have a proven track record in teaching Welsh medieval history'). It might be necessary to justify very carefully why such a specific set of criteria is deemed necessary, especially if the US Department of Labor knows there's actually a glut of good medieval history teachers and researchers already in the USA. But mostly US employers only headhunt overseas for specific skills to complement existing ones, or to bring in someone so prestigious no one is going to be able to object to a brain-drain so obviously to the advantage of the USA.

JOB HUNTING

Jobs as a result of specific advertisements have the advantage of someone in your corner to prepare the paperwork demanded by the US authorities. Removal expenses and help with finding a house and car may be available too (if only on a semi-informal basis).

Once the job's accepted, though, there's little or no choice as to which part of the country you'll have to live in. Having no job to go to does at least enable you to consider a wide range of possible places. Nevertheless a bird in the hand remains better than two in the bush.

Check out the travelling

An extended visit if you have no job arranged could enable you to see not just a particular city, but to check out feasible commuting. Freeways may imply swift movement between, say, downtown Washington DC and central Baltimore, but rush-hour traffic may in practice suggest otherwise. Riding the buses may show how slow public transport really is unless you can live and work near an express route (or a stop on the underground if you are considering one of the few cities to have one).

Checking out the area

An extended visit can be used to:

- check out whether or not an area appeals
- check out whether housing costs are appropriate
- check out schools, public and private.

Think in terms of why you are considering the USA:

- Can your love of the Rockies be met by living in Boston?

- Could you afford to ski if you lived in New Orleans?

- You may love New York City's television, but could you live with only three stations in the mountains of North Carolina?

- You may relish the cultural diversity of the USA but what if you were to find yourself stuck in an almost all-white, Bible-belt town on the one hand or the racial battlefield of the South Bronx on the other?

It's very risky going to the USA for the first time *after* arranging a job. Ideally a month is needed to get the feel of the country, including at least a week at the proposed job location and a week in the surrounding area. A car is essential for getting about except perhaps in New York City, Washington DC and San Francisco. If you want to visit the suburbs away from public transport routes a car is still essential.

Beginning to job hunt

Job hunting is hard enough at the best of times. Trying to do it at a distance can be next to impossible.

- A reconnaissance trip to start with can pay off handsomely if only to get you a toe in the water.

- A *lot* of letters will have to be written. This is true in the UK, and it's going to involve a far higher failure rate doing it from overseas, so you'll need to send off that many more enquiries.

- You'll need as large a source of names and addresses as possible. This book can only hope to start you off. You'll need to do considerable detective work in your own field to dig out more.

- Read 'Selling to the Americans' in James Hogan (ed) *Exporting to the USA*, Market Link Colchester 1988–89 for a useful overview of US business culture.

The rest of this section takes a look at some of the careers and fields of employment within the US economy today, with some general words of advice, and addresses. For the current US phone number ask British Telecom for International Directory Enquiries (153 for the USA). If you have a specific address and it sounds as though you would actually make the call they will ask the US operator to search for the number (using the American son of Ma Bell computer, so it shouldn't take too long). Also useful:

- *National Business Telephone Directory*, published by Gale Research Company of Detroit Michigan since 1956 (available in large city reference libraries).

- *National Fax Directory 1998* also by Gale (has addresses, faxes and phone numbers for 180,000 fax users across the USA). Published annually.

Useful places to find US employer information:

- City Business Library, 1 Brewers Hall Garden, London EC2 (Tel: (0171) 638 8215 for opening times).

- CIEE, 52 Poland Street, London W1V 4JQ (open for directory consultation 9.30–5.30 Monday–Friday).

Self-employed business opportunities

The US can provide significant entrepreneurial advantages for the self-employed. But as at home it is going to be very hard work, probably more so:

- US attitudes towards work mean people expect more of you.

- You'll be operating in a new set of business and tax laws (often more demanding than in Britain, contrary perhaps to expectations).

- You'll need to adapt to a new and often bewildering set of commercial ethics, and there'll be a whole new set of trading conditions, expectations about delivery dates and lines of credit.

Will it be worth it? Only you can say so. If you make a go of it the profits can be very substantial. But the hectic race has its losers too, and the US has little in the way of a safety net.

A few addresses that may be of interest:

- National Retail Merchants' Association
  100 West 31st Street, New York, NY 10001

- Insurance Information Institute
  110 William Street, New York, NY 10038

- National Association of Realtors
  N Michigan Ave, Chicago, Illinois 60611-4087.

Silver lining time: Though failure is very harsh in the USA many would maintain that business failure is not necessarily terminal. Being bankrupt is not like having an anti-social disease. Many people start right over again, and are admired for it. Only those who once down are prepared to stay down are really deemed beyond the pale. The sin is not *falling* down, but *staying* down.

Business and office jobs

As service industries continue to grow in importance and as computerisation seems to create even more jobs (though not usually for those losing the older jobs) periodic shortages of particular skills are often met by overseas recruitment. The quality press often carry advertisements from US firms, or on their behalf by UK-based recruiters. For those chosen the bureaucratic hassles will be minimised and company lawyers will smooth the way providing necessary supporting documentation for any visa application.

For more general information on recruitment it may be worthwhile writing to the following:

- National Association of Accountants
  10 Paragon Drive, Box 433, Montvale NJ 07645-1760

- American Bankers' Association
  1120 Connecticut Avenue NW, Washington DC 20036

- American Institute of Certified Public Accountants
  1211 Avenue of the Americas, New York NY 10036

- American Federation of Information Processing Societies
  1815 N Lynn St, Arlington VA 22209

- National Association of Public Insurance Adjusters
  300 Water St, Suite 400, Baltimore, MD 21202

- Insurance Information Institute
  110 William Street, New York, NY 10038

- National Secretaries Association
  2440 Pershing Road, Suite G-10, Kansas City, MO 64108

- Institute of Internal Auditors
  249 Maitland Ave, Altamonte Springs, FL 32701-4201

Media and the arts

Unless you are an artist of international renown able to obtain an H-1 visa it is very difficult to enter the USA to take part in its world famous communications industry. H-2 visas are only available for artists who will not be taking work from Americans. Artists visiting for concert tours need special arrangements with US Equity to ensure they come under reciprocal agreements arranged with British Equity. Visits and performance tours can and are arranged, not just by impresarios with legal departments to smooth the hassles but by various US agencies. The US Department of the Interior, for instance, arranges international festivals for traditional musicians from overseas.

Some skilled or gifted people enter this field by ways of placements as part of their postgraduate degrees in US colleges. Entrance to such courses is, however, competitive, especially where financial assistance is needed, and funds sufficient for the issuing of a non-immigrant student visa must be available *prior* to applying for a visa (see the later section on student visas).

Assuming that you are not wanting to be reunited with family already in the USA, that you are not an anti-communist refugee, that you don't have lots of money to invest, and that you aren't an artist of sufficient renown, you will need to be accepted by a US employer able to prove the post has been unsuccessfully advertised with the USA. This means in practice that only professional people already well established in their careers will be recruited, and so eligible for entry to work.

Remember: Sarah Brightman and then Jonathan Pryce were not deemed to be of sufficient renown by US Equity and the INS to appear on Broadway.

If you consider that you are capable of getting the right entry and work permits here are some addresses you may find helpful:

- Society of Illustrators
  128 East 63rd Street, New York, NY 10021

- Professional Photographers of America Inc
  1090 Executive Way, Oakleaf Common, Des Plaines, Illinois 60018

- Photo Marketing Association International
  300 Picture Pl, Jackson, Missouri 49201

- Printing Industries of America
  1730 North Lynn Street, Arlington, VA 22209

- American Society of Interior Designers
  608 Massachusetts Ave, NW, Washington DC 20002

- American Institute of Graphic Arts
  1059 Third Avenue, New York, NY 10021

- Graphic Artists Guild
  30 E 20th Street, Room 405, New York, NY 10003

- Industrial Designers Society of America
  1142 East Walker Road, Great Falls, VA 22066

- Society for Technical Communications Inc
  1010 Vermont Ave NW, Suite 421, Washington DC 20005

- American Federation of Television & Radio Artists
  260 Madison Ave, New York, NY 10016

- National Association of Broadcasters
  1771 N Street NW, Washington DC 20036

- Federal Communications Commission
  1919 M Street NW, Washington DC20554

- American Federation of Musicians
  1560 Broadway, Suite 600, New York NY 10036

- Software Publishers Association
  1101 Connecticut Avenue NW, Suite 901,
  Washington DC 20036

- US Equity (Actors' Equity Association)
  165 West 46th Street, New York, NY10036

For those with electrical/electronic skills:

- Communication Workers of America
  1925 K Street NW, Washington DC 20006

- Institute of Electrical & Electronic Engineers
  1828 L Street NW, Suite 1202, Washington DC 20036

Education, caring and social services

A desire to get rich quickly will not propel you into this line of work. Also, such public jobs depend heavily upon government spending programmes as so many are directly tied to federal programmes (and so federal budgets). With money (outside the military budget) increasingly tight the job situation is not rosy. Furthermore many jobs will require US qualifications to work in the USA.

Many people from overseas will only enter these fields if eligible for residence on other grounds. Once within the US job market, however, foreign professionals may be able to gain credit for courses overseas, or must be prepared to enter related jobs, such as legal paraprofessionals, library technicians or teachers' aids.

Some useful addresses:

- American Society for Information Science
  8720 Georgia Ave, Ste. 501, Silver Spring MD 20910-3602

- Legal Paraprofessional, American Bar Association
  541 N. Fairbanks Ct., Chicago, Illinois 60611

- Council of Library Science
  University of Mississippi, University, Mississippi 38677

- National Recreation and Parks Association
  2775 S. Quincy Street, Suite 300, Arlington, VA 22004

- National Education Association
  1201 16th Street NW, Washington DC20036

Engineering and science

Jobs are very competitive, so looking for a US job in these fields means looking for US firms that are actively recruiting overseas. Professional journals and magazines which carry such recruitment advertisements can be found in large public or university libraries – see their current acquisition section (ask at main desk, and don't worry: members of the general public are usually welcome to use such specialised materials).

US recruitment agencies will also pinpoint their efforts upon certain areas of the country. If an aerospace firm closes down, US firms hoping to attract away skilled labour will advertise locally, even open local recruitment offices. Of course it is the most modern skills they seek, held by people with at least 20 years' work left in them. The industrial cities of the USA already have far too many of their own approaching their fifties with skills no longer needed anywhere.

For information on US careers contact JETs Guidance, 1420 Icing St, Alexandria VA 223124. The publication to see is Peterson's *Engineering, Science & Computer Jobs*.

A few addresses that might be useful:

- American Institute of Aeronautics and Astronautics
  370 L'Enfant Promenade SW, Washington DC 20024

- American Society for Agricultural Engineers
  2950 Niles Road, PO Box 410, St. Joseph, Michigan 49085

- National Aeronautic Association
  1815 North Fort Myers Drive, Suite 700, Arlington, VA 22209

- US Energy Department
  1000 Independence Ave NW, Washington DC 20585

- American Institute of Biological Sciences
  730 11th St NW, Washington DC 20001-4521

- American Institute of Chemical Engineers
  345 East 47th Street, New York, NY 10017

- American Society of Civil Engineers
  345 East 47th Street, New York, NY 10017

- Institute of Electrical and Electronic Engineers
  345 East 47th Street, New York, NY 10017

- Institute of Food Technologists
  221 North LaSalle Street, Chicago, Illinois 60601

- Society of American Foresters
  5400 Grovenor Lane, Bethesda MD 20814

- American Geological Institute
  4220 King St, Alexandria, VA 22002

- American Institute of Industrial Engineers
  25 Technology Park, Norcross, Atlanta, Georgia 30092

- Instrumentation Society of America
  400 Stanwix Street, Pittsburgh, Pennsylvania 15222

- Marine Technology Society
  1828 L Street NW, Washington DC 20036-5104

- American Society of Mechanical Engineers
  345 E 47th St, New York, NY10017

- American Meteorological Society
  45 Beacon Street, Boston, Massachusetts 02108

- American Congress on Surveying and Mapping
  Woodward Building, 733 15th Street NW, Washington DC 20005

- American Institute for Design and Drafting
  3119 Prince Road, Bartlesville, Oklahoma 74003

Health care services

The shortage of doctors and nurses has significantly increased the need for technicians who can take over routine health care duties such as blood tests and dispensing medicines. The bureaucracy necessary to operate the complex private and public health care programmes, plus the growing number of older people, adds up to more health care jobs at many levels.

Once within the health care profession this is a career field that offers good salaries and good conditions. Health jobs offer steady work with few lay offs, as well as health care benefits, a most useful perk in a country where the high cost of health insurance can be a major drawback.

Most medical jobs require US training, but due to the pressures upon administrators to find suitably trained people it may be possible to gain significant credit for professional qualifications gained from recognised establishments overseas.

Nursing

To practise professional nursing in the USA you must pass a licensing exam in one of the states, or the District of Columbia. If you are already an SRN or SEN, passing an examination by the Commission on Graduates of Foreign Nursing Schools (CGFNS) is first necessary. In fact a CGFNS Certificate is required if you wish to secure a non-immigrant occupational preference visa (H-1), or to obtain an immigrant occupational (third) preference visa and a work permit from the US Labor Department regional office.

Information on taking the exam in the UK is available from:

- Commission on Graduates of Foreign Nursing Schools,
  3624 Market Street, Philadelphia, Pennsylvania 19104.

Addresses of state boards of nursing can be obtained from:

- National Council of State Boards of Nursing,
  303 East Ohio Street, Suite 2010, Chicago, Illinois 60611.

Expect higher pay and a higher social status in the USA, with more responsibility in emergency units if the doctor is not on the floor at the time. However, in less dramatic circumstances be prepared to refer to superiors even over nursing items, due to the fear of the institution being sued if improper treatment is given. Some aspects of nursing will be very different. British nurses can find obstetrics frustrating in the USA. US midwives have a shorter training than in Britain, and generally defer more to obstetricians, who do the actual deliveries rather than remain in the background unless a complication develops. Generally US nurses have less interaction with their patients. Doctors give instructions: nurses carry them out, and know their place. Likewise in geriatric medicine it is important to be aware of different medical ethics in operation. It is rare for the financially solvent but terminally ill, however aged, to be allowed to die without being first subject to levels of medical intervention most nurses would not want for themselves but which they are required by their employers to carry out to avoid malpractice suits by patients' relatives.

Paid training opportunities in the USA are made available from time to time via the Central Bureau for Educational and Vocational Exchange (CBEVE) for qualified or experienced foreigners aged 21–30 willing to work with mentally handicapped Americans. Couples are encouraged to apply. Contact, with a 9" by 12" stamped-addressed envelope:

- AYWO-HS Practical Training Exchange Program
  Seymour Mews House, Seymour Mews
  London W1H 9PE
  Tel: (0181) 445 0736

Some useful addresses:

- American Association of Chiropractors
  2025 I Street NW, Washington DC 20006

- American Chiropractors Association
  1701 Clarendon Boulevard, Arlington VA 22209

- American Dental Assistants Association
  666 North Lake Shore, Chicago, Illinois 60611

- American Dental Association
  211 E Chicago Avenue, Chicago, Illinois 60611

- American Dental Hygienists Association
  444 North Michigan Ave, Chicago, Illinois 60611

- American Hospitals Association
  840 North Lake Drive, Chicago, Illinois 60611

- Emergency Medical Service Branch
  National Transportation Safety Board
  800 Independence Ave NW, Washington DC 20594

- American Pharmaceutical Association
  2215 Constitution Avenue, Washington DC 20037

- American Association of Medical Assistants
  20 N. Wacker Drive, Suite 1575, Chicago, Illinois 60606

- American Society for Medical Technology
  330 Meadowfern, Bammel, Texas 77401

- American Medical Record Association
  John Hancock Centre, Suite 1850, 875 North Michigan Avenue,
  Chicago, Illinois 60611

- National Association for Practical Nurse Education & Service
  1400 Spring St, Ste. 310, Silver Spring, MD 20910

- American Nurses' Association
  600 Maryland Ave SW, Ste. 100, Washington DC 20024-2571

- American Occupational Therapy Association
  1383 Piccard Drive, Box 1725, Rockville, Maryland 20852

- Association of Operating-Room Technicians
  110 West Littleton Boulevard, Suite 201, Littleton, Colorado 80120

- Association of Operating Room Nurses
  Highpoint Office Bldg, 2170 S. Parker Rd., Ste. 300
  Denver, COL 80231-5711

- National Academy of Opticianry
  514 Chestnut Street, Big Rapids, Michigan 49307

- American Optometric Association
  243 N Lindbergh Boulevard, St. Louis, Missouri 63141

- American Physical Therapy Association
  1111 N. Fairfax Street, Alexandria, Virginia 22314

- American Society of Radiologic Technologists
  15000 Central Ave. SE, Albuquerque NM 87123-3909

- American Association for Respiratory Therapy
  7411 Hines Place, Dallas, Texas 75235

- American Association of Orthodontists
  401 North Lindbergh Boulevard, St Louis, Missouri 63141-7816

- American Osteopathic Association
  142 E. Ontario St., Chicago, Illinois 60611

Recruitment drives are held from time to time in the UK, and are accompanied by considerable media interest, so opportunities may present themselves to anyone ready and willing to relocate. But beware: US salaries may seem very high, but if you couldn't afford to move from Birmingham to London because of the high cost of living in the south-east you may not be able to afford housing in New York City either. But a move from London to rural Minnesota might be very profitable.

Any move by a single person to the USA (if only for a year or so) may be worthwhile just for the experience. And of course many single people going over to work in the USA also marry an American, whatever their original plans.

For a guide to job hunters and recruiters see Matthew Cunningham, *The International Recruitment Guide & Directory*, International Venture Handbooks, Plymouth 1996.

UK-based recruitment agencies include:

- Angel International Recruitment (0171) 583 1661
- British Nursing Association International (0171) 629 9030
- Grafton International (01232) 242824
- Medic International (0181) 568 4300
- Miller, Brand & Co Ltd (0171) 377 5661

For carers for the elderly placements:

- Private Care Association
  801 Princeton Ave. NW, Suite 426, Birmingham Alabama 35211

- Association of Homes for the Ageing
  1129 20th Street NW, Suite 200, Washington DC 20036 (see their 'Jobmart' job listings)

Service industries

As people have more money and more leisure time, service industries, particularly those dealing directly with the general public, grow and grow in number and importance. Many service jobs, though, are poorly paid, recruiting non-unionised teenagers, as in fast-food outlets. These jobs may be available on a casual basis, but are not career jobs, nor are such jobs available for foreigners without resident status. However, some services do require specialist skills, such as the rescue and police services. Unfortunately such public services are often geared to government spending levels. In certain parts of New York City public services have been subjected to 'planned shrinkage'! If you have already served in the fire service contact:

- International Association of Firefighters
  1750 New York Avenue NW, Washington DC 20006

For information on police opportunities write to the state police department of any state you are interested in, which will probably be located in the state capital (*eg* Albany for New York, Tallahassee for Florida, or Sacramento for California). There is no federal police force (unlike the Mounties in Canada) as law and order is very much a state responsibility (as it remains for each country in the European Union, with which the USA should perhaps be more properly compared). Alan Whicker presented a British police officer's view of both the service and his Los Angeles 'beat' on his 1986 television series (see *Whicker's New World*, once a Book Club choice now turning up in secondhand bookshops).

Transport
Employment is expected to increase for highway and air jobs, but continues to decline for railway work. Sales and reservation jobs are now much like any other job that deals directly with the general public within catering or tourism. Most jobs are therefore only available for those already US residents. Aircraft mechanics need a licence from a Federal Aviation Administration (FAA) approved school, plus considerable experience, usually gained in the US military. Except for overseas applicants with highly unusual skills this field is essentially closed to people who don't already have US residency.

A note of warning: if you are thinking of investing money, time or effort in any commercial trucking enterprise, please get professional advice. Moving furniture in a VW bus for friends or acquaintances is one thing, but getting into long haul trucking may soon bring you up against the International Teamsters (at best) or the Mafia (at worst). Neither organisation tends to encourage people moving onto their turf.

Contract work
Contract work is advertised in the UK press primarily as available for

engineering and electronics persons, ranging from a few months to a couple of years. Employment is on US terms (with minimal holidays) but at very good rates of pay even by US standards. Fixed terms are usually necessary for immigration regulation purposes. Beyond the end of the contract there is no security, and you will have to have one eye always on the next contract opportunity, which may mar the travel time between contracts. It'll play havoc with family life.

Good news
- good pay
- experience of USA
- formalities undertaken by employer
- fares paid
- nomadic
- travel between contracts

Bad news
- fixed term
- you may not be able to stay on
- can't change employer
- can't visit beforehand
- hard on family life
- you may be reluctant to spend money if no further job is in sight

For an exploration of the possibilities of contract work see Rod Briggs *Working on Contract Worldwide*, How To Books, Plymouth 1996.

APPLYING FOR A JOB

Applying for any job, especially one overseas, demands great care. You are presenting yourself, so take your time. You only get one bite of the apple. Show your draft copy to someone, whether a careers adviser, a relative in business, or just a friend. Their comments may be all the feedback you'll get, and so may be invaluable.

How well you fill in an application form is generally crucial: it is usually the first contact with an employer. The overall impression created by a completed form will precede you to any further interview. In the competitive job market today, the importance of well presented and well thought out applications *cannot be over-emphasised.*

The job hunter's perspective
From the job seeker's perspective application forms are a huge hurdle:

you generally have to complete a great many just to get one interview; it can be very time consuming; and they often ask the most awkward and difficult questions. But there is no escape from them if you hope to find a job.

Think of applications as a challenge – a means of presenting as positive and interesting (but truthful) picture of yourself as you can. Make sure the employer will want to find out more about you.

The employer's perspective

From the employer's point of view application forms are vital selection documents. Most employers cannot interview all applicants, so half or more are usually eliminated through this initial screening. Application forms provide an economical basis for deciding which candidates are most likely to meet their criteria. Their decisions will be based not only on what you write, but also on *how you present it*.

Presenting your application form

The effectiveness of your application will depend largely upon your prior preparation. You cannot expect to sit down 'cold' with any application form and do justice to yourself there and then. Prior work is essential.

Assess yourself

Many questions will focus on you as a person:

- What have you gained from your education/training/career so far?
- Why do you think you would make a useful member of their firm?
- What are your main strengths and weaknesses?

Thorough self-analysis and relating your skills, interests and background to the demands of the job are vital steps in the application process, enabling you to present a convincing case for yourself.

Research

Research the job and the particular employer before filling in the forms. You need to find out as much as you can about both the organisation and the job. Lack of such homework is almost always evident and a common basis for rejection at this stage.

Types of questions

Although forms vary, and range from one side of foolscap concentrating on factual information, to booklets requiring almost a total life history, they usually ask for the following information.

Personal details and educational background

Make sure all the information is accurate and nothing relevant has been omitted. It is usually best not to list failures unless specifically asked to do so or unless they indicate a gap in your life that cannot otherwise be accounted for. Try, however, to be positive wherever possible. If you feel you must say how far you fell make sure they know how soon you came back up to try again and to succeed.

Interests, extra-curricular activities and positions of responsibility

Selectors will deduce quite a lot from what you do (or do not do) with your spare time. They will be particularly interested in positions of responsibility and evidence of initiatives. This is particularly crucial when applying for your first ever job (when you cannot offer practical experience). Do you seem to be an active, social type or more of a loner? Are you a single-minded specialist or an all rounder? Is there evidence of leadership abilities, of being able to work well in a team? The main thing is to try and write positively about your activities – whatever they may be.

Work experience/previous jobs

Employers are interested in any work experience you have had. When describing your employment include a brief description of the duties involved. Try and demonstrate what you gained from this experience, such as working under pressure, with the general public, out of doors, shift work, *etc*. Particularly if you are applying for your first job do not leave anything out. Anything and everything can count as useful experience.

If you are further along with your career you can be more choosey. Even here, though, vacation work twenty years ago might be worth mentioning, if for instance it was in the USA (and so the company knows that early on you showed initiative, and that you have already had some experience of living in the USA).

Job choice/career aspirations

Almost all application forms will have some questions aimed at drawing out your motivation for the particular job, and for determining your longer-term career aspirations. It is vital that you communicate interest in the job and the organisation, backed up by whatever concrete evidence you can use.

Knowing precisely what the company has to offer is crucial (you must read the recruitment literature carefully). Relate your needs, interests and aspirations to what they say they need. Indicate what specific factors have influenced your career choice and why you think your combination of experience, qualifications and personal attributes is appropriate for the job in question.

Open-ended questions

These can include:

- What have been your main achievements in life?

- What initiatives have you taken and what have you been able to accomplish?

- What difficulties and disappointments have you met and how have you tackled them?

Such questions may seem very intimidating at first, particularly since most of us have had relatively ordinary careers, unpunctuated by momentous accomplishments, events or turning points. However difficult such questions may seem, try to see them as an opportunity to portray something interesting and positive about yourself and to demonstrate your ability to communicate clearly and concisely.

Employers are generally more concerned with what an experience meant to you personally, how you dealt with it, or what you gained from it, than the actual event itself. Thus, persevering with months of boring assembly line work rather than going on the dole could be more relevant than going to climb Mt Everest (if, for example, you were killing time before going to take a business management course).

It is useful to think about what the employer is trying to get at by asking this type of question. There is no standard or correct answer. You need to write about your own experiences!

Additional information

Many forms have a space for anything additional you feel you could usefully tell them. There may be something you thought they would want to know but don't seem to have asked for. Perhaps you could mention foreign travel, expeditions, or special qualifications that might suggest the sort of person you are. Maybe you could use this opportunity to explain why you were made redundant. You may be able to write something distinctive that will make you stand out from the general run of the mill applicant. If your area of responsibility was increasingly profitable but was undermined by an asset-stripping take-over then say so. You may get no other chance to explain why you are looking for work.

Questions to be raised at interview

This gives the interviewer advance notice of questions you might want to ask and gives the selector a further opportunity to assess the quality of your thinking about the job. Never leave this section blank. And never ask just about salary and holiday matters. Think carefully about what you have read in the company literature. Are there gaps in what they have said about the company? Perhaps you still feel you need to know about the range of training they will provide? The likeliness of career progression? Do not be afraid to ask challenging questions.

Referees

If you have recently completed formal education one of these should be an academic referee. The second should be a previous employer or someone (not a relative) who knows your career well, and can comment upon your performance, particularly if it is not possible to ask your present employer for a reference (if you don't want it to be known that you are applying for jobs elsewhere). Always consult referees before naming them, and make sure that they have a good idea about what you are applying for.

General guidelines

- Try to approach the firm as *positively* as possible. It is important to be truthful, but you will have to **sell yourself** and convince the employer that you really want the job and have the ability and potential to succeed at it. Don't make claims you cannot substantiate, but remember, no points are given for modesty.

- Do all the necessary preparation – **assess** yourself, **research** the job and the company and **relate** your attributes and aspirations to the demands of the job.

- Before writing anything, **read the form carefully** to get the feel of what to put where and how much space you have.

- Follow all the **instructions** carefully – mistakes will be interpreted as an indication of carelessness.

- **Make a draft version of what you intend to write.** This can be done on a photocopy of the application form. It is particularly important to draft out answers to open-ended questions and, ideally, to put the draft away for a day or so before returning to it with a fresh eye.

- Use **black ink** (many photocopies may have to be taken).

- Pay particular attention to **neatness** and **spelling**. Selectors will not be well disposed to applications that are untidy, difficult to read or filled with spelling errors. Type, unless specifically asked to write in your own hand.

- Make sure the **layout** is clear and attractive. First impressions are important.

- Do not leave any unexplained chronological **gaps**.

- Answer **all the questions**, unless not applicable.

- Relate what you write to the precise **requirements** of the job.

- Always keep a **photocopy** of completed applications. They will be necessary at the interview stage (you'll need to see what you told them beforehand!).

- Many of the questions asked at **interviews** will be based on answers you have provided on the form. Before an interview it is vital to think about how your response might be further developed.

- If you need **help**, ask a friend or colleague. They can help you think through the difficult questions and can advise on the overall impact your application makes.

Curriculum vitae (CV)
Some very detailed application forms (similar to those for university entrance) do not require a separate CV, but with most applications you should send one along. Known as a **resumé** in the USA it is a personal, one-page statement of:

- who you are
- what you have done already
- what qualifications you have
- what you have to offer.

- It should be set out in a generally acceptable format, must be typed, and should be carefully spaced so that the layout draws the reader's attention to essential information in a methodical and logical fashion. The usual British format is as follows:

Personal	Nationality, age, date of birth (spelled out in full), marital status, address, telephone numbers (work and home), relevant extra information (hobbies, association memberships). However, US laws to combat discrimination restrict the types of information that can be included in applications (date of birth, marital status and driving licence record) so do not include details that will render your application invalid.

Work experience   Names and addresses of past employers, dates of employment, positions and responsibilities held, with reason for leaving. Don't distinguish between paid and unpaid work experience.

Education   Dates and schools, colleges, universities attended, examinations passed (with dates and grades), with any other qualifications. Mention any awards, honours or scholarships.

- It's usual to set out present positions first and then work back. If a column for dates is kept clearly visible on the left this should be quite clear to any reader.

- If you have little or no employment to record (if straight from college) place the education section before the employment section.

- If you are sending out multiple applications use the best copier you can afford. It may be worthwhile to visit a copyshop rather than rely on doing it yourself in a coin-in-the slot machine. For isolated applications send an original rather than a copy.

Remember: US students have long typed all their work so the quality of your competition's CV will be very high. If in doubt pay for your CV to be professionally typed and copied. At the very least use a template from a Desktop Publishing (DTP) package such as Microsoft's *Publisher*.

Sending off applications

- **Type** your covering letter on good quality A4 paper, and send it in an appropriately sized envelope with your CV. Neatly type the envelope using the correct zip code. It is usual in the USA to place your address in the upper left hand corner of the addressed side of the envelope. Use the correct value stamp and an airmail sticker. The use of a commemorative stamp on a well-produced envelope may well catch someone's eye in a pile of applications.

- If you wish for confirmation of receipt of your application, or wish for items to be returned, or further information to be forwarded, always send either sufficient postage stamps (saved from last year's Florida holiday or bought from a stamp dealer!) or sufficient International Reply Coupons (available at your post office).

For more information see Appendix E (Job Applications) in Roger Jones, *Getting A Job in America*, How To Books 5th edition 1998 for suggestions on tailoring applications to US guidelines.

Offered a job?

Before accepting any job abroad make absolutely certain you are aware of all relevant factors:

- Are your professional qualifications acceptable in their existing form in the USA?

- Who will be responsible for getting the appropriate papers, yourself or the employer?

- What is the length of the contract? Is there a probationary period?

- What is the salary and when will the first payment be made, and in what form?

- Who is responsible for deductions?

- What vacation entitlements are there in the first year?

- What relocation help is available? If so, when and how much?

- What accommodation arrangements are there, for how long and at what cost?

- Will commuting be necessary? Is public transport feasible?

- What sickness provision is there for self and for family? When does it take effect?

- What pre-conditions exist? Will you be asked to sit any in-house examinations, undergo medical tests?

If you are offered a job it may well be necessary to accept or reject it quite quickly. The more versed you are in the problems of moving the easier it will be to concentrate upon the essential factors upon which you'll make your decision.

COMMUTING AS AN OPTION

Rather than change countries it may be easier to commute between Britain and the USA. Academics, journalists and certain businessmen may find living in both countries feasible.

Points to consider may include:

- costs of maintaining two bases
- costs of air fares
- time involved in travelling
- tax liability
- immigration standing.

All these points need careful consideration, else you could find yourself committed to far more travel and far greater costs than initially anticipated.

Two bases

There are several options worth thinking about:

- *Home in the UK and staying with US friends*
  You can't stay too long, or you'll outlive your welcome. Paying for a spare room may solve this problem. You'll avoid US local taxes and the problem of leaving your US base unoccupied (and thus vulnerable) for long periods.

- *Home in the UK and own place in US*
  If this involves owning in the UK and renting in the USA you may get tax advantages from your UK home as your 'principal residence' and the rented flat as a business expense. This is easier than the other way around, as it leaves a Briton with an existing relationship with the Inland Revenue. Avoid starting any relationship with the more strict Internal Revenue Service in the USA. Better the devil you know...

- *Base in the UK, with long-stay hotel accommodation in the USA*
  This could be right for you, but only if you intend to stay put, say in New York City or Los Angeles. Otherwise you'll be humping stuff around the USA. But for a month or so long-stay rates can be attractive, being much lower than daily rates. At worst you could try staying at a basic level at the YMCA or YWCA, though security for business materials while you're out at work might be worrying. A half-way solution might be to rent an efficiency room from a motel, which would include a kitchen besides the usual facilities.

Cost of air fares

If you are self-employed these costs can start to eat into profits, even if you are able to claim them as business expenses for tax purposes.

You may well not want to wait for cheaper standby places, nor can you travel to and fro wedged into a tourist seat too frequently. Eventually you'll need to travel at some expense if only to get some sleep and to minimise jet lag. Concorde back from Washington DC or New York City is ideal, but pricey.

Other costs would include:

- getting to and from the airport
- long-stay car parks
- shipping over goods and materials.

Travel times

Few will live in the lee of Heathrow or Gatwick nor will a US base necessarily be near to JFK or Newark. The journey from Birmingham to Heathrow is tortuous with luggage, though easy by motorway. What do you do with the car at Terminal 4? Flying down from Birmingham International may be more convenient, but may raise your travel costs by 20 per cent. British Airways now fly directly from Birmingham to JFK from which connections can be made, especially convenient if by USAir, BA's partner in the USA.

Do you want to have a three-hour motorway drive home after arriving at Heathrow from New York City? If you'd flown Concorde then Heathrow would be only halfway home!

Tax liability

Though US-UK treaties ensure that you'll only be taxed on the same income once, each country will want it to be in their system. The rule of thumb is that you'll be taxed in the country where you spend most of your time. The United States IRS uses a complicated formula to calculate a notional definition of where you live, or as bureaucrats prefer to put it: where you have a 'substantial preference'! (see box.)

If there's any doubt where you live then both bureaucracies will read their own regulations to their own fiscal advantage (wouldn't you?), may change the rules from year to year, and may redefine what is meant by a permanent base, the indicator of where you intend to be taxed.

'Substantial preference'
In theory it's quite simple:

31 days in the USA this calendar year and 183 days in this year plus the last 2 years, but counting only a third of last year's days, and counting only an eighth of the previous year's.

Got it?

A worked example:

In 1999 you spent 100 days in the USA and these are counted in full	100
1998 is the previous year, of which 100 again were spent in the USA but only a third count	$33^1/_3$
Plus 80 days for 1997, where only an eighth count	10
	$143^1/_3$

So, though you spent more than 31 days in the USA in 1999, you stayed only $143^1/_3$ in 1997–9 rather than the 183 that would have made you liable for US tax.

Easy, isn't it!

If at all possible keep your residency status the same from year to year, so that you only have to deal with one pack of wolves at a time (remember the military nightmare of a war on two fronts).

For the US view of tax details and so forth see the IRS booklet No. 518 *Foreign Workers, Scholars and Exchange Visitors*. For the British equivalent leaflet ask for IR58 from your local tax office.

For an unofficial but authoritative British view see *The Expatriate's Guide* by Andrew Burgess, an ex-Inland Revenue officer who moved on to become the director of financial planning at Neville Russell Accountants, 246 Bishopsgate, London EC2M 4PA. This is a most useful guide for those interested in the tax consequences of living and working in the USA. It is well thought out, with good headings and an index to help you find your way through the issues. Phone (0171) 377 1000 for details of the guide's availability.

Immigration standing

US regulations assume that you are either a visitor or an immigrant. Exceptions get very messy and confused. Many people, afraid of falling between two stools, hire a lawyer specialising in immigration matters, though this can be expensive, and is no guarantee of a satisfactory outcome, especially if the lawyer is mainly used to dealing with people who want to get permanent residency status. Most people would get by with the normal commercial non-resident B1 visa. Academics, for instance, usually get the B1-2 visa valid for multiple entry that would allow visits and commercial trips. This is because they would be working for UK-based employers (colleges and publishers).

If you want to work for a US-based employer you will need an employment visa or residency status (the famous so-called Green Card). This is much harder to get, of course, unless you can arrange to be hired by, and paid by, the UK subsidiary (or even a UK parent company).

INVESTING IN THE USA

For people with more than their lives and families to invest in the USA investment may or may not involve actually moving to the USA. Either way it needs expert advice. Selling your thriving fish and chip shop here, packing the money into a suitcase and going through US customs and immigration as a tourist (it's been done) is not advisable. There are too many tales of people coming sadly and very badly unstuck, investing in motels that then go bust as the new freeway opens and takes all the passing trade elsewhere (haven't they seen *Psycho* or *The Postman Always Rings Twice?*). Don't buy a college town bar just as the state's liquor laws change to stop students under 21 drinking. Too many small investors end up washing floors, dishes and windows, one-step ahead of the Immigration and Naturalization Service (INS), not to mention the Teamsters or the Mafia if they think you are muscling in on their patch.

Finding out information

For more specific and detailed information see the appropriate *Daily Telegraph Guide* by Peter Farrell, *How to Buy a Business*, published by Kogan Page of London. Though certain specifics may age the general approach necessary to such a major transaction surely doesn't. Another vital guide is Paul Chaplin's *Choosing and Using Professional Advisers*, also published by Kogan Page.

If property investment is proposed an essential work of reference is Nigel A. Eastway and David Young's *Expatriate Tax and Investment Guide*, published in London by Longman. Besides dealing with the joys of double taxation, capital gains and capital transfer taxes, this otherwise general source of information specifically presents a section tailored to the needs of those people with an eye on the United States.

Penetrating the US market

The behaviour of UK firms well illustrates how difficult it is to penetrate the US market. UK retailers have been badly mauled by trying to impose British retailing formats and techniques upon US consumers. Laura Ashley's costly investment in the USA almost destroyed the company. It had to close its 150-store US chain just to survive. American shoppers just didn't go for the English look. Marks and Spencer took over Brook Brothers in the late 1980s, but in a complex deal that involved access to specific shopping malls found that their long-term interest in gaining access to the convenience food market was fraught with difficulties. Not all malls are modern with access to the market niche desired. Learning the hard way can be an expensive option. Dixons, likewise, found its US subsidiary a money pit. Sock Shop found collapse followed initially massive expansion. If such enterprises cannot read the US market, with all their support services, what chance a small business going it alone?

Getting help with a sales campaign

For the manufacturer who wants to explore the possibilities of investing in a sales campaign within the USA the British Overseas Trade Board now known as the DTI should be approached on (0171) 215 5000. The DTI can provide seed corn grants for market research, and can provide help with stands at trade fairs overseas. They do, however, tend to insist that suppliers seeking to penetrate the US market do so from a tested and tried basis with local and European markets. The US market should be approached from strength rather than speculatively.

Meanwhile consult:

- *Exporting to the USA*, James Hogan (ed.), Market-Link International, Colchester.

- 'Setting up business in the US' in the American Chamber of Commerce (UK) volume *Anglo-American Trade Directory* for advice and contact numbers.

Using a US-based trading company

The entrepreneur who sees the US market as impenetrable except from within may well be missing an equally appropriate option. For those with no wish to leave home for more than the occasional and very necessary business trip the very thought of emigration may so repel that any further interest in the US market may die as well.

But markets overseas are ever more critical. The more specialist the product the more commercially necessary will it be to sell it within the USA. Lacking the knowledge of international corporations and the financial ability to buy it in (as would a larger concern), the small entrepreneur may consider the US market as inaccessible as a weekend climber finds Mt Everest. What is needed is a proven, low-cost guide for the small entrepreneur into this potentially most lucrative of markets. 'Trading posts' now provide such a guide.

The US economy continues to suck in not only consumers and electronic goods from overseas, but increasingly seeks foreign ideas, techniques and materials. Research and development (R & D) concerns servicing the space, semiconductor and electronics industries are looking not just for British experts to move to the USA but also to buy, license or even fund those techniques deemed essential if the USA is to survive its huge trade deficit.

This new generation of intermediaries is more active on behalf of customers, rather than being just a computer clearing house. Matching products with R & D customers, trading firms actively join suppliers in selling their product to the market, coupled with overseeing the actual processes of importing, distribution and after-sales support. A specialist staff would handle all sales and marketing in return for exclusive distribution rights. The trading company buys only from suppliers whose product reliability is excellent. The trading company then sells to US end users with suitable credit ratings. Trading companies thus act as a risk-taking buffer between the supplier and the buyer, profiting not on a commission basis, but on the difference between their buying and selling prices.

So successful has this procedure been that US blue chip customers such as Bell, Exxon, Hewlett Packard, IBM, MIT, NASA and Texas Instruments now use such trading companies for specific products. The management approach is to focus upon universities, government and corporate research rather than geographical regions (the latter being more appropriate for consumer rather than technological products). The time scale is extended to ensure both products and suppliers are carefully chosen, with an overt emphasis upon sound and proven technology, strong management and a whole-hearted commitment to both the product and the customers.

Seeking sales of over $1 million per annum companies need to be able to fund a high entry cost, up to $250,000. But to place a qualified and committed company representative over in the USA could cost over half this sum, with no legal backup: an expensive way to send rarely effective brochures that could have gone in the post, if not straight in the bin.

For more information contact the American Chamber of Commerce (UK), 75 Brook Street, London W1Y 2EB. Tel: (0171) 493 0381. Their *Anglo-American Trade Directory* contains information on entering the US market, acquiring a US business, finding US premises and hiring and firing guidelines (euphemistically listed as 'Human Resource Advice').

This massive initial cost will, of course, exclude most UK companies from even considering going it alone, never mind in tandem with a trading company. Other options do exist:

- the brochure blitz

- the phone call campaign

- the personal contact

- the transatlantic trip

- buying in skills from local colleges and universities

- co-operation with bodies actively promoting US investment in the UK, such as **Business Link Staffordshire**, Civic Offices, Riverside, Stafford ST16 3AQ. Tel: 0345 202122.

- co-operation with agencies promoting British exports in the USA, such as the **Department of Trade and Industry** on (0171) 215 5000 in London or (0121) 212 5000 for the West Midlands.

WORK AND THE INFORMATION HIGHWAY

The research for this book has involved not just working in the USA but searching out directories in many libraries, turning pages in search of that illusive piece of information. Soon, though, such data searches will start and finish at my desk: an information revolution is at hand. I already contact US colleagues more by computer than by phone and fax. Recent reviews of public libraries insist they should provide public access to the electronic highway, the Internet. Most university students already log onto a network computer to research their papers and write their dissertations. But this revolution is more than just efficient ways of accessing books or writing essays. The revolution coming our way allows us to search for information anywhere in the world. I can already access the US Library of Congress, the US National Archives and even the CIA. Soon most public agencies will make data bases available for all of us, if not for free then at a price the market will bear. Books such as this already focus more on how to find out about living and working in the USA than actually on how to live and work. If you seriously want to be part of the USA you will have to join the information highway to find the necessary information. Once you are connected people and institutions will actually come and find you; already the daily White House press release arrives in my electronic mailbox, whether I like it or not: electronic junk mail has already arrived.

Further reading

There is a regular small business column in the financial section of the *Guardian*. General business climate and conditions in the USA are increasingly important in the weekly *Economist* (as an ever large proportion of its readership is American). There is always, of course, *The Financial Times*. Knowing your way around the *FT* makes going through back copies much easier for large parts can safely be ignored so long as relevant sections are carefully monitored. Also search out:

- American Chamber of Commerce (UK) *Anglo-American Trade Directory*

- James Hogan (ed), *Exporting to the USA*, Market-Link, Colchester

- Gary Hoover, *Hoover's Handbook of American Business*, William Snyder, £18 annually

- *The American Almanac*, William Snyder, £13 annually in hard copy, or on CD-Rom as part of Microsoft's *Bookshelf* (1996 edition).

Some contact numbers:

- US International Marketing Center   (0171) 629 4304
- American Chamber of Commerce (UK)   (0171) 493 0381
- US Embassy Commercial Reference Library   (0171) 499 9000
- United States Information Service (USIS)   (0171) 408 8053

For a more detailed guide to practical job-hunting in the USA consult another book in this series, *Getting a Job in America* by Roger Jones (How To Books, 1997), which contains useful copies of immigration and taxation forms (forewarned is forearmed).

Financial health warning

Investing overseas is fraught with danger and may only be for those who can afford to lose everything. Most foreign investors just do not appreciate the cultural difference between home and the USA. US consumers are particularly price and brand sensitive, while insisting upon regular changes in the products offered ('this year's line'). Unless you can address brand recognition costs you really shouldn't approach the US market. It takes successful companies decades sometimes to get a substantial return on their investment, and they can be caught out by serious exchange rate fluctuations.

9
Money Matters

CASH

Payment is made with cash far more widely than in the UK, despite the widespread use of credit cards, charge cards, personal cheques (checks) and travellers' cheques.

Beware:

- All US banknotes (bills) are **green**, the same size, and have similar layouts (though a different president's face appears on each denomination). Watch though for the new forge-proof $100 bills.

- You may come across the following sign: 'Legal tender not accepted.' It means just what it says. Payment is to be prepaid token or by card (credit or charge). It's all part of the war against crime: no cash means there's nothing to steal.

PERSONAL CHEQUES

Personal cheques are far less convenient than in the UK. They are subject to more scrutiny and more delay than you have ever met before. Personal cheques can usually only be used locally within the area served by your bank. Unfortunately your bank may well turn out to be far more local than you might have expected from its name as 'First National Bank of...'.

To use a cheque it must be overprinted with your name, address, telephone number, account number, and in some places your driver's licence number. *And* you'll need local identification (ID). And to write $11.60 write eleven and $\frac{60}{100}$ dollars.

What's ID?

This usually means a driving licence at the very least. It'll be asked for whenever you use any form of cheque, even travellers' cheques! Don't bother trying to explain to the clerk that travellers' cheques are as good as cash if signed at time of use. You'll be shown the sign that hangs everywhere 'all checks must have ID'.

> Once, in the Smithsonian Institute bookshop in Washington DC, an American Express dollar travellers' cheque was refused with reference to just such a sign (since taken down), and the clerk wanted local identification. The cheque wasn't accepted until a five-year-old, almost expired, US government ID was produced (a relic of a previous spell working in the capital).

The reason cheques cause so much hassle is quite simple. Cheque theft is endemic. Furthermore, if you leave a retailer with a cheque that bounces (and there are no guarantee cards to ensure payment up to a certain level) they'll want to find you to cover the value of the cheque, plus their administrative costs, plus the penalty payment the bank charged them. You may see signs warning you that a bounced cheque will cost you $10. As current accounts cannot go into the red the possibilities of going into cheque bouncing territory is high if you'd been used to the more casual situation in Britain. When, in 1992, a hundred members of Congress were found to have bounced cheques a national scandal ensued!

Overdrafts are generally frowned upon. In some states you are guilty of a felony if you write a cheque for more than you have in your account: you are trying to spend money that is the bank's not yours. Overdraft protection is available whereby an account likely to go into the red is topped up automatically (from another account or from a credit card).

CREDIT CARDS

Credit cards are more widely used than in Germany, but, surprisingly not as widely as in the UK. Most stores and petrol stations will accept VISA or Mastercard but there are still enough places that won't accept either card to make things tricky if you run out of petrol or need accommodation in out of the way places. Check beforehand if you can. Also, you may have to pay a surcharge for using a credit card.

Don't be surprised if the clerk hands you back not just the credit slip top copy but also the carbon. A few years back there was a rash of carbon-based frauds. Retrieving used carbons from bins gave thieves customers' credit card numbers, which were then used to order goods by telephone. Many people now expect to be offered the carbon for disposal.

Creditworthiness

Creditworthiness is different from what you're used to. It is *illegal* in many states to go unexpectedly overdrawn. If the bank were to honour your cheque it would be giving you its own money, so you would have spent what doesn't belong to you. If, on the other hand, the bank won't honour your cheque you have just attempted to defraud the retailer stuck with the bouncing cheque. Either way you are deemed to be beyond the pale. And your creditworthiness will disappear, which may hurt you when it comes to buying a car, or just trying to obtain a credit card.

Credit card companies require an indication you won't do a bunk and disappear after a shopping spree, so they may check your bank, your employer and commercially available bad-debts lists. If you are self-employed and live in a trailer then credit won't be available.

DEBIT CARDS

A short trip, up to a semester long for students paying fees in other ways, may call for a debit card withdrawing cash as required from Automated Teller Machines (ATMs) which, as at home, are now everywhere. Beware of withdrawing small amounts as each withdrawal involves a 1.5 per cent handling fee (and depends upon having money in your UK account).

BANKS

Banks are organised somewhat differently than in Britain, and this affects how they operate and the services they provide. Don't deposit any money in an uninsured bank. Many lived to regret doing just that in the 1930s Great Depression. The federal government set up the Federal Deposit Insurance Corporation (FDIC) to guarantee deposits (and so minimising the chance that there would ever be a dangerous loss of confidence in the financial system among small to medium savers). The maximum insured individual deposit continuously rises. By the mid-1980s it had reached $100,000 (more than most of us will ever have in the bank!)

SAVINGS AND LOAN ASSOCIATIONS ('THRIFTS')

Savings and loan associations are the nearest equivalent to British building societies. Loans have traditionally been fixed interest (good if you finance a property when the rates are low, not so good if they were very high), though loans are often refinanced if rates change substantially, or if house prices rise so high you are undermortgaged and so find you can raise more money on the property (say for an extension, a pool or even to go back to college). By 1990, though, half all new loans were on a flexible rate. If depositing make sure the association is insured by the savings and loan version of the FDIC, the Federal Savings and Loan Insurance Corporation (FSLIC).

MORTGAGES

American-style mortgages differ from traditional British ones in that the loan is linked with the property rather than with the borrower. That is, US mortgage levels are more directly based upon the collateral value of the property than is the case in the UK where the lender is more interested in the borrower's ability to repay irrespective of the potential of the property. American concern for the collateral value of the real estate explains why mortgages can be passed on to the next purchaser, providing some with a more efficient way of entering the housing market than starting a huge new mortgage that will be front loaded with interest payments rather than reducing the principal. Americans do not share the widespread British assumption that all mortgages must be as long as possible. Indeed the standard British 25-year mortgage reflects merely a long-standing concern for interest rate cycles among building societies. The downside is that US lenders, like new British banks, are more directly geared to seeking out profitable business with minimal risk, so they tend not to be very sympathetic to lenders in financial trouble.

Borrowers who run into trouble with their US savings and loan can easily lose their home, but unlike in the UK the lender will not pursue them through the courts for any shortfall between the value of the property and the outstanding mortgage debts. US lenders only lend what they can realise from the collateral view of the property, and if they misjudge its redeemable value that's their problem not the borrower's. It makes lenders more circumspect, though, about giving loans in the first place. The losers are those with lower incomes and jobs with poor security wanting mortgages on property they can afford but for which they cannot get a loan: Catch 22.

PENSION PLANS

Pension plans depend upon how long you intend to stay in the USA. If you are going to return home in a year or so you may just have to accept that all your required pension payments will be for nought. If your company can transfer them all well and good. If you leave the USA with all taxes paid you may be able to claim your US social security payments back, but only if you can show that you have taken no deductions, have paid tax at the flat rate, and will not be returning to the US to live. Students on an F visa may be able to do this, but it may well be cheaper for long-term visitors to pay as little tax as possible and to pay their social security knowing they'll get nothing for it. Students should consult their foreign student office at their university.

For those more affluent visitors who pay both tax and social security a tax accountant may be needed to get the best deal. And if you hear Americans talk about how rapidly support for the IRA is growing remember that in all probability they are referring to **individual retirement accounts** which involve tax-free savings earmarked for retirement. Such accounts enable people to move between jobs with no pension loss (so long as they can keep making the payments).

HEALTH INSURANCE

Health insurance may well be a major fringe benefit of a job offer. Few companies, however, offer full coverage for the employee and the rest of the family. You need to know precisely what the cover includes. Pre-existing conditions will, of course, be excluded, but beware of ceilings on payments for treatment. Cover will often only be for 90 per cent of costs up to say $10,000 and 100 per cent over that. Pregnancy may not be included, nor will dental and optical charges. Check when the cover comes into force – it might not be until six months into the job. Ask:

- When does the cover start?
- Who's covered?
- What's included?

It is essential to know what the situation is beforehand so that you can arrange bridging cover before you leave Britain. And you had better get those details in writing in case there's any dispute when push comes to shove. Illness can be emotionally devastating. In the USA it can also destroy the financial security of a family, and often does. Catastrophic illness can destroy the family just as much as the patient. At least be insured!

Medicare

The USA is the only G8 country with no basic medical insurance for all. Instead private schemes compete with a jerry-built structure of private, state and federal systems – some overlap, others leave gaping, unbridgeable holes for the working poor.

Medicare is the nearest thing the USA has to Britain's National Health Service, but it applies only to the aged (not to be confused with **Medicaid**, a joint federal and state health care programme for the poor). Medicare pays hospital bills less certain deductibles for the first 60 days only. Then the patient typically has to pay:

- $150 per day for one month
- then $300 per day for the next two months
- and then *all* the bills from then on.

To cover the gap between what Medicare pays and the bill some people will have taken out **Medigap** insurance, but this still only covers five months of Medicare cover. After that everyone is on their financial own.

Over 30 million patients rely on Medicare each year (of whom over 800,000 pay over $2,000 for Medicare during treatment). Life-savings are threatened by any catastrophic illness, or just the need to be in a nursing-home, which costs about $30,000 per person each year (of which only about 2 per cent has been covered by private insurance).

Warning: extras to the above include:

- outpatient drugs
- extra physicians' charges
- eye glasses
- dental costs.

It is not unheard of for surviving partners to be left with $10,000 worth of debt upon the death of the sick loved one. This is paid off like a mortgage (say $100 per month, with, if lucky, the balance due at the death of the surviving partner from whatever is left in the estate).

Health care is increasingly costly. A family of 2 adults and 3 children paying $2,500 a year at the end of the 1980s would be paying $5,000 a year by 1993 for Blue Cross Insurance cover. Not surprisingly about 40 million Americans have no health insurance at all but are nevertheless not poor enough to qualify for Medicaid.

TAXATION

A necessary summary of a necessary evil:

Is there a US version of PAYE?
Yes, but it is calculated in a way quite different from that traditionally used in the UK. The system goes something like this:

- You estimate what your allowances will be for the coming year.

- A proportion of your salary is excluded from tax on this basis and the rest is taxed at a variable rate plus a flat fee according to income.

- At the end of each tax year you fill in the tax form with the actual (not estimated) allowances. Tax actually due is compared with tax actually paid, and either you pay them or they pay you.

Any good news?
At least the tax year is the calendar year, though the infamous 1040 tax form doesn't have to be submitted until April, to give time for information to be collated.

If this sounds a complicated routine, in practice it's actually worse, as the allowances actually allowable are open to dispute.

Any useful short cuts?
- There is a short form for those lucky people with no complications (for instance, no deductions for things like mortgage interest).

- Most people find it pays to use the long form, which means getting professional help or spending at least 17 hours filling it in (officially it should take 2¾ hours). You'll see tax accountants as often as car exhaust and tyre companies on the edge of shopping malls. The major chain (H & R Block) is as well known as any fast-food firm.

Will it get any simpler?
Reagan's popularity with ordinary voters was partly based upon his promise to simplify government, which for most people means easing not just their tax burden but the burden of doing their taxes. Reagan also promised to do something about national debt. He did – he enlarged it as never before.

Needless to say tax reform has not materialised, though there is a new W-4 form designed to help calculate withholding levels. Paradoxically the new form is 4 pages long, twice the size of what it replaced!

What can I as a foreigner do to simplify my tax?
The criminal justice system never got to nail Al Capone. The tax people did, though, and sent him away for a long time for not paying tax on his illegal income. It makes you think. No wonder Americans are often heard saying only two things are certain in life: death and taxes (though not necessarily in that order!).

The IRS **audit** taxpayers. Audit is a word that conjures up fear and loathing across the USA. The IRS can ask for all written evidence to support your claim for tax allowances for the previous seven years.

Most taxpayers' returns are not scrutinised – the volume of returns wouldn't allow it. *But* the IRS do undertake *random* examinations of tax returns, and if anything untoward turns up then an audit may result. Many Americans liken this to shooting hostages, but mostly tax returns are so honestly completed only people pulling a fast one will suffer from an audit.

Does the IRS deal with all income taxes?
The IRS is the *federal* tax gatherer. Each state is entitled to tax as it sees fit. Most, but not all, do. This means that you have to fill out state *as well* as federal tax forms, though the state forms are usually simpler, shorter and information from the federal form can often be reused (and may be

cross-checked if there's a feeling you are trying to defraud the system).

Any other taxes?

For the first three years working in the USA you can continue to pay UK National Insurance Contributions. After that you are liable under the Federal Insurance Contributions Act to contribute to the old-age pension fund and to Medicare (generally for those over 65, or disabled veterans). Reckon on about 8 to 10 per cent of salary for these deductions. You must have paid for 40 quarters to be eligible. Many payments from these funds can be made available anywhere, and some people retire back to Ireland or to Poland to get the most from their pensions.

Individual states may have their own social welfare taxes, such as a disability insurance scheme taking off another 2 per cent or 3 per cent from salary.

And, of course, while your overall tax burden may well be lower than in the UK, even when you've added federal and state payments, you'll still have to pay for your private health and pension plans. The total outgoings from your salary may end up being very familiar to those from Britain (though less than from such countries as Sweden or the Irish Republic). The good news, of course, is that with an initially higher income you hope to be ahead at the end of the day.

In short: if at all possible avoid being liable for US taxes by continuing to pay UK taxes. Though UK taxes are somewhat higher it's worth the extra to avoid entanglements with the US Internal Revenue Service, whose penalties are greater if you fall foul. Remember they got Al Capone...

Just because you live in the USA does not necessarily mean that you can avoid a tax liability in the UK. If you are within the UK for 183 days in any one tax year the Inland Revenue will consider you liable for UK tax. Furthermore, if, over a three-year period, you spend an average of 90 days a year within the UK you will be deemed liable. And as we go to press these guidelines are being tightened up so get professional advice. Unless you have a full-time job outside the UK you could also become liable if you have and use 'available accommodation' here in the UK. Of course, if your property is let out and you have no access to it during a return to see the family that doesn't count. But if a non-working spouse comes home s/he could be considered a resident for tax purposes if using a residence that can be used at any time, such as a 'granny-flat'.

Taxation at a glance

The graph in Figure 2 showing relative rates for six countries provides interesting comparisons. Figures include all compulsory payments to federal, state and local governments for 1990.

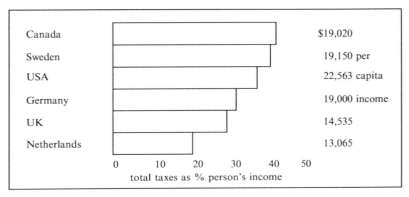

Fig. 2. Comparative tax rates.
Sources: *The World Almanac 1992: Statistical Abstract of the United States 1990*

These figures should be interpreted with some caution. Sweden and Canada may have higher rates than either Britain or the USA, but Swedes may still be materially the most well off, so beware assuming that tax rates are critical. If you are sick the USA may well help you become bankrupt the fastest.

Where can I read more on this?

Andrew Burgess, *The Expatriate Guide,* Neville Russell Accountants, 246 Bishopsgate, London EC2M 4PA. This well thought out guide outlines the tax consequences of living in the USA. It's written by an ex-Inland Revenue accountant. It may enable you to decide whether or not your financial position needs professional advice or not.

Michael A. Eastway and David Young's *Expatriate Tax and Investment Guide*, published by Longman, is useful too.

There are also magazines for expatriates which may be of interest:

- *Resident Abroad*, 102–108 Clerkenwell Road, London EC1M 5SA. Tel: (0171) 251 9321.

- *Nexus*, Expat Network Ltd, International House, 500 Purley Way, Croydon CRO 4NZ. Tel: (0181) 760 5100.

9
The Children and Their Education

...It is often the children who truly lead their elders to America, the sons who take their fathers to their first baseball game or shepherd them to their first rock concert to give them a real sense that they have a stake in America's future.

Henry Grunwald, editor-in-chief, *Time Magazine*
(born in Austria, arrived in the USA aged 17)

Many if not all people emigrate for their children. Safe within their family children are amazingly resilient. They'll pick up the language in weeks not years. They'll play with any child who'll play with them. They'll accept wherever they are as normal. They seem to possess a secret weapon unavailable to their parents.

Parents may be as ambivalent towards the USA as Americans are about them. Parents may keep one eye open towards the old country, following its progress, watching for it on television and in the papers. Their children, however, will not. They live in and for the present, which is now the USA. Where parents need gumption, courage and ambition plus the will to make it, their children will have all that and more besides, with no homesickness, no sense of alienation from things American and no feelings of exile. So great may be this feeling of moving forward that parents too may get left behind, seen as old-worldly, accent-ridden, out of touch. A national spelling contest was once won by a 13-year-old Tamil student!

Placing a child in the US educational system will be one of the major implications of moving to the USA with a family. Even if you can afford and want to place your children in the private sector there will be remarkable contrasts both with what you remember from your own days at school and from what is going on in Britain today. You may find surprisingly little difference if you are moving from a stable middle class school to one in an equivalent part of the USA, but if you are moving a child from a small rural British primary to a large suburban American school the culture shock experienced (not least by yourself) may be immense, just over this aspect of the move. Prepare your child, and thus yourself for the move.

- Talk it though with your child.

- Get to talk with the teacher responsible for your child's pastoral care (who may or may not actually teach them).

- Make sure the school knows the background, educational and otherwise, that your child has experienced to date.

- Take as active an interest in things like the Parent-Teachers' Association (PTA) as you can to keep track of what's going on in the school. This may be particularly necessary if you are not a church-goer (where many parents will meet, discuss their children and generally keep in touch).

- Don't expect your child's schooling to be like yours was. It wouldn't have been even if you were still back in the UK!

- Don't despair: your child could still return to the UK for third level education if necessary (though this would place a different and perhaps even more unanticipated pressure upon the family, and not necessarily a financial one at that).

THE US EDUCATION SYSTEM

The USA actually has two parallel education systems: one private and one public. In the public sector, which involves about 90 per cent of all pupils and students, control has traditionally been vested in state and local authorities under the general supervision of State Boards of Education, usually appointed by the Governor, though sometimes elected. Each state is divided into school districts, over 16,000 throughout the whole USA, each administered by school boards either elected or appointed locally.

Education is therefore far more locally controlled even than it used to be in Britain. This means that by and large rich areas run well-funded schools, poor districts poorly funded schools. However, a widespread concern for civil rights and the belief in the need for a high minimum level of general education has led to the provision of federal funds for the improvement of educational facilities, though not always in the most needy of areas.

Regional variations
Education is by far the greatest item of expenditure for state and local governments, averaging about a third of total spending, being generally lowest in those states where average earnings are depressed. Though southern states have, with some reluctance, come to regard the provision of high quality public schooling for all children regardless of race as an

urgent social necessity their generally lower incomes mean that they cannot always afford to improve their educational system.

In rural America, particularly in the West, the level of expenditure is partly dictated by the scattered nature of settlement, making educational costs quite high. Cultural characteristics are also quite important. Minnesota's liberal German and Scandinavian traditions have included considerable support for the adequate funding of education. In the Dakotas, by contrast, a decrease in general levels of prosperity has been reflected in a serious decline in proportionate support for education.

Racial integration

After the Civil War, southern whites were unable to accept the social, economic and political implications of the freeing of the slaves. They were supported by the US Supreme Court which declared that segregation was permissible, provided that facilities for black people were equal to those for whites (though they rarely were so). In 1954, though, the Supreme Court reversed this 'separate but equal' doctrine, declaring that separation was itself a form of inequality. Federal action followed to integrate the education system. After the 1964 Civil Rights Act Congress cut off funds to any school district that failed to provide fully integrated education.

Between 1966 and 1967 the once racially segregated public school system of the South was turned around, most dramatically in those states initially most segregated. In the northern states the problem has been focused within the huge cities where segregation, though it surely existed, had not been backed by the force of law.

However, concern with the changing official position has obscured two very important trends: within much of the South white children are now sent to privately funded and segregated schools, often called 'academies', leaving the officially desegregated public schools to the black children, thus defeating the object of federal policies; and across the North the movement of much of the white population to the suburbs has left officially unsegregated but often totally black schools in the inner cities of huge conurbations. Here the only way to achieve integration has been to bus children from one school district to another, a policy much at odds with the established tradition of neighbourhood schools.

Though the practice of '**bussing**' black children away from their local schools to preserve segregation had long been established the introduction of bussing to integrate schools came as a rude awakening to many white parents, particularly in those areas that thought the new standard applied only to the South. Widespread resistance followed, and still smoulders. Black students trying to enter once all-white schools have been subjected to verbal abuse and even to physical violence, with law and order only being restored with the arrival of the National Guard.

This kind of lawlessness should not, however, be permitted to over-shadow the amount of social change that has come about, especially in the South. The segregation of so many black children in poor, inner city schools remains, however, a much more intractable issue for American society.

A BEGINNER'S GUIDE TO US SCHOOLS

As if the practical issues of getting a child into school aren't enough, going to school in the USA may turn out to be quite different from the equivalent experience in Britain. There is no national curriculum as at home. Furthermore the history, geography and literature taught may well change quite dramatically. Religious instruction and prayers are actually forbidden in the public, tax-supported, system. Other ceremonies like the pledge of allegiance will incorporate your child from day one, and there's little that you can or should do about it.

Children start school at age 6, and pass through 12 grades, finally 'graduating' at 18. The term 'K-12' is often used. It means kindergarten through high school. After that there are community colleges (usually a further two years) or universities (four years). All institutions of learning at whatever level are commonly called 'school'. And *public* schools are

Two US variants			British variant
	kindergarten	kindergarten	infants year 1
1 2 3 4 5 6	elementary school	grade school　　1 2 3 4 5 6 7 8	2 3 primary 4 5 6 juniors
			year 7 8
7 8	junior high		9
9 10 11 12	high school	freshman sophomore junior senior	10 11 lower sixth (12) upper sixth (13)
1 2 3 4	university freshman sophomore junior senior	two year community college	first second final postgraduate

Fig. 3. School years compared.

just that, schools run for the general public from the public purse.

The groupings of years together in the same school varies from district to district as in Britain (as anyone who has moved into or out of a middle-school district will realise), but the following routine would be widely recognised (a couple of variants are compared to one English norm in Figure 3).

Grade or elementary schools (grades 1 to 6 or 8) are for those aged 6 to 10 or 13, and usually resemble their British primary equivalent (though without the uniforms so beloved of middle class schools in the UK).

The real contrast will come in both **Junior High** (grades 7 through 8, ages 10 to 13) and **Senior High** (grades 9 through 12, ages 14 to 18) where an amazing lack of discipline and petty rules so prevalent in Britain will be both exciting and frightening, especially for the British pupil making the transition halfway through the system. Younger children will take it more in their stride. For older pupils the lack of discipline will resemble that of going to college, with all its opportunities for individual discovery and the pitfalls of having to work it all out for themselves.

Academic grades

These appear straightforward:

A – very good worth 4 points
B – good   3
C – average   2
D – poor   1
F – fail   0

Grades such as these are given for every essay (paper), exam and course taken, and the grades points average (GPA) calculated (hence 'he's a genius, got a straight four-oh in his senior year'). All grades are internal, and are in comparison to the appropriate peer group. They cannot be compared to GCSE exam results at all. Most grades are from continuous assessment, including marked exercises and short tests rather than lengthy final examinations.

Graduation from high school may be all that's technically required for a place (self-financed though) at the local state-funded college. For entrance to a private college further assessments will probably be required, plus recommendations from teachers.

A few choice words on maths standards

A January 1987 US National Research Council symposium noticed that three new studies showed US school students ranking low among the twenty or so nations considered in mathematical skills (even though US-based standardised scores have actually risen since 1980). This is especially so in geometry and calculus. Only 20 per cent of college-bound US students have ever taken any calculus, deemed essential in applying for any maths degree course elsewhere.

Why such a poor US showing?

- Most Americans see maths (US = math) ability as innate rather than learned, so if it seems difficult it is because the student is pushing against a locked and bolted door and no amount of teaching or time will ever change anything, so it's best to shift attention to something else.

- US schools generally stress broader, more 'creative' skills such as reading and writing rather than the maths skills emphasised in other countries.

- The use of 'tracking' (assigning students to ability levels) tends to reinforce both good and bad evaluation, with the poorer student giving up completely.

- 'Spiralling' in the curriculum has failed to provide an adequate system for developing advanced skills; spiralling involves an initially light introduction to maths, returning later to the same concepts at supposedly increasingly sophisticated levels. But in practice it has students revisiting the same material again and again, covering much the same ground at about the same level, with boredom setting in all around.

- All-purpose teachers, especially at early grades, are used rather than well-trained maths specialists.

- Geometry and algebra are only introduced after students are more than halfway through the 12-year programme, whereas elsewhere the ideas have already been introduced, if only very generally, much earlier.

Girls v. boys

Programmes over the last twenty years to undermine the gender stereotypes as to who is supposed to be good at maths and science seem to have started to raise everyone's standards.

A 1998 study clearly shows that girls have at last caught up with boys in maths achievement, a goal long sought after by educational reformers.

Who runs the schools?

The decentralised administrative system of the USA deeply influences the public schools. They are run not by counties but by specially constituted **school boards**, who have to raise money locally from taxes.

By and large school boards in well-to-do areas have the money to maintain the schools, pay attractive salaries, and suitably equip the libraries and laboratories. In poor areas the converse happens. Government grants are available in target areas (say if a school is next to an airforce base which influences the student intake and may overburden the local tax base).

Federal monies may be available for remedial programmes, but by and large schools reflect the local tax base. As this shifts so does the quality of the schools.

General points worth considering

- *Size*

  Often much bigger than (traditionally at least) in Britain. A graduating year may reach 1,000. Hence the number of yellow school buses out on the roads!

- *Assembly*

  In British 1944 Education Act sense assemblies don't exist in the USA. The US Constitution requires the separation of State and religion, so religious observances far from being required are forbidden (and would be deemed divisive).

- *Sport*

  Low key, which may be a surprise given the high profile nature of much school competitive sport. Most effort has traditionally gone into the school teams, so 'jocks' used to get most of the attention. Women now participate in a wider range of sports than ever before, which may help explain the success of school soccer (and it's less expensive and less dangerous than American football!).

- *Uniform*

  Unheard of in all but a very few select private schools pretending to be British prep schools or else pseudo-military academies (like most of continental Europe), though recently proposed by Clinton.

PRIVATE EDUCATION

Across the whole range, from kindergarten to graduate school, private education parallels the public system. This is based upon two things:

Money

The first factor is the desire to *buy* a better education for the children. As in Britain a bought education is not necessarily better than what is publicly available, but so long as people are looking for conspicuous consumption *and* an edge over other people the private schools will continue to have a social cachet if nothing else.

The east coast tends to have two main variations:

- the military, usually but not always, southern-based school where military style uniforms, discipline and hygiene are imposed upon a chosen few

- 'prep' schools, preparing students for college, usually prestigious 'Ivy League' ones (hence the term 'preppy' for an American Sloane Ranger).

Both types are rare out west, being seen as too European, and thus more suited to a supposedly decadent east.

Religious principles

Since religion is excluded from the public schools by the US Constitution, private schools based on religious principles have developed, with 'Parochial' schools like you'd find in the UK, through to fundamentalist academies which might be a little too vigorous for British tastes, even for those of a religious persuasion themselves.

Unfortunately too many parochial schools, especially in the South, are merely attempts to create all-white schools given that the public schools have been racially integrated.

There are other schools, such as those run on experimental lines for usually well-to-do liberal progressive parents with lots of money to spend.

GROWING UP IN THE USA

In the whole range of everyday activities things won't be quite the way they were back home. Moreover, your children will not be yours for very much longer. This would be equally true if you had stayed where you were. But taking them to the USA and immersing them in American society means that it may well seem all that much more dramatic. The values, habits and expectations they pick up will be from people who do not necessarily share the same cultural background, even more so than had you stayed at home. Rather the children will come back to you ever more American as each day passes. And while there will be good things about this, aspects of which you will approve, there will also be things of which you may strongly disapprove.

Getting a job

It has long been taken for granted that middle class children get some kind of job as early as possible, if only around their own yard (that is, the garden). Children are after all in training for an adulthood of getting and spending.

Babysitting is often a daughter's first experience with the great world of work. If you have young children you'll find that local junior high school students will expect to babysit for you (as they will expect you to buy Girl Scout cookies from them in due season). The babysitter may well bring her young sibling along with her (so doing two jobs at once). These even younger would-be earners may well return in due course ready and eager to haggle with you over garden chores you might have been expecting that you or your children would do as a matter of course. Watering the lawn and flower beds is a great favourite for those too young to babysit but not too young to spend. Television assures an intimate knowledge of every possible product aimed at children whether clothes, foods, drinks or toys. If you live in a condominium apartment complex where the children may not be able to offer gardening services they will still find ways of earning money, if only watering the plants and feeding the cat when you are away.

By high school mere babysitting will have been supplemented by working in the local ice-cream parlour, fast-food outlets, dog-walking, bagging-up or even cashiering in local stores. It is all good preparation for 'working your way through college', and through life come to that.

US children seem to grow up quickly. In this they are generally encouraged by families, neighbours and friends. If you believe that everything should be in its due season you may be seen as sheltering your children from the harsh facts of life. Children are introduced very early to that most American of claims: 'there is no free lunch.'

How to respond?

- Talk things through with your children. They may actually prefer to get paid for mowing the lawn (like their friends) rather than have a set amount of pocket money come what may. The children have to live with their friends, just as you have to live with new colleagues and neighbours. Though no-strings pocket money may sound great it may not be as good as doing what everyone else at that age does.

- Your children will want to be exactly like their US friends, rather than like you. They will say the pledge of allegiance along with everyone else even if you are only in the US for a fixed period. After all, as grown-ups you wouldn't want to be excluded from the Fourth of July party just because you are foreigners!

What can I read about US education?

There's not a lot available outside the USA. You may be able to order the following couple of critical exposes, both by a (not the) David Owen, *High School*, Viking, New York 1981 and *None of the Above* (the title echoing the last choice of a multiple-choice test), Houghton Mifflin, New York 1985. For an extremely jaundiced view of being an American student see Allen Bloom's *The Closing of the American Mind*, Simon & Schuster, 1987. For a work of more careful scholarship try Amy Gutman, *Democratic Education*, Princeton University Press 1987.

For an extremely detailed, place by place, outline of America's school districts see the Education section of David Savageau and Richard Boyer, *Places Rated Almanac*, Prentice Hall, New York, 1993. For a most useful introduction see David Hampshire's *Living and Working in America: A Survival Handbook*, 1995.

GOING TO COLLEGE

Where once upon a time twelve years of schooling was supposed to be enough to give the immigrant and native alike a sufficient leg-up to do well in the US job market, and thus in life, a further four years of college is a minimum prerequisite these days. A further two years of postgraduate work are also highly desirable. This is due to the growing sophistication of the job market and the corollary that twelve years of schooling prepares people for very little these days. Compared to British sixth-formers most American high school seniors are a couple of years behind academically.

Student optimism

Middle class American students display a far greater sense of optimism than their British equivalent. They may seem to talk about ozone depletion, the greenhouse effect and AIDS, but their unselfconscious optimism seems to surround them with a protective shield. For them their good will defeat anyone else's evil. They may be publicly cynical about the 'system', but they will never doubt that this century belongs to the USA. They are on the winning side, the side of democracy, even while buying ever more Japanese goods.

Such myopic optimism may seem little more than the positive thinking of a prosperous society, but it also comes from the kind of education they receive. Debate as understood in the UK is quite rare for school children. The political system that they learn about in Civic classes, and which they follow through the congressional hearings on television (Watergate to Irangate), is quite different from that in Britain.

Congress's role is to act as a check upon the executive. On the floor of the House of Representatives members do not argue, that is debate by a series of arguments laid out to sustain an internally consistent line of thought. Rather members make speeches that will get into the papers, or if they are lucky, get onto the TV news back in their home state. Students themselves don't debate as such but hold arguments that are often little more than rows, people talking past each other.

'Really educated people'

By the time high school students have moved on to college they often come over as amazingly erudite. Talk to them and you feel you are talking to really educated people, even if you can't quite put your finger upon what it is they have been educated in. But they are amazingly aware, interested, studious even (if there's a test due). They have courses in subjects that British high-fliers have only heard of: nutrition, family dynamics, even 'world history'. And their more traditional courses seem so well focused upon the 'now' of it all: feminism in George Eliot, Stonehenge as a proto-computer, or Chinese history (since Nixon let them be friends and business-partners with this particular group of 'Reds'). Everything comes to be channelled towards tomorrow's big chance. It's all very professional. No knowledge for knowledge's sake, or even as a hobby (leave that for retirement). All are being educated for the job market whether coming to it from the humanities, the social sciences or the natural sciences. On the other hand colleges run courses that would seem bizarre elsewhere, such as bagpiping as part of a BA at Pittsburgh's Carnegie-Mellon University (in association with the university pipeband, a legacy of Carnegie's Scottish roots).

College entrance tests

High school graduates wanting to go to college have no standardised examination results like A-levels to offer the college of their choice. The grades of each school cannot be usefully compared one with another. To cope with this many students take SATs, that is **Scholastic Aptitude Tests,** held by the Educational Testing Service for those who want to go somewhere other than to their local state college. By the late 1980s over 1½ million students were taking SATs each year. And this despite the repeated criticisms made of such tests.

- A perfect SAT score is 1,600 (800 mathematical/800 verbal skills).US norm is 897 (461 and 426).

Evidence from cramming courses suggests that SAT scores can be raised by 100 to 175 (even up to 250 for very exceptional cases), though ETS organisers maintain that cramming can only produce more modest improvements of 14 to 26 points.

At worst SATs are accused of testing nothing but a student's ability to take the SATs themselves. At best they are seen as assuming all students share a common white, upper-middle class, suburban point of view. The existence of cramming colleges that teach, for instance, the meaning of the hundred most commonly tested word definitions (for example: enigma and apathy) suggests claims that SATs test only aptitude rather than any particular body of knowledge are shaky. Still, be aware that such tests, warts and all, do exist. Scores vary from place to place. Students seem to score better if they come from cold-weather states, though distance from 1940s A-bomb test sites has been a factor (statistically at least!).

There is an equivalent for those graduating from college, the **Graduate Record Exam (GRE)** a three and a half hour test of verbal, quantitative and analytical skills, costing $76.00. Foreign applicants are asked to take such tests at various UK centres but foreign student offices may waive standardised tests for well documented foreign applicants, though may require a GRE Subject Test, costing $56.00.

It is vital to have all transcripts, certificates and exam results available for the US school or college. Most higher education institutions in Britain can supply results with a note of explanation written for US schools and colleges (originally designed for US students doing their ritual 'junior year abroad' at a British college).

Standards

The traditional British put-down of the American high school graduate and the self-satisfied observation that their first two years at college raise Americans to about A-level standard should not blind the British arrival to the fact that US graduates, those who complete the four years at college, are at least as competent as their British equivalents, or put another way:

- it's easier to get into college in the USA,
- but just as hard to get out.

In most states publicly funded colleges admit state residents who have graduated from high school. This means that first-year undergraduate classes are *huge* (200–300 per lecture, 30–40 per 'discussion group' where the lecture and this week's chapter and exercises are gone over in more detail). Exams are set so that vast numbers of students (usually a pre-set percentage) will fail.

Electing a major

Those who survive this in-house selection of the first couple of years 'elect a major', that is declare to the college which subject they want to specialise and so graduate in. They then proceed to choose from the college catalogue those courses that when added together constitute a degree programme. Each course is usually self-contained, with tests and exercises most weeks, with a longer term paper (essay) plus a final, written exam at the very end of the course. Each course successfully completed provides credit plus grades, markers on the way to graduation.

Graduating

At the end of the programme, which is supposed to last four years (but can last as long as the money and stamina remain available for weaker or poorer students), those with the highest grade point averages may graduate *Summa cum Laude* (excellent), *Magna cum Laude* (very good), or on the *Dean's List* (good).

College terms

Terms are generally called **semesters**, of which there are two, Fall and Spring, each lasting about 14 weeks, with some places having a break about midway. At the time of 'spring break' thousands of students swarm south to the beaches. The papers go wild with talk of 'sex and drugs and rock'n'roll' in places like Fort Lauderdale, Florida.

Semesters run from late August to Christmas, and January to May. For those who missed or failed a course and wish to catch up, shorter, more intensive 8-week courses are offered between two semesters in **summer school**, when staff, often on auto-pilot, teach again at great speed what they've just taught earlier in the year, but for extra money.

Some colleges (US = 'schools') have 3 quarters, like the old British term system. The fourth quarter is summer school.

Fees

Publicly financed state universities and community colleges charge reduced tuition fees for people from within that state. All others pay 'out of state fees', which can be hefty. This naturally encourages students to stay within their own state.

But remember that most states are the size of countries elsewhere, so many still have to leave home to go to college. Even with cheap tuition there are still 'nominal' registration fees, health centre fees, sports centre fees, all of which must be paid at the beginning of the semester (and don't forget that parking lot fee too!).

And of course if you want to live on campus in a **dormitory** (hall of residence) you will have to pay a residence fee for accommodation, and these are not grant-aided. Over four years even a 'cheap' college education can be expensive. How, then, do students manage it?

- Living at home may be necessary just to survive. For parents this means supporting an adult until they are at least 22!

- Part-time work, which can mean anything, just to raise cash for books, clothes, *etc*, even where parents provide the accommodation. In college towns most menial and service jobs, such as in fast-food outlets, are held by students.

- Work-study, where government or the college provides students with menial work for low pay.

- Loans, repayable upon graduation, whether governmental or commercial.

- Many go to local two-year 'community colleges', transferring to the more expensive universities for only the last two years of study.

Financing a college education

Ronald Reagan once starred in *She's Working Her Way Through College* in which a burlesque star tries to better herself by going to college, promoting the US ideal that students should be both willing and able to work their way through college, so becoming free of both parents and the State. The reality today, however, tends to be otherwise. By the late 1980s less than 4 per cent of the average student's financial package came from work as against just under 45 per cent grants and almost 52 per cent loans. The soaring costs of college and diminishing federal support means that commercial loans are becoming ever more necessary.

Work-study programmes provide help with fees in exchange for working in the college itself. Almost a million students nationwide work on federally funded work-study programmes, but the maximum is 12 hours per week during term time, the pay is the legal hourly minimum, and as it involves mostly washing floors, dishes and serving food hardly amounts to vocational training.

Some universities hire their own students to do the menial work. Each year, for instance, the University of Minnesota hires 17,000 of its students for up to 29 hours each, with a yearly pay bill of about $70 million. But with financial pressures bearing down upon college budgets at least as hard as upon individual students there's always the temptation to cut down upon financial support except for those in dire need or for those sporting or high-flying students likely to bring credit to the college. Everywhere the need for student loans seems on the rise.

Loans are becoming even more necessary. The best are at fixed low-interest rates not repayable until after graduation. In the past these have tended to be governmental, or underwritten by government, but so many people disappeared after graduation and never paid up that the authorities have tried to end these altogether. **Commercial loans**, preferably based upon parental collateral, are ever more important. By the late 1980s students and their parents borrowed over $10,000 million. This all places graduating students under great pressure to get good well-paid jobs as soon as possible, with many socially necessary but not so well-paid jobs (including college teaching!) being far less attractive than well-paid legal and commercial jobs. This skewing of the job market is getting quite serious in places.

Tuition costs $4–12,000 per 9-month academic year plus a further $7–12,000 per academic year for living costs.

Private colleges

Many world famous US universities are private foundations, but be sure to distinguish between those of social status and those with high academic standing. The most prestigious universities in popular standing are the **Ivy League** (Brown, Cornell, Dartmouth, University of Pennsylvania, Princeton, Columbia, Yale and Harvard), so called because of their 'ancient', ivy-on-the-wall, standing. Together with once all-girls colleges such as Vassar and Smith these form a self-sustaining first division, though for many this rests upon high social-standing as much as upon world renown.

The Massachusetts Institute of Technology outside Boston is at least as world renowned as Harvard, but like other institutions such as Stanford on the West Coast, has a 'boffin' image. There are also a large number of often quite small, sometimes experimental, colleges right across the country.

All tend to be expensive. 'If you need to ask the cost you can't afford them' is a pretty good rule of thumb. Expect to pay $8–20,000 per 9-month academic year (plus $7–12,000 living costs per year)

Community colleges

These are two year post-secondary, mostly vocational colleges funded out of the public purse, attended by almost half the 18-22 age group. Good grades can be translated into a transfer to the state university system. Community colleges are the unsung work-horses of US further education.

How to choose a college?

If you decide to send your offspring to a US college, rather than fly them back to the UK for a British education (which may be cheaper and possibly better if you choose well) it is very much a question of detective work, asking other parents of college-age children, reading prospectuses (**catalogs**) and if possible visiting the campus and appropriate departments. Do you really want your 18-year-old to go to a state university, living at home, commuting every day (along with maybe 10,000 other drivers) onto a campus of 35,000 students, where classes will be in vast lecture rooms seating 300 at one go, being taught in classes of about 35 students a time by overworked and underpaid postgraduates (**teaching assistants**)? The same university might be just the place for postgraduate work after graduation elsewhere. Graduate classes will be of about a dozen, with sustained personal contact with senior staff over several years, with access to facilities only a vast state university library and laboratories could offer.

'It's all Greek to me'

The film *Animal House* may have introduced the notion of **fraternities** (for men) and **sororities** (for women) to a British audience. Fear not, such excesses as portrayed there are as likely as the school rebellion in the British film *If*. Nevertheless, it's useful to know something about these institutions, if only to know what to avoid:

- **Greeks** – members of societies so called because of their use of three Greek letters, such as Delta Beta Phi.

- **Frat house** – houses owned by Greek societies, usually on the edge of campus, providing room and board for members.

- **Rushes** – recruitment of new members, which can involve recruits passing through initiation rites (often masonic by way of Monty Python).

- **Honor societies** – undergraduate societies that recruit students with excellent grade averages for social and academic functions (rather like subject-based societies at British universities, but nationally based, as with the Geographers' Gamma Theta Upsilon).

- **Greek week** – a week for 'fun' activities run by fraternities and sororities (resembling a rag week in the exuberance, high-jinks and potential for mayhem).

10
Opportunities for Young People and Teachers

SHORT-TERM OPPORTUNITIES

There are many easily found packages for those with money to spend: visit any good travel agent. For those who need to work their way across there are basically two routes:

- Work over here and spend over there – see David Leppard, *The Directory of Summer Jobs in Britain*, available from Vacation Work Publications, 9 Park End Street, Oxford (annually).

- Work overseas and spend time and money in the USA – see David Leppard, *The Directory of Jobs and Careers Abroad*, also available from Vacation Work Publications, or Roger Jones, *How to Get a Job Abroad* (How To Books, 4th edition 1995). Susan Griffith covers the ins and outs of working overseas, including the USA, in *Working Your Way Around the World* (8th edition) 1997. For a guide specifically geared to the USA see Roger Jones, *Getting a Job in America* (How To Books, 5th edition 1998).

The most usual and still highly popular jobs in the USA are:

- summer camps
- au pairing.

It is quite possible to arrange jobs unaided by specialists, but it's likely to be more convoluted, time-consuming and risky. You can find information on US summer jobs in:

- US newspapers
- US magazines
- via US contacts
- by writing to US branches of groups you may deal with over here, such as the YMCA, YHA, Scouts.

If you do get a job this way you'll have to pay your own ticket (which might be a financial blow) but you'll get to keep your final pay: it'll be yours, which wouldn't be the case if you've used a broker (like Camp

America). You may be able to negotiate a better deal than you'll get if you go through an agency. But you may be ripped off, exploited, sacked or worse. You take the risk (and it may well pay off).

If you've little room for manoeuvre you may have to go through an intermediary. At least that way your papers will certainly be in order. The leading intermediaries are **Camp America** and **BUNAC** – The British Universities North American Club.

SUMMER CAMPS

If you are a student, a teacher or a nurse and are over 18 then Camp America or BUNAC may be able to help you arrange a 9-week job in the USA teaching sports, arts and crafts, or camping and other outdoor skills in US summer camps. Jobs in camp maintenance are also available.

Being a camp counsellor

This is a demanding job, but for the right people summer camps can be both challenging and fun, an incredibly rewarding way to experience a slice of American life. Specialist counsellors need specific qualifications and experience in a particular field or activity, such as swimming or archery. General counsellors need experience with children in a leadership role. Counsellors are assigned to a cabin of about six children and, along with other counsellors, take responsibility for their welfare. The camp will expect counsellors to set a good example, ensuring that the children keep themselves and their cabin (or tent) clean, that they follow the camp routine and have a great but safe time. The children may experience homesickness or other personal problems and the camp counsellor needs to be a mature friend (like a big brother or sister) as well as an impartial adviser. Earning their respect can be difficult, so it is vital counsellors are sure of their own strengths and weaknesses beforehand. Applicants need to be flexible, adaptable and positive enough to adapt to living and working abroad, which may include working in camps isolated from the rest of the world, with a limited social life given there will be few evenings off; plus rules and regulations to be kept (curfews and no alcohol), dealing with difficult children, coming to terms with the 'rah-rah' atmosphere of many camps and the mosquitos and other creepy-crawlies. You may also find that not only is the setting a little more isolated than you thought, but the job involves doing over and beyond what was initially expected.

Applications

Applicants must be in full-time study or training doing a degree level, tertiary (HND, 2 year BTEC, NVQ4/5) or postgraduate course in

England, Scotland or Wales. Northern Ireland students may apply for a similar programme through USIT.

Benefits include the right paperwork for US Immigration, free or cheap return flight, board and lodgings, insurance cover, pocket money and free time for your own travel plans at the end of the job before flying back home. Contact:

- **Camp America**, 37A Queens Gate, London SW7 5HR. Tel: (0171) 581 7373. Web site: *www.camp-america.com*

Camp America typically places over 4,000 applicants in summer camps in the USA, finding places for 85 per cent of British applicants. Though round-trip fare is included you will be required to provide an initial £25 deposit on application, and a further £25 when placed, plus £115 compulsory insurance, plus £14 visa handling fee. If you are one of the unlucky ones for whom no place is found the initial deposit is refunded.

- **BUNAC**, 16 Bowling Green Lane, London EC12 OBD. Tel: (0171) 251 3472. Web site: *www.bunac.org.uk* (or contact by email on bunac.easynet.co.uk). Members (£4 fee payable) have access to special summer employment lists, summer camp jobs, and the necessary J-1 visas through three authorised programmes. Gap year students with a confirmed university place will be considered.

- **BUNACAMP** for camp counsellors. For a £59 registration fee BUNAC arranges placements, and pays for your flight (being reimbursed by the camp). You get a J-1 visa, a return flight, board and lodging, plus about $400 in hand salary.

- **KAMP** for kitchen and maintenance jobs. Other details are essentially the same as for BUNACAMP. Costs not included in your registration are: travel to and from the required orientation sessions, US visa processing fee (currently £30 for British/Irish nationals), medical/ accident/baggage group insurance policy (approximately £93), and a medical examination if required by your camp (expect £25–55 more) and your holiday time after camp. It is a US Immigration Service requirement that you take at least $400 in cash or travellers cheques. Reckon to take at least $400 more just in case.

- **WORK AMERICA** for those who wish to arrange their own summer job. You are eligible for BUNAC's cheap flights, but would get to keep all your salary rather than have most of it reimburse BUNAC for your fare (as in BUNACAMP). You need a definite job offer or a personal sponsorship plus $400. If you have no definite sponsorship you need about $700 to qualify for the visa. A BUNAC brochure explains all.

- **International Camp Counsellors Program**, council of YMCAs, 640 Forest Road, London E17 3DZ. Tel: (0181) 520 5599. Apply by 31 January each year.

When?

The US summer is somewhat earlier than that in the UK so you'd need to plan accordingly. Summer starts when school gets out, which can be as early as the third week in May. Summer camps are well underway by the end of June, so you should be able to leave Britain no later than the middle of June. As summer formally ends with the first Monday of September (Labor Day) summer camps end by about 26 August. Then you'll have time to travel until you're due back in Britain.

How can I find out what it's like?
- Ask around at college.
- Write to **Camp America/BUNAC**.
- Attend various **Recruitment Interview and Orientation** meetings.
- Read *Exchange Programs within the USA* leaflet from Educational Advisory Service of the Fulbright Commission, Fulbright House, 62 Doughty Street, London WC1N 2LS. Tel: (0171) 404 6880. Fax: (0171) 404 6834.

What do I need to apply?
- A character reference.
- A curriculum vitae (CV) stating your skills, qualifications, and what you've done that makes you suitable for the job.
- Three good passport sized photographs.
- Any sporting, teaching or professional certificates you can produce to support your application.

Are gap year students eligible?

Those of you with an unconditional offer of a university/college place are eligible during the summer preceding your first year studies not during the gap year itself. Canada may accept gap year students from the February before starting higher education (see BUNAC's *Work Canada* brochure).

AU PAIRING

British au pairs have traditionally been in great demand in the USA, even where cheaper local or Mexican help is readily available. This has something to do with the snob value of having someone from Europe, someone a little bit exotic but who speaks English. Any British accent is deemed high class and so desirable (at least among the class of people who want and can afford to hire au pairs). Applicants must have childcare experience (NNEB an advantage), non-smoker, full driving licence, aged 18–25. Expect $139 per week pocket money plus flight plus 2 weeks' holiday and medical insurance. Since the Woodward case be prepared for considerably more conscientious vetting of credentials by both families and US Immigration officials at the port of entry.

How do I find out what's it all about?
- Mark Hempshell *Working As An Au Pair*, How To Books, 1998.

- Write to Au Pair Childcare Department, 37 Queens Gate, London SW7 5HR (Tel: (0171) 581 2730) for **Camp America**'s brochure.

- **EIL Ltd**, 287 Worcester Road, Malvern, Worcester WR14 1AB (Tel: (01684) 562577. Fax: (01684) 562212) runs a similar programme called Au Pair Homestay for 18–26 year olds.

- **Pre-select Staff Agency**, 924 Stratford Road, Springfield, Birmingham B11 4BT (Tel: (0121) 702 2100) is the UK office for a Utah-based au pair registry. By post please enclose large SAE with two 1st class stamps.

Can I do it without such help?
- The US authorities are tightening up their response to US residents hiring people who lack the necessary papers to work in the USA. In practical terms it's unlikely that people staying on after a holiday would ever be found out, but you would have to be prepared to live in something of a limbo, and if you do get caught you may find that deportation will mean you won't be allowed to re-enter the USA again.

- Camp America and EIL provide a fully legal service based upon 18 years of dealing with the appropriate US paperwork.

- They also have the contacts built up over the years.

- You might be able to find a suitable employer from this distance, but even if you made contact you are taking a far greater risk than when going through an agency that in effect acts as a vetting process, for both employer and employee.

- If you organise everything yourself and things don't work out who can you turn to? Camp America has US contacts.

- If you do everything for yourself and it works well you will of course stand to make more money: your employer won't have any agency fees to pay.

What do I need to apply?

- Three good passport sized photographs.
- A character reference.
- A curriculum vitae (CV) setting out what you've done, what skills and qualifications you have.
- Any sporting, teaching or professional certificates you have to support your application.

Alternatives?

- Mark Hempshell, *Doing Voluntary Work Abroad*, How To Books, 1998.

- David Wood Worth (ed.), *The International Directory of Voluntary Work*, Vacation Work, Oxford.

- **Winant Clayton Volunteers Association**, 38 Newark Street, London E1 2AA. Tel: (0171) 375 0547. Organises 3 month programmes (June–September), including 3 weeks for travel before returning home, for volunteers in their community work programmes in New York City, Boston and Washington DC. Once in place volunteers receive room and board and pocket money. Expect to contribute about £800 including all travel, though grants may be available for needy applicants with practical experience of working with people (voluntary or professional sectors). UK residents only, minimum age 19. Interviews are held in late January and early February.

- **Mountbatten Internship Programme**, 13 Muffats Lane, Brookmans Park, Hatfield, Herts, AL9 7RX. Tel: (01707) 661870. Email: Mountbatten.programme@virgin.net. Web site: *www.mountbatten.org* Provides work experience opportunities in New York City for school-leavers who wish to defer going on to higher education for a year and would like practical experience in business. Apply before taking A-levels and be prepared for an interview. Don't forget to ask the institutions to which you are applying how they would respond to your deferring entry for a year.

STUDENT INTERNSHIPS

Many students benefit from work experience during their academic studies. Enquire from schools liaison officers at higher education fairs, open days for applicants, or at interview as to opportunities that exist for work in the USA during your course of study. There are several schemes:

- **The International Association for Exchange of Students for Technical Expertise** (IAESTE). Internships provide practical experience in agriculture, architecture, commerce, engineering, science and technology (but NOT medicine) during the long vacation (or exceptionally as part of a sandwich course). Student applicants must be from institutions which are already affiliated to the scheme, and applications should initially be focused through the college's appointed representative. Work experience in the USA is over-subscribed, but any application that can offer an equivalent UK traineeship will be enhanced. The UK side is co-ordinated by the Central Bureau, Seymour Mews, London W1, though initial enquiries should be through your local careers service.

- **The GB National Committee**, UKIN House, Phipp Street, London EC2A. (Tel: (0171) 739 9847) co-ordinates international management training for students of economics and management with at least 2 years of full-time study already completed. Applications are initially through a local representative, details from your local careers service. Applicants only prepared to go to the USA rather than also consider an alternative venue may not be considered, though a preference for the USA may be expressed.

- **The Mountbatten Internship Programme** also provides internships with multinational corporations, advertising, legal and financial institutions for graduates in secretarial studies, management, accountancy or business studies. Tel: (01707) 661870 or view Web site *www.mountbatten.org*

- **Bunac OPT** (Overseas Practical Training) offers those over 18 an opportunity to spend from 3 to 18 months in the USA as an intern or trainee. The snag is that you have to arrange your own placement (education, social sciences, library science, counselling and social service, management, business, commerce, finance or health-related occupations). Bunac provide the screening, help, and access to the necessary J-1 Exchange Visitor Visa.

You may also find the following of interest:

- *Working Holidays* published annually by the Central Bureau for Educational Visits and Exchanges, 10 Spring Gardens, London SW1 2BN. Tel: (0171) 389 4004.

- *1999 Internships*, Writer's Digest Books, F&W Publications Inc, 9933 Alliance Road, Cincinnati Ohio 45242.

- *Directory of International Internships*, Office of Overseas Programs, Michigan State University, East Lansing, Michigan 48824.

- *Advisory List of International Educational Travel and Exchange Programs*, Council on Standards for International Education Travel,

1906 Association Drive, Reston, Virginia 22091.

There are three organisations that can help with the necessary paperwork, though they do not themselves arrange traineeships, placements, or internships.

- **The Council on International Educational Exchange** (CIEE), 52 Poland Street, London W1V 4JQ. Freephone 0800 7319076. Tel: (0171) 478 2000. Fax: (0171) 734 7322. Email: InternUSA@ciee.org. Web site: *www.ciee.org* This is the major supplier of the necessary authorisations for those undertaking placements arranged as part of the course requirements for British degrees. Students must return to the UK upon finishing their placements, and so should take the US experience mid-course not after graduation or as a gap year activity. Write for work study booklet.

- **The Central Bureau for Educational Visits and Exchanges**, 10 Spring Gardens, London SW1A 2BN. Tel: (0171) 389 4004. Involved with the UK/US Careers Development Programme which allows UK nationals aged 19–35 to work in the USA for up to 18 months. Participants must secure their own placements and have a couple of years' experience or appropriate professional qualifications. There is an application fee of £45, and a processing fee of $800 payable either by the trainee or their US employer. The Hotel and Culinary Exchange is an equivalent system geared to those who have completed, or are presently studying, a hotel or catering course with suitable work experience. Job placement assistance is available, but would slow down any application considerably. An application and a processing fee will be charged to successful applicants.

- **The Educational Advisory Service of the US-UK Fulbright Commission**, 62 Doughty Street, London WC1N 2LS Tel: (0171) 404 6994 (open to the public 10.30am–1.00pm and 2.00pm–4.30pm Monday–Friday). Provides information, and can supply a leaflet outlining exchanges, internship and trainee opportunities and regulations. Excellent Web site (*www.fulbright.co.uk*) with most documents you could need, and a Frequently Asked Questions (FAQs) section. Particularly good for MBA-linked opportunities.

WORKING IN WASHINGTON DC

Thousands of young Americans regularly work in the offices of the US Congress. An estimated 19,000 more swell the staff of political think-tanks, lobby groups, media and business institutions, or work in the State Department, the White House, or elsewhere in the administration. These high-fliers enjoy positions of prestige that will place them on the road to further privilege. The bad news is that these **interns**, as they are known, are paid little if anything. The pay-off comes in the experience, the connections and their enhanced CV (or resumé as they'd say). It is an investment in their future whether or not they envisage a future in politics or public administration.

Increasingly students are placed in **programmed internships** by their own college working through college representatives permanently stationed in the capital. Students get course credit towards their degrees in exchange for writing a report on their experience. The best programmes are carefully scrutinised by academics knowledgeable in the ways of Washington politics to ensure that interns are more than office dogsbodies. With the local University of Maryland alone providing 600 interns per year there is demand and supply far exceeding anything found in British local government or even Westminster. Congress alone employs about 5,000 interns per year, who gain first-hand experience of the legislative process, lobbying and wheeler-dealing.

The American University in Washington DC organises intern programmes for about 500 students per semester, of which about 10 per cent come direct from foreign universities. For the 1995 Fall Semester the total cost was $8,260 (including $3,350 for tuition and $3,120 for board and lodging), the availability of which must be proved on the F1 student visa application. If you wish to transfer your course credit to your British degree programme there is a further $5,000 fee! The good news is that the programme provides 3 days of tuition per week and 2 days of internship in a wide range of public or private agencies and businesses associated with the capital's main activity: government (lobbying, reporting and legislating). For details write to David C. Brown, Dean of the Washington Semester Program, The American University, Tenley Campus, 4400 Massachusetts Avenue NW, Washington DC 20016-8033 (or Fax 202 895 4960).

Competition for political internships is fierce. There are over 200 applications for each place in a senator's office. Preference is given to people from the home constituency, particularly those already known to the senator or representative in the election campaign that brought them into office.

Interns answer the telephone, answer constituents' mail (using word processors, for letters and machines that 'sign' outgoing constituency mail), may attend meetings of Congress to prepare memos and report on matters of concern, and may get to draft position papers based upon library research.

Non-governmental options go through a clearing house: **The Washington Centre**, 1101 14th Street NW, Washington DC 20005,

(202) 289 8680, which ensures a quality placement, laying on courses and seminars for over 600 colleges. It ensures that no more than 20 per cent of the intern's time is spent on mundane clerical work. The think-tanks are privately sponsored research and policy monitoring institutions such as the conservative **Heritage Foundation**, 214 Massachusetts Avenue NE, Washington DC 20002, Tel: (202) 546 4400, which has 17 summer programme places each paying about £120 a week, or the (liberal) **Institute for Policy Studies**, 1901 'Q' Street NW, Washington DC 20009, Tel: (202) 234 9382. Another avenue would be the *Student Guide to Mass Media Internships* published by the School of Journalism, Boulder, Colorado, which lists 2,000 different internships in the USA (newspapers, magazines, television, radio, and publishing). Hands-on experience prior to a formal job-search would be good for the old CV.

Few British students participate, but doing an exchange year in the USA may make it possible via your US college's own programme. Some British students with family connections in the USA have worked 'on the Hill' as it's called, but without remuneration. British students in the USA as 'resident aliens' may be able to work in the office of their local representative as part of a US-based degree course. If still interested in working on Capitol Hill contact:

- The Intern Program Director, US Congress, Washington DC 20515.

APPLYING FOR SUMMER JOBS

Before an employer can employ a foreigner s/he must be willing to obtain, fill out and submit all the necessary US government forms. Remember the basic rule is that foreigners cannot take jobs in the USA. The paperwork makes a case for exceptions to this general rule. It means time and effort for the employer, for little if any immediate gain if people already in the USA could be readily hired. But as a student there are special arrangements to provide temporary permission to work – so the employer doesn't have to worry so long as the foreign student has the right visa.

Dealing with such organisations as BUNAC, Camp America, or CIEE can help with the paperwork as:

- they are familiar with what's needed
- they deal with US contacts also familiar with the problems
- US authorities will only issue work visas through authorised organisations such as these.

Even if you arrange something on your own it may help to obtain the kind of advice available only through groups such as BUNAC or Camp America.

It helps to understand what is involved. As a general rule there are only three types of visas suitable for foreign students who will be returning home after their summer employment:

H-2 'Temporary Worker'

This requires a US employer to obtain a 'labor certificate' from the local state employment service. The US Department of Labor requires evidence that:

- a real job exists
- reasonable effort has already been made to fill the job from within the USA
- no qualified US resident has applied.

> **Example:** Camp Manhattan takes a lot of Canadian children for whom a French-speaking canoe instructor is always hired. This year though, despite advertising in college newspapers since October, no suitable applicant has applied. Then a British canoeist who's just spent a year at a French college applies. The camp wants to hire him, and is prepared to do the paperwork. Certification would be granted as a legitimate case has been made.

H-3 'Industrial Trainee'

Here no labor certification is required, but any application must include:

- a detailed training plan
- a training/on-the-job breakdown
- an explanation as to why this training cannot be obtained in the applicant's home country.

> **Example**: Camp Manhattan prides itself on the quality of its management, and especially its own camp counsellor in-house training programme. A British student who's worked in a British day camp writes asking if she can join their programme for residential experience. The Camp organisers could submit the necessary details for an H-3 visa, *but* it might well be rejected if the Immigration and Naturalization Service believe it's just a fiddle to get someone's British girlfriend into the USA for a paid summer job.

J-1 'Exchange Visitor'

These visas are *only* available for applicants participating in educational programmes specifically approved by the US government. Approved

Exchange Visitor Programs are granted only to US sponsoring organisations such as US government agencies, colleges, hospitals and private educational organisations.

The **Council on International Educational Exchange** has for all those wanting something other than camp counselling or au pair work a J-1 authorisation for a summer 'work-travel' programme. This programme permits students to work on any job they can find (though not to undertake practical training such as medical internships). No extensions or visa changes are permitted. Details of this Work and Travel USA (WAT USA) Programme are available via their excellent Web site *www.ciee.org*, which has specific details on summer job availability. There is a freephone: 0800 731 9076, or Email watusa@ciee.org.

J-1 summer camp placements are authorised for the International Camp Counsellor Program of the YMCA (356 West 34th Street, 3rd floor, New York, NY 10001), with an 8 week limit, and must involve counselling or skills instruction rather than kitchen or office jobs.

Paid practical training is organised via a number of sponsors who have J-1 programmes such as the International Association of Students in Economics and Business Management (AIESEC), 14 West 23rd Street, New York, NY 10010, and the International Association for Exchange of Students for Technical Experience (IAESTE) Trainee Programme, c/o Association for International Practical Training, 1040 Little Patuxet, Suite 320, Columbia, Maryland 21044. The maximum length of practical training time for any one person is 18 months.

What happens now?

- H-2 and H-3 visa applications, if successful, will lead to the US Embassy being so informed, where the visa will be issued to the student presenting a valid passport.

- J-1 applications, if successful, lead to sponsoring organisations issuing a 'Certificate of Eligibility' (IAP-66) to be taken, plus passport, to the US Embassy.

- Upon entering the USA the immigration inspector will issue form 1-94 upon which the visa type and maximum stay date are recorded.

How difficult is it?

The process takes time. Securing a visa can take up to six months, so start early, at the beginning of the academic year. When contacting prospective employers let them know which visa you are seeking, which sponsoring organisation (if any), and which forms they would need to submit, if any.

A word of warning

The summer officially ends on Labor Day (first Monday in September). Colleges and schools start back in the last week of August. If you don't intend to return to Britain before the end of September (say for a British university term or semester) you may have difficulty persuading US officials that intending to return that late in the year isn't incompatible with being a student. You'll need to explain when term starts (and that your term didn't end until early July rather than late May).

FURTHER OPPORTUNITIES FOR STUDENTS

Undergraduate study in the United States

Colleges vary in quality of education provided, prestige, location and costs. There are two major systems, the private and the public. The former are deemed more prestigious, cost considerably more, and claim to offer a better education. In Maryland, for instance, the private John Hopkins University fees stand at over $16,000 per 9-month academic year, whereas the public state university charges 'only' about $8,000. Out of state students (and that includes those from abroad) are charged a special 'out of state' rate, a surcharge ranging from 25 to 400 per cent. Understandably very few British students attend college for their whole undergraduate programme. Most British undergraduates attending colleges in the USA do so as part of the British degree programme. Just as language students have to spend time abroad so students taking American Studies degree programmes offer, some even require, their British students to spend a year or a semester (half a year) in the USA. Such programmes involve two sets of costs:

- Fees – these continue to be paid for by your British local educational authority (LEA) and the student (normally £1000 year) if the course counts towards your British degree. Many UK institutions arrange exchanges, balancing their outgoing British students with incoming US ones, so that the LEAs continue to pay UK fees even while you are in the USA and the student pays their home institution as if they had not gone abroad.

- Travel – discretionary, and so at the whim of charge-capped LEAs. You will probably have to pay this yourself (just as if you lived in Inverness but went to Exeter University).

You need to explore who will pay for health insurance and emergency repatriation, though such matters are usually part of the package negotiated between participating colleges. For advice on insuring your belongings, particularly computer equipment or musical instruments, contact the Advice Service, PO Box 172, Bowness Avenue, Headington,

Oxford OX3 0AL.

When applying for details of American Studies degrees in the UK ask whether there is a required semester in the USA. Increasingly other degree programmes offer study time in North America. Keele students, for instance, can apply to go to Maryland if they are political scientists (the campus is 12 miles from the White House) or Ball State if they are historians. For a highly informative leaflet on one university's offerings contact the North America officer at Lancaster University (Tel: (01524) 592035).

For a scholarly exploration of the college experience see:

● Ernest L. Boyer, *College: the Undergraduate Experience,* Harper, New York, 1988.

For two vast over-views of admissions, enrolment, costs and financial aid at 2,000 accredited colleges and universities see:

● *The College Handbook Foreign Student Supplement* available from College Board Publications, Box 886, New York NY 10101 ($14.95 plus $2.95 for shipping).

● James & Max Birnbaum, *Comparative Guide to American Colleges for Students, Parents and Counselors,* Harper Perennial, New York, 15th edition 1991 ($40).

The Institute of International Education, 809 UN Plaza, New York, NY 10017 provide a *Guide to Scholarships, Fellowships and Grants* package which includes a leaflet on 'Costs of US Institutions of Higher Education' and 'Specialised Study options – a Guide to Short Term Programs for Foreign Nationals'. However, the best source of US information in the UK is probably:

● The Educational Advisory Service
The Fulbright Commission, Fulbright House,
62 Doughty Street, London WC1N 2LS
Tel: (0171) 404 6994
Web site: *www.fulbright.co.uk*

For British students where the existing degree programme does not involve studying in the USA it might be worth contacting:

● Study Associates International Ltd (Academic year in the USA)
Wilmerhatch Lane, Epsom, Surrey KT8 7EH
Tel: (01372) 275005

Costs of such arrangements have risen dramatically in the early 90s, and quoted costs may not even include travel costs.

For a general introduction see Teresa Tinsley's *How to Study Abroad,*

How To Books, 3rd edition 1995.

Most UK colleges and universities have a careers library that should stock a wide range of continuously updated published materials on studying in the USA.

Student visa holders

The 1990 visa regulations now allow foreign students who have successfully completed their first year of study to take off-campus jobs for up to 20 hours per week during term time (previous regulations had insisted all jobs must be on-campus). Out of term time the hours restriction is lifted. To ensure that such a job does not undercut US workers' wages any employer offering foreign students employment must attest that the position has already been offered to US workers for at least 60 days, and that foreign students and US workers are being offered the same wages for the same work. If the Department of Labor decided that these conditions are not being met the employer will be barred from employing foreign students.

A note of warning: the present arrangements were originally set to remain in force only until 1995. Whether these new arrangements are retained depends upon whether the US authorities continue to believe the regulations are enabling foreign students to graduate, or are merely being used as a way around the immigration regulations.

POSTGRADUATE DEGREES

In the US the word postgraduate is always shortened to just graduate. Large universities usually offer both Master's and Doctoral pro-grammes, though smaller institutions might only offer graduate courses to the Master's level. If you would like to carry straight through at the same institution you need to check up on this very early in the process.

Master of Arts (MA)

MA programmes are designed primarily for students who wish to acquire a further degree but who also wish primarily to make their career within the world beyond education, whether in business or government. Courses generally last one year for full-time students, a minimum of two years for part-timers. Programmes are by taught courses followed by either a thesis or at least two research papers. The programme provides a firm theoretical and methodological foundation for either moving on to the doctoral level, or for a move out into the wider job market, which increasingly requires an MA rather than a BA, as more and more people complete the first degree.

Doctor of Philosophy (PhD)

PhD programmes are more complicated than in Britain, usually requiring considerable high-level taught courses (which might be in statistics, computing, languages or philosophy irrespective of the main field) before progressing to the preparation of a lengthy research dissertation. It is usual for the PhD stage to take at least three years after the two years spent on the master's degree, a total of at least five years, with the writing up often taking a further couple of years. As most people will be in employment in order to pay the bills by this time it can be very difficult to complete, especially if work takes you away from your university to live elsewhere, and if growing career and family demands gradually ease the PhD to one side. Beware: completion must be within a pre-set timetable, and unlike the UK situation cannot be extended almost indefinitely.

For a useful introduction read 'The American doctoral programme' in E. M. Phillips & D. S. Pugh, *How to Get a PhD*, OU Press 1987.

How to apply

If you wish to apply for (post-)graduate work in the USA you should first write to the **heads of departments** you might be interested in asking for general details. Technically you should write directly to the Director of Graduate Studies at each institution asking for forms and additional information, but procedures seem to be more relaxed for foreign applicants.

Be prepared to write to a wide range of universities, and don't be bothered by the vast number who never even reply. A dozen letters for two or three replies might not be unusual. Twenty initial enquiries is not unusual. Those that do reply are usually taking your application seriously.

In theory you should be prepared to supply:

- Three letters of recommendation.

- Graduate Record Exam (GRE) scores (1,000 minimum). For details contact Educational Advisory Service, 62 Doughty Street, London WC1N 2LS. Tel: (0171) 404 6994. The Fulbright Commission Web site has considerable details on GRE-specific matters.

- College records ('transcripts') of all previous academic work showing a grade point average of at least 3.0 or equivalent (B+ for coursework, plus 2.1 degree).

- Proof of proficiency in English, usually waived for applicants from English-speaking countries.

- Proof of sufficient funds to pay all fees and expenses for at least one year. This is vital.

Universities that deal regularly with certain foreign countries' applicants may waive the need to take a GRE exam and may automatically assume you will need to apply for financial aid both to get the visa and of course to stay alive.

For anyone wishing to be considered for financial aid all applications, letters of recommendation, *etc*, *must* be received by the US institution by 1 February (for entry the following August) and preferably earlier. Most university career advice centres should be able to discuss opportunities and ways of approaching US institutions, and may well have copies of US catalogues (prospectuses). The available guides include:

- *Postgraduate Study and Research: A Guide to Higher Degree Study and Financial Support at Home and Overseas* is a useful introduction to the general issue of postgraduate study, including the USA. It is published by Association of Graduate Careers Advisory Services, and available from the Central Services Unit, Crawford House, Precinct Centre, Manchester M13 9EP. Tel: (0161) 273 4233.

- *Postgraduate Study in the United States* published by the Educational Advisory Service of the Fulbright Commission, 62 Doughty Street, London WC1N 2LS. Tel: (0171) 404 6994. This is probably the best source of specifically US information for UK applicants. Most items are available on *www.fulbright.co.uk* pages, one of the best sites available for updated information on studying in the USA.

Most students wishing to further their studies in the USA will probably start with their own institution's careers service who should have the above guides, and may well have others such as:

- *Peterson's Guides to Graduate Study* (6 volumes) published annually by Peterson's Guides, Princeton, NJ.

- *Directory of Graduate Programs* (4 volumes) Educational Testing Service, Princeton, NJ.

- *Graduate Study in the United States: A Guide for Prospective International Graduate Students*, Council of Graduate Schools, Washington DC 20036-1173.

Often the initial response to seeing this volume of information is growing dismay. Fortunately the Educational Advisory Service has recognised this and now provides ways through the problems of information overload:

- Talks to prospective students. These are often given as part of the annual 'milkround'. Watch careers service notice boards (or ask!).

- An excellent, informative summary 'Postgraduate Information Pack'.

- Listings on graduate study in particular fields.

- A one-page schedule for applying.

- A two-page summary of tuition costs across the US.

- A two-page summary of awards for postgraduate study and research in the United States.

- A set of videos outlining the application procedures, and providing information on moving to the USA.

- A Student Specification Form, which, when filled in with details of what courses and institutions you are interested in, can, with the use of Foreign Student Information Clearinghouse (a computer software program), provide listings, for a fee, of suitable institutions and courses worth following up. Forms can be obtained from careers offices or from the EAS.

- A pre-departure orientation in late June (£10).

The EAS encourages attending their London office in person, Monday–Friday, 10.30am–1.00pm and 2.00pm–4.30pm. Forms can be picked up and videos watched, plus advice given in person. Much of their material is supplied annually to British university careers service libraries where it should be on file.

FUNDING GRADUATE STUDY IN THE USA

Costs
State universities offer graduate education for fees that are considered 'moderate' compared to those of private, ivy-league ('Oxbridge'-style) universities. Typically residents of that state pay about $3,000 per academic year (two fourteen-week semesters). Non-residents (US or foreign) pay considerably more, anything up to 400 per cent in some institutions. Academic fees alone may well then be prohibitive for the self-financing foreign student, never mind the need to have some $8–12,000 for living expenses to get an entry visa. As examples the University of Maryland at College Park charges $9,494 for a foreign graduate student in political science for an academic year. The private Johns Hopkins University charges $18,800 – almost double. Now you know why I went to Maryland not Johns Hopkins!

Working your way through college
Americans expect to work their way through college, but as an outsider

you will be expected to pay your way with funds from overseas, at least for the first year. New visa regulations now permit students in good standing to work from their second year on to graduation on or off campus. Most foreign students who are not independently wealthy or bringing with them a UK scholarship will need to consider an assistantship, that is, teaching undergraduates on campus.

Assistantships

The good news is that most universities offer their graduate applicants assistantships, foreign applicants included. As a graduate assistant you will be paid a regular 10-month stipend each year, plus a waiver of fees (which may double its value). You may have to be frugal to live off such a stipend. Be prepared to share a flat, perhaps even a room, and don't expect to be able to run a car. For that you will have to teach extra courses during the summer vacation, or given the new visa regulations, find off-campus work. The stipend though has to be earned: it is no sinecure. You will have to teach first year undergraduates in large introductory classes, under the supervision of a professor, assemble reading lists, grade papers, invigilate exams, conduct lab classes and help out on field courses if appropriate, plus act as the professor's research assistant (or dog's body) for no more than twenty hours per week, all alongside your own studies. It is a very busy life, but it pays the rent, avoids paying fees, and is sufficient proof accepted by the Immigration & Naturalization Service (INS) that you have the necessary wherewithal to support yourself, so enabling the visa to be issued with a minimum of fuss. About one-third of foreign MA students have some form of assistantship, two-thirds of foreign doctoral students.

In the long run assistantships provide an excellent academic apprenticeship, each year involving ever more responsibility. Doctoral students may well take full responsibility for a course they have previously helped teach under the careful supervision of a senior member of staff, for which they will be paid at the top of the assistant salary scale.

Colleges vary in quality of education provided, prestige and crucially location: a California stipend may be almost twice that of somewhere in the Midwest but may provide only the same material standard of living. For some people Los Angeles might be intolerable at any price. For a lone British postgraduate, without friends and family for support, Los Angeles without a car might be far less satisfying than a Midwestern college town with less money, where you could walk to work, save up for a car, and visit the big cities with new college friends as and when chances present themselves. And what is the cost of living anyway? Do you expect to have your own flat immediately upon arrival or would you share? But would you share a room with a fellow student? Would you walk or hitch-hike to work? Are you on your own, or with a spouse not allowed to work by visa regulations?

- Location of research materials or study area may mean a high stipend college is not where you want to be.

- Computer connections mean for certain resources you can be almost anywhere and still gain access to your research material.

If you are single, able-bodied, and prepared to be flexible upon your arrival, getting a graduate stipend should solve not just your visa problems but keep a roof over your head. And if that doesn't always work out many graduates have made long-standing (though supposedly temporary) nests in their office on campus – while intending to look for somewhere else of course! For a married student survival is possible, but can be financially very tight and demoralising for the non-working partner.

The advice of experience is: **go**, if at all possible. It's worth it for the experience. And with an academic department as your base, a place to live in, people to share with, old cars to borrow or even to buy, things always turn up via the grapevine. Americans are proverbially hospitable, and no more so than when they hear of someone at the office sleeping in a bag on the floor or walking to work from an unfurnished apartment. For further funding information see:

- *Funding for US Study: A Guide for Foreign Nationals*, Institute of International Education, New York, NY.

- Commonly Asked Questions about Postgraduate Admissions *www.fulbright.co.uk* particularly 'what are my chances of getting financial aid?' and 'what are my chances of being fully funded by a university?'

POSTGRADUATE SCHOLARSHIPS

There are several well-known UK scholarships specially available to British postgraduate students wishing to study in the USA: **Fulbright, Thouron** and **Kennedy**.

Fulbright scholarships

These are available for travel and maintenance for British UK-based postgraduates for 'a year of advanced research in the United States'. Applications must be submitted by late October each year. Details and application forms available from July each year.

- Fulbright Commission, 62 Doughty Street, London WC1N 2LS. Tel: (0171) 404 6994. Enclose A4 stamped and addressed envelope. Details available from *www.fulbright.co.uk*. This is an excellent and essential site for any prospective postgraduate student considering the USA.

Thouron awards

The Thouron-University of Pennsylvania for British-American Student Exchange offers five awards covering maintenance and fees for study at the University of Pennsylvania (in Philadelphia). Closing date is early November each year. Details can be obtained from:

- The Registrar, Thouron Awards, The University of Glasgow, Glasgow G12 8QQ.

Kennedy scholarships

These are for postgraduate study at Harvard or the Massachusetts Institute of Technology. Twelve scholarships exist to cover tuition, health care, travel and maintenance, providing an allowance of $15,500 (1998–99). Prospectus and application forms from:

- The Secretary, Kennedy Memorial Trust, 16 Great College Street, London SW1P 3RX. Tel: (0171) 222 1151. Enclose 9 x 6³/₄ SAE.

Closing date for applications is mid October.

Post-doctoral awards

Awards for scholars already holding a doctoral degree or of similar standing are listed in a flier available from the Fulbright Commission, 62 Doughty Street, London WC1N 2LS. Tel: (0171) 404 6880. Web site: *www.fulbright.co.uk*

Harkness fellowships

These are for UK-educated professionals dealing with health provision, education or urban management, approximately 21–40 years old on 1 September of the year of application, which must be made by 8 October for interviewing the following February. For full application materials write to:

- The Harkness Fellowships, Harkness House, 28 Bedford Square, London W1CB 3EG. Tel: (0171) 631 0411.

For a list of *Awards for Postgraduate Study & Research in the US* see the information pack produced annually by the Educational Advisory Service, 62 Doughty Street, London WC1N 2LS which contains details of some further 14 award schemes available to UK citizens or look up their excellent Web page (on *www.fulbright.co.uk*).

OPPORTUNITIES FOR TEACHERS

Teachers wishing to spend time in the USA might like to consider a scholarship specially geared to their needs, or a post-to-post exchange with someone. For a general introduction see:

- Roger Jones, *Teaching Abroad*, How to Books, 3rd edition, 1998.

Start by contacting the British officer of the Council on International Educational Exchange (CIEE) for information on School Partners America, High School Study Visits, Teaching Visit USA and their general support for UK-US exchanges. Tel: (0171) 478 2007. Fax:(0171) 734 7322.

Teacher scholarships

These are organised by the English-Speaking Union to enable participants to explore their field of study within the USA and to become more broadly acquainted with American life. There are two main sets of scholarships:

- the Walter Hines Page Scholarship for 8-week term-time visits (October to May)
- Chautauqua Institution Scholarships for a 9-week summer school-based tour.

Other Page scholarships for shorter (4-week) visits are sponsored by teaching unions and associations such as NASWT and NUT. There is, fortunately, an introductory leaflet which gives details of where to apply. Write to:

- The Director of Education, The English-Speaking Union, Dartmouth House, 37 Charles Street, London W1X 8AB. Tel: (0171) 493 3328.

Applications usually have to be submitted by the end of November for the following year, and short-listed candidates are interviewed in February. Those elected will be expected to contribute £50 to £200 depending on the dollar–pound rate on the 4-week scholarship (where the grant would be about £500). Hospitality in the USA is provided by the US branch of the ESU.

Post-to-post exchanges

These are organised by the **Central Bureau for Educational Visits and**

Exchanges, a UK government agency responsible to the various British departments of education. Their aim is to develop contacts, co-operation and exchanges between British teachers and teachers overseas.

The scheme is open to all qualified British teachers from nursery schools through to universities with five or more years' experience, of which the final two years must have been with the same school or college. Posts can be exchanged for a full year, or for a term. Applications for a year's exchange have to be completed by early December, or by the end of June for spring term visits.

Exchanges are organised centrally. If a high school geography teacher from North Dakota applies to the US organisers just as another such geography teacher from Inverness applies, the Central Bureau would try to arrange for them to swap jobs, perhaps even accommodation, subject to both teachers being accepted as suitable. As this might be a very hit and miss way of getting an exchange it has been suggested informally that teachers *already* in contact (say after a holiday trip or via friends and relatives) might like to submit a statement to both sets of organisers saying a link has already been established. This is the way university teachers usually swap jobs on this or on other such schemes.

Teachers return to their post upon returning home. They are seconded to full salary with all rights safeguarded. The visit counts as service for all purposes, including incremental credit. Grants from central government also cover return travel and any necessary extra cost of living allowance (a British salary will not go very far in the USA, especially not if the exchange is for central New York City!).

In addition the US authorities give each teacher a free insurance policy for sickness and accident during the period of the exchange (as the US visiting teacher in Britain would be eligible for NHS treatment).

Applications for the US/UK Teacher Exchange Schemes can be obtained by sending a 12" by 9" stamped addressed envelope, along with your name, home and institution addresses, with a note on subjects taught to:

● Teacher Exchange (USA) Central Bureau for Educational Visits & Exchanges, 10 Spring Gardens, London SW1 2BN. Tel: (0171) 389 4004 for details.

Teachers (and others) interested in meeting a wide cross section of Americans might usefully contact the US wing of **Servas**. The name is esperanto for 'we serve'. Contact US Servas Inc., 11 John Street #407, New York, NY 10038. Tel: (212) 267 0252. Fax: (212) 267 0292 (or email usservas @igc.apc.org).

School exchanges

For those teachers hardened by years of school trips, camps, outward bound and field trips the ultimate organisational experience might now be available: a UK/US school exchange. After matching, school pupils from the UK live in the homes of their US partners and attend the link school for four weeks. The US pupils return the visit either in the summer or in the autumn terms. It is hoped that once established links would continue between the two communities, a form of educational twinning almost.

Contact the various Central Bureau offices (see above for addresses). English and Welsh schools should contact the London Office, Tel: (0181) 486 5101, Scottish schools the Edinburgh office, Tel: (0131) 447 8024, Northern Irish schools the Belfast office, Tel: (01232) 664418. Also: phone CIEE about their School Partners America programme on (0171) 706 3008.

School visits

School and college groups are increasingly going to the USA just as earlier generations once made their first trip across the English Channel. Usually one leader will go free for every 20 fee-paying students. A week in New York City or Washington DC will cost each student about £400 for flight and accommodation.

For details:
- **UK Connection** on (0171) 351 6882 for details.
- **New World Travel**, Discovery House, Lamberts Road, Tunbridge Wells, Kent TN2 3EH. Tel: (01892) 515363.

Higher education exchanges

Full-time academics may also be eligible for Fulbright grants for head-for-head exchanges lasting a full academic year. Travel and subsistence expenses may be approved for those initiating exchanges of younger staff. Closing date is usually 1 November. Information and application forms are available from either:

- **The British Council (Higher Education Division)**, 10 Spring Gardens, London SW1A 2BN. Tel: (0171) 930 8466.

- **The US/UK Education Commission**, 62 Doughty Street, London WC1N 2LS. Tel: (0171) 404 6880.

For information on a scheme which recruits teachers for inner city programmes from the ranks of the newly graduated without any previous teacher training, contact **Teach for America**, PO Box 5114, New York, NY 10185. Tel: 001 212 789 9302.

GAP YEAR OPPORTUNITIES

A break before college has become increasingly popular, and if spent usefully can be highly advantageous: students arrive back more confident and mature. But for the US the gap year can be a problem. Most visa regulations require student applicants to be mid-course. A place on a course a year hence may not be sufficient. After all, you have no investment you wish to complete by returning to the UK as would a student approaching their final year.

If you are going to college and wish to consider a gap year off it can be a worthwhile investment to visit the college to talk to the recruitment officers and course tutors. Don't rely on being able to talk in any great detail with any of these people on an advertised Open Day. Thousands of would-be students attend these occasions and you may never find a specific person, with the best will in the world. But particularly if you intend to take a gap year visit the college where you intend to study upon your return, if only to give yourself a mental image of what you would be missing if you start reconsidering the wisdom of returning to college at all. And when you do visit phone ahead so that the college can arrange for specific people to be available to talk about the implications of a gap year. Let the college know precisely what you want to talk about so they can be prepared to brief the right people. And of course a gap year in the USA may be much more attractive to certain departments than others.

For general information:

- *The Gap Year Guidebook* Peridot (£8) can help with job hunting in the UK, to raise funds for an extended US visit.

- *A Year Between* Central Bureau for Educational Visits & Exchanges (£8).

- *Go For It* Lennard (£8).

- *A Year Off...A Year On*, Careers Research & Advisory Centre, 2nd Floor, Sheraton House, Castle Park, Cambridge CB3 0AX (Tel: (01223) 460277).

- Nick Vandome, *Spending a Year Abroad*, How To Books, 3rd edition 1997.

- Mark Hempshell, *Planning Your Gap Year*, How To Books, 2nd edition 1998.

11
Staying or Returning

REMAINING IN THE USA

Most visitors to the USA, whether long or short stay, will at some point consider the possibility of staying on permanently, making the USA home, if only in the medium term. You'll need to consider:

- career implications
- family reactions
- implications for health care and retirement
- possible status – resident or citizen.

Career implications

Only you can judge how good an idea staying on could be for your career prospects. It is possible to get locked into your US-based career structure without giving adequate consideration to moving sideways back into the UK. Who wants to get off a moving staircase if it's going steadily upwards? But remember: career implications are only one reason for staying or returning, even if they seem the most obvious.

Family reunions

These need careful consideration, both for the immediate family, presumably with you in the USA, and those back home such as ageing parents. Whereas the side of the family back in Britain will probably be stoical (they may have assumed you'd gone for good when you set off originally) your family in the USA will react in terms of their immediate needs, fears and expectations. Most children will have settled down quite quickly and will not want to move anywhere, certainly not back to a country they hardly remember. But remember, they would not want to move to the next town if they were still back in Britain, so you need to consider how much weight the grown-ups should give the views of the children. But do let them have their say, and explain why you intend to overrule them if necessary.

Perhaps more critically you'll need to ask certain questions about the family staying on:

- What are their US-based career prospects?
- Will college be an affordable option in the USA?
- Will you want them to become US citizens?
- Should you give them the option to return home at, say, 18 to make up their own minds?
- What if they return to the UK and stay on?

Health care and retirement

You'll probably just continue with your existing health plan, but what of retirement? The US social security system is getting very fragile, with no prospects of improvements as more and more people reach retirement age and the US budget deficit grows ever larger. The pensionable age is being gradually raised, but with economic restructuring pressure on people to retire earlier and earlier continues. The US military has helped promote the belief that after 20 years' service, at whatever age, it's time to retire, or at least take a pension *and* start another career. Ever more people are opening an Individual Retirement Account (IRA). This will allow you to supplement any government pension, but if you attempt to use the money before the agreed term you'll lose most if not all of the tax benefits. As IRAs proliferate the information about them grows. See a trusted accountant!

A word of warning: your health plan was for a limited stay (with a return to the UK always a possibility if things got dire). Is your health plan now adequate if you want to stay on a different basis? It's worth checking it out. Ask other people who've stayed on whether they changed their health care plan, or if not, do they wish they had.

Citizen status

Though the green card no longer exists, permanent status does. If you want to change your status consult a lawyer specialising in this field, though initially you could have a look at something like American attorney Richard Fleischer's *Applying for a US Visa* (How to Books/ International Venture Handbooks, 1993). Marrying a US citizen is the most popular reason for staying on in the USA, and it's the way that certainly makes the paperwork easiest if you arrived on a non-immigrant visa. And you won't have to return home before applying! Failing that you'll need to gain status as set out earlier in this book. Your employer will probably be the most important factor, emphasising skills needed for the US economy, and that the job won't deprive an American of a job.

Should you adopt citizenship?

For many people publicly disavowing their country of birth is one step too far. Whereas it was presumably easy for Germans fleeing the Nazis in the 1930s, for those not in exile it's probably a much more difficult decision. Fortunately taking US citizenship doesn't cancel British citizenship, except as far as the USA is concerned. British law accepts dual citizenship. US law doesn't. And if you think this is a lawyer's quibble it's worth recalling that the 1812 war between Britain and the USA was over just this point (Britain press-ganged US citizens on US vessels on the high-seas saying they were still British and there was a war on against France, *etc*).

If you do take US citizenship and lose your British passport for an American one you could still re-enter the UK and settle down back home again. Strictly speaking you don't even need a British passport to re-enter Britain, just some means of identification (I have used an RAC card at Heathrow before!). You'll forfeit US citizenship if you take out a British passport or run for office outside the USA (as would *any* US citizen).

There might still be a joker in the pack that you've not considered when considering permanent residency and citizenship: **military service**. Once legally settled into the US all men over 18 must register (see notices on how to do this at your local US Post Office). Once the Vietnam War ended, the draft (conscription) ended. The USA now has a professional, full-time army (despite a revolutionary heritage that considered anything other than a citizens' part-time militia a start down the road to tyranny). But in times of international stress things can and do change. Even in peacetime it is an offence not to register. It is even possible that anyone liable to the draft who came back to the UK to avoid it would be liable to be handed over to the US authorities under the appropriate Visiting Forces Act. Remember that US draft dodgers went to Canada or Sweden *not* the UK during the 1960s!

COMING BACK TO THE UK

Returning to the UK can be as great a decision as going away in the first place. For many it's even more difficult: new roots have been put down, it's always easier to stay put, and home starts to appear like the foreign country it has actually become.

What's changed?

- the government (or not as the case may be)
- the currency (coins for English £1 notes)
- TV channels (all day TV, extra channels)

- motorway network (which can be disorienting)
- the cost of everything (£2 a pint, payable with a single coin)
- very (too?) American?
- European Union integration (passport and courts)
- house prices (US urban costs in the UK southeast).

Some things haven't changed:
- the unpredictability of the weather (three fine days then a thunderstorm)
- London taxis
- draught stout (but at what a price!).

And so on. These are what await someone returning now after only a couple of years in the USA. What will have changed if and when you get back in five or ten years?

When you are away change will continue as ever, and you'll have to meet it all at once if you return. If you'd left in 1971 and kept in touch only by telephone, Christmas cards, a quick dash back for a funeral, plus British television programmes on the PBS network, what would Britain of 1998 look like? Answer: a foreign country.

How to make contact back home

You'll need to explore as wide a variety of approaches as possible:

- Put the word out that you are interested in returning home for the right job. Let your contacts know you are thinking of moving back if the right slot opens up. Here having kept in touch will pay off. Come back to conferences (even if at your own expense) to keep a high profile, to let colleagues in your field know that you haven't fallen off the edge of the world, and perhaps as vital, to remind prospective employers you are still interested and keeping in touch.

- Read the British newspapers (as available in large universities) for any idea of what's coming vacant, who to contact (even if you are too late for particular jobs).

- Write to friends and contacts to widen your circle. Email is a godsend here.

- Approach UK agencies with a CV – they may be looking for someone with US experience.

US taxation

You'll need to prove to the IRS you'll be leaving with no tax debt. If you leave fully paid up you'll be due a tax refund in due course, unless you left at the very end of the tax year. Leaving at the right time can be as advantageous to your tax situation as getting married at the right point in the tax year used to be.

UK National Insurance
If you've been out for more than three years you'll need to re-establish yourself. Employers will usually do this for you.

UK Immigration
Technically returning British citizens don't need a passport to enter the UK. Crossing from the Irish Republic to Northern Ireland you may not even see border control (though you might have to negotiate a security check point). At international airports you'll get through with either a UK or US passport, though if you are obviously not returning as a tourist, UK papers, such as a birth certificate, may ease your way. An American spouse with a US passport coming in with a British spouse should get the paperwork sorted out with the UK authorities in the USA, but usually it's easier for a US passport holder to enter the UK as a 6 months tourist, changing status as per the procedure outlined by the:

- **Home Office Immigration & Nationality Department**, Lunar House, Wellesley Road, Croydon CR0 2BY. Tel: (0181) 686 0688. Calls taken in rotation, closing at 4.00pm. First try the Home Office Web page: *www.homeoffice.gov/ad/hpg.htm*

UK government leaflets HC169 and HC503 explain the rules in detail. A fiancé(e) can enter this way, but if you apply for fiancé(e) (rather than tourist) entrance you'll need to provide written proof of a planned wedding within *three* months, and the visa will be for a maximum of three months.

UK Customs and Excise
There's no need to provide the detailed listing necessary on entering the USA, but be honest and don't try to bring in restricted items (especially pets). Personal effects over 6 months old will come in duty free. If you feel someone is trying to use you to bring illegal substances into the UK there's a free UK number provided by HM Customs & Excise (0800 59 5000).

Pets
If you need to ask how much it costs to bring a pet over and to have it go through quarantine you can't afford it (a happy, helpful hint offered by our Embassy in Washington DC). By mid-1990s reckon on at least £1,000 for the quarantine alone, plus the cost of the flight. Quarantine is for 6 months, though visiting is permitted after the first two weeks.

RETURNING HOME

You can move home, find a large supermarket nearby, drive on the motorway to work, and hardly notice you've changed countries. But spirits will cost about twice as much as in the USA, blue jeans a lot more, and petrol even more again. You'll miss your US friends of course, but enjoy remeeting your British ones. You'll enjoy good shoe shops, with width fittings for children, a range of beers, but the couldn't care less attitude of so many shop assistants will be a delight you'll soon realise you hadn't missed at all. Eating out will be less frequent, though you'll probably do it more than your British friends. The weather may be a bit of surprise, especially the lack of both long standing snow or stable hot weather.

Salaries will seem low: they generally are. People in the middle income bracket are less well off in the UK. Those lower or higher may well be better off. But holidays will probably be twice those you had in the USA. Being able to visit the continent will of course mean cheaper foreign holidays – but EU regulations have still not reduced air fares to levels comparable to those within the USA.

Families that hated going to the USA may well hate returning. US sport, fast food, late night shopping and the swimming pool in the sunshine may all seem like paradise lost, especially for teenage children or a spouse whose career progress has been broken yet again. Fortunately pre-teen children adjust well given love, attention and food. Teenagers are something else. Moving away from friends, especially a first love, can be traumatic, especially if tackled heavy handedly.

Children will have to change schools so it will help to move in sync with the natural breaks in the school year, preferably between years, ideally when a change of school would be involved anyway. If your child started school in the USA they'll be behind comparable British children, if only for having started later.

Coming back to go to university might not be a good idea without considerable organisation. Scottish students starting at English or Welsh universities with a school education one year shorter can have major difficulties, especially in technical subjects. How much less prepared will students from the USA be! Better try for British A-levels via a college of further education before applying for university. Arriving at university after such a bridge can be very profitable. And older students generally get better degrees.

If you have been on a mutual academic or teachers' exchange slotting back in again may take no time at all: children return to their old friends and a new teacher, your own car may seem much smaller than you remember (and perhaps more worse for wear) and various changes in the house, garden and neighbourhood will gradually make themselves known. But if you have been away for several years on contract or secondment you need to consider:

- US and UK tax consequences – in the year of return you may actually be eligible for tax rebates!

- UK capital gains liabilities on US investments sold off on returning home

- renewed National Insurance liability (including the implications of having missed paying in for several years)

- regaining any tax advantages on any long-held life assurance policies.

For an excellent summary (though now rather out of date) of the financial implications of your eventual return to the UK, see Harry Brown's *Working Abroad: The Guide to Fiscal Do's and Don'ts*, Northcote House, Plymouth, 5th edition 1986. For a more recent guide try Jonathan Golding, *Working Abroad: Essential Financial Planning for Expatriates & Their Employers*, How To Books/ International Venture Handbooks 1995. For the cultural implications see Robert Chesshyre's *The Return of the Native Reporter*, Viking, London 1987.

US English

American English sprang originally from British English, and in certain ways and in certain areas retains its heritage in a form far more traditional than generally found in Britain. The speech of Appalachia can be traced back to the hills of Ulster, the Scottish borders, and the West Country. And a US performance of Shakespeare's plays is likely to involve pronunciation and intonation far more familiar to the Bard himself than anything he'd hear in Stratford today. British English has moved on from its Elizabethan stage. Only in the peripheral areas of the English-speaking world can the older, most truly Anglo-Saxon forms be found.

But US English moves on too. The simplicity of Anglo-Saxon usage has been its downfall. It simply doesn't sound sophisticated enough in an increasingly cosmopolitan age. There isn't, after all, a truly Anglo-Saxon word for 'sophisticated'! So Americans have sought to improve their standing by 'improving' their English, by which they mean using long words in ever more complex patterns. It has something to do with the rise of meritocracy, the professionalism of so much of American life, but mostly the need to sound as if you are at the cutting edge of science and progress. If regional accents in the USA carry no indication of social standing then vocabulary and syntax will have to do so instead.

A little simultaneous translation from Shakespeare may show what's involved:

Original:	Modern USA:
It is a tale	It is in narrative form
told by	vocalised by
an idiot,	an individual of arrested mental development
full of	emphasising the
sound and	audio and
fury,	hyperindignant components
signifying	possessing
nothing	no meaningful insight

The impact of Latin-based words and Germanic-sounding sentences has been enormous. Today there's also computer terminology. Memories *download*, people *interface*, surely classic cases of GIGO (Garbage In, Garbage Out). School Latin will finally be of some use to help get to grips with all the prefixes: *counterurbanization*, *exurban*, and don't forget *post-industrial*.

The American language is indeed flexible and dynamic. You can even make things seem better by your choice of terms. Don't have a family row: enjoy an aggressive interpersonal interaction. You don't like the idea of hiring a cleaner? Then hire a domestic hygiene specialist. And that wasn't a pay-cut. That was a downward income adjustment. Video clips of MTV (the video channel) are not repeated regularly, rather they are made to withstand 'heavy rotation'! At Universal Studios Hollywood no one is sick after the T-Rex attack and 85ft waterfall plunge, they suffer 'protein spillage'. And remember: when house hunting you should be wary of living downwind of the effluent treatment plant.

A few place pronunciations:

Peru (Indiana)	PEEroo
Cairo (Illinois)	KAYroe
Versailles (Kentucky)	Ver sales
Maryland	Mairal'nd
St Louis	Synt Lewis
Michigan	Mishegan
New Orleans	New Orluns
Syracuse (New York)	Sirracuse
Des Moines	De Moyn

Glossary

The first Americans had... to invent Americanisms, if only to describe the unfamiliar landscape, weather, flora, and fauna confronting them.

AAA. American Automobile Association ('triple A').

apartment. Flat.

appraisal. Valuation.

area code. Dialling (STD) code.

ATM. Cashpoint machine.

baggage. Luggage.

bathroom. Toilet (WC) but also known as 'the john' (from seventeenth-century English); 'the head' (naval bulkhead); 'wash-room'; 'comfort station'; or 'restroom'.

billion. Thousand million.

biscuit. Scone-like roll.

bomb. Fail (not success).

broiled. Grilled.

brownbag. (as in 'we'll brownbag it'). To work through lunch with each person bringing their own packed lunch (traditionally in a brown bag).

burbs. Suburbs.

busy signal. Engaged tone.

BYO. Bring your own (bottle).

cable. Message. Telegram (now 'telemessage' in UK).

call collect. Reverse the charges.

can. Tin (food).

Canuck. Canadian (derogatory).

chaser. Long drink (usually beer) to follow a spirit.

check. Bill (restaurant).

checking account. Simple bank account with cheque book.

checkroom. Cloakroom (but not a WC).

close out. End of range sale.

closet. Cupboard (usually built in).

coach class. 2nd or tourist class.

comfort station. Roadside toilets.

community chest. A local fund for neighbourhood charities.

community college. Publicly funded college for local people offering vocational or pre-university courses, similar to further education colleges in Britain.

condominium ('condo'). Flats sold to sitting tenants, or purpose built with housing association-like tenancy but commercially run.

cookie. Biscuit.

cook out. Barbecue.

corn. Maize.

Daylight Saving Time. Summer time.

detour (on sign). Diversion.

diaper. Nappy.

direct drafting. Direct debit.

divided highway. Dual carriage-way.

Dixie. The South (south of Mason-Dixon line).

draft, the. Conscription.

dual citizenship. Having citizenship of two countries at once (illegal for US citizens).

duplex. A two-floored apartment.

easy over. Eggs fried both sides.

El. The elevated railway (in Chicago).

elevator. Lift.

expressway. Motorway.

fall. Autumn.

fanny bags. Bum bags.

faucet. Tap.

FDIC. Federal Deposit Insurance Corporation (government agency insuring bank deposits).

fender. Bumper.

FHA. Federal Housing Administration (agency that insures new construction mortgages).

fifth. Bottle of spirits (one fifth US gallon).

first name. Christian name.

food stamps. Coupons bought by poor people at below face value for use in food shops at face value.

garage sale. A car boot sale in one's own driveway.

garbage can. Dustbin.

gas. Petrol.

gearshift. Manual transmission.

general delivery. Poste restante.

GI Bill. Popular name for Serviceman's Readjustment Act (1944) entitling veterans to post-discharge benefits, especially payment of college fees.

go, to. Take away, carry out.

GOP. Republican Party ('Grand Old Party').

green card. Permit to live in USA (no longer green).

happy hour. Half-price drinks in late afternoon.

help. Servants (particularly a southern euphemism for black servants).

hockey. Ice hockey (not field hockey).

hood. Bonnet of car.

hose. Tights.

HOV. High occupancy vehicle.

icebox. Refrigerator.

IRA. Individual Retirement Account.

IRS. Internal Revenue Service.

INS. Immigration & Naturalization Service.

JAP. 'Jewish-American-Princess' (or any spoilt rich girl).

jay walking. Illegal crossing of street.

jello. Jelly.

jelly. Jam.

klutz. Socially inept person.

lavatory. A wc.

levelized billing. Budget payment plan.

limey. A Brit.

line. Queue.

loaded. Drunk.

long distance call. Trunk call.

mailgram. Telemessage.

Martini. 3 parts vermouth, 1 part gin + olive.

men working. Road works.

mezzanine. Floor between main floors.

micro breweries. US 'real ale' producers.

night letter. Overnight telegram (now 'telemessage' in UK).

NORAID. Northern Irish Aid (IRA fundraiser).

NRA. National Rifle Association (major gun lobby).

observatory. Viewing platform.

Okie. Farmers from Oklahoma (who fled to California in the 1930s).

one way (ticket). Single ticket.

outage. Power loss.

overpass. Flyover.

pants. Trousers.

pavement. Road surface (tarmac).

penny sale. Special offer where second item costs only 1c (essentially two for cost of one).

person to person. Personal call.

phone booth. Call box.

plaza. Open square.

poison ivy. Similar to Virginia creeper (but poisonous).

preppy. Lifestyle associated with young people of social elite.

railroad crossing. Level crossing.

rain check. A promise to take up an invitation at a later date.

ramp. Motorway sliproad.

range. Cooker.

realtor. Estate agent.

redcap. Porter (airport or railway station).

redneck. Right-wing blue-collar worker.

roadway. Carriageway.

robe. Dressing gown.

roundtrip (ticket). Return.

rotary. Roundabout.

RV. Recreational vehicle (motorised caravan).

school. Any institute of education (especially university).

SEC. Securities and Exchange Commission (stock exchange watchdog).

sidewalk. Pavement.

soccer. Football.

soda. Any fizzy drink.

special delivery. Express post.

stand in line. Queue.

store. Shop.

straight. Neat (liquor).

streetcar. Tram.

subway. Underground railway/tube.

sunny side up. Eggs fried without being turned over.

sweats. Tracksuit.

tag. Car number plate.

3.2 beer. A fairly weak beer with 3.2 per cent alcohol (legalised from 8 April 1933, the end of Prohibition), still often the only beer legally available in certain states.

toll-free number. Free number (1-800 prefix).

traffic circle. Roundabout.

trailer. Caravan.

tramway. Cable car.

treaty investor. A substantial investor seeking residence on a non-immigrant basis, and coming from a country with a reciprocal treaty.

trunk. Boot of car.

turnpike. Toll road.

TVA. Tennessee Valley Authority (regional development agency and power company in southern Appalachians).

two weeks. Fortnight (a term rarely used in the USA).

twofers. Two for the price of one.

underpass. Subway (pedestrian only).

unlisted number. Ex-directory.

VA. Veterans' Administration.

veteran. Anyone honourably discharged from the US forces (including coastguard).

VCR. Video (cassette recorder).

Wash up. Freshen up (hands and face, not dishes).

WASP. White Anglo-Saxon Protestant.

windshield. Windscreen.

wire. Telegram (now 'telemessage' in UK).

WPA. Work Projects Administration (a make-work agency in the Great Depression).

yield (on sign). Give way.

yuppy. 'Young upwardly mobile professional' hence 'buppy' is a black yuppy).

zip code. Numerical post code (5 or 10 digits).

Statutory Public Holidays

New Year	1 January
Martin Luther King's Birthday	16 January (most states)
Washington's Birthday	22 February
Memorial Day	Last Monday in May (46 states)
Independence Day	4 July
Labor Day	First Monday in September
Columbus Day	Second Monday of October (32 states)
Veterans' Day	11 November ('Armistice Day')
Thanksgiving	Fourth Thursday in November
Christmas Day	25 December

Beware: public holidays are state not federally authorised. Most states give all the above holidays, which are also enjoyed by federal employees throughout the USA. Lincoln's Birthday is observed in northern but not southern states.

For a listing of public holidays and other observed days (from Armed Forces Day via Mother's Day to United Nations Day) see the inside front cover of *The World Almanac* published annually by Funk & Wagnalls.

Consulates in the USA

Australia
- 611 N. Larchmont Blvd, Los Angeles Tel: (213) 469 4300.
- 1601 Massachusetts Ave NW, Washington DC. Tel: (202) 797 3159.

Canada
- 1251 Ave of the Americas, New York, NY. Tel: (212) 586 2400.
- 501 Pennsylvania Ave NW, Washington DC. Tel: (202) 682 1770.

Ireland
- 515 Madison Ave, New York, NY. Tel: (212) 319 2555.
- 2234 Massachusetts Ave NW, Washington DC. Tel: (202) 462 3939.

New Zealand
- Suite 530, 630 5th Ave, New York, NY. Tel: (212) 586 6060.
- 37 Observatory Circle NW, Washington DC. Tel: (202) 328 4800.

South Africa
- 50 N. La Cienega Blvbd, Ste. 300, Beverley Hills, CA. Tel: (213) 657 9200.
- 326 48th St E, New York. Tel (212) 838 1700.
- 3051 Massachusetts Ave NW, Washington DC. Tel: (202) 232 4400.

UK
- 225 Peachtree St NE, Suite 912, Atlanta, GA. Tel: (404) 524 5956.
- 1 Samsome Street, Suite 850, San Francisco, CA. Tel: (414) 981 3030.
- 845 3rd Ave, New York, NY. Tel: (212) 752 8400.
- 3100 Massachusetts Ave NW, Washington DC. Tel: (202) 462 1340.
- 3701 Wilshere Blvd, Ste. 312, Los Angeles, CA. Tel: (213) 385 7381.

State Tourist Offices

Most of the tourist offices listed below are part of each state's own administration which is not necessarily based in the largest city. For instance, Albany is the capital for New York, Annapolis for Maryland, Harrisburg for Pennsylvania. But with modern electronic phone and computer links the actual office can be physically almost anywhere. Often the only public presence will be at freeway rest areas on entering the state where there will be a supply of maps and brochures for the visitor to take away.

State	Numbers	Web site
Alabama	(334) 242 4554	www.travelfile.com
Alaska	(907) 465 2010	www.touch-alaska.com
Arizona	(602) 255 3618	www.arizonaguide.com
Arkansas	(501) 682 7777	//1800natural.com
California	(916) 322 1396	www.gocalif.ca.gov
Colorado	(303) 892 1112	www.colorado.com
Connecticut	(203) 566 3977	www.state.ct.us/tourism
Delaware	(302) 739 4271	www.state.de.us/tourism/intro.htm
District of Columbia	(202) 789 7000	www.washington.org
Florida	(904) 488 5607	www.flausa.com/index.html
Georgia	(404) 656 3590	www.georgia.org/itt/tourism
Hawaii	(808) 923 1811	www.hawaii.gov/tourism
Idaho	(208) 334 2470	www.visitid.org
Illinois	(312) 793 2094	www.enjoyillinois.com
Indiana	800 289 6646	www.ai.org/tourism
Iowa	(515) 225 2323	www.icvba.org
Kansas	(913) 296 2009	
Kentucky	(502) 564 4930	www.tourky.com OR www.state.ky.us/tour.htm
Louisiana	(504) 342 8100	www.state.la.us.crt/tourism.htm
Maine	(207) 289 5710	www.visitmaine.com
Maryland	(301) 269 3517	www.mdisfun.org
Massachusetts	(617) 727 3201	www.mass-vacation.com
Michigan	(517) 373 0670	www.michigan.org
Minnesota	(612) 296 5029	www.state.mn.us/explore/index.htm
Mississippi	(601) 359 3297	www.mississippi.org

Missouri	(314) 751 4133	www.missouritourism.org
Montana	(406) 449 2654	www.travel.mt.gov
Nebraska	(402) 471 3796	www.visitnebraska.org
Nevada	(702) 885 4322	www.nevadaweb.com/ct
New Hampshire	(603) 271 2343	www.visitnh.gov
New Jersey	(609) 827 6230	www.state.nj/travel/index4.html
New York	(518) 474 4116	www.state.ny.us
North Carolina	(919) 733 4171	www.commerce.state.nc.us
North Dakota	(701) 224 2525	www.ndtourism.com/howto.html
Ohio	(614) 466 8844	www.ohiotourism.com
Oklahoma	(405) 521 2406	www.otrd.state.ok.us
Oregon	(503) 373 1200	www.traveloregon.com
Pennsylvania	(717) 787 5453	www.pavisnet.com
Rhode Island	(401) 277 2601	www.ritourism.com
South Carolina	(605) 734 0129	www.prt.state.sc.us/sc
Tennessee	(615) 741 2159	www.gotennessee/com
Texas	(512) 462 9191	www.tdoc.state.tx.us
Utah	(801) 533 5681	www.utah.com/home.htm
Vermont	(802) 828 3236	www.travel-vermont.com
Virginia	(804) 786 2051	www.virginia.org
Washington	(206) 753 5600	www.tourism.wa.gov
West Virginia	(304) 348 2286	www.state.wv.us/tourism
Wisconsin	(608) 266 2161	www.tourism.state.wi.us
Wyoming	(307) 777 7777	www.state.wy.us/tourism

Most of the above Web sites are run by the state office for tourism and travel, though some states have no such office leaving such matters to the private sector. In this case the private equivalent Web page has been listed.

Since the closure of the United States Travel and Tourism Administration (USTTA) there has been no central source of tourist information for the USA in Britain. The *Visit USA Association*, however, is a non-profit organisation representing US states, airlines, hotels, car-hire firms and tour operators. Call 0891 600530 (50p a minute) for their 'Essential Travel Planner to the USA', a guide to their members' services. For the southern states contact *Travel South SA*, PO Box 300, Peterborough PE1 5RB. Tel: (0171) 603 2622. In the absence of a US government travel agency, individual states are increasingly represented in the UK. Though originally aimed at the travel trade these offices are increasingly dealing with the general public:

- **Alabama Bureau of Travel & Tourism**: 31 Blackwell Road, Barnt Green, Worcestershire B45 8BT. Tel: (0121) 445 4994.

- **Arizona**: Tel: (0181) 651 3636.

- **Capital Region USA**: for the Virginia, Washington DC and Maryland area. PO Box 52, St Leonards on Sea, East Sussex TN38 9TY. Tel: 0345 697236.

- **Colorado**: 2 Maxstead Road, Hemel Hempstead, Hertfordshire HP2 7DX. Tel: (01442) 232901. For details of an information pack call (01564) 794999.

- **Florida**: Roebuck House, Palace Street, London SW1E 5BA. Tel: 0891 600 555. Be prepared for a three-minute recorded menu of options (costing £1.50 daytime) followed by a suggestion that you take your enquiry to a travel agent or send money for an information pack. This number is *not* an enquiry service per se but a contact point for receiving material on general Florida issues.

- **Georgia Department of Industry, Trade & Tourism**: 31 Blackwell Road, Barnt Green, Worcestershire B45 8BT. Tel: (0121) 445 4554.

- **Hawaii Visitors Bureau**: PO Box 208, Sunbury on Thames, Middlesex TW16 5RJ. Tel: (0181) 941 4009.

- **Illinois Bureau of Tourism**: 20 Barclay Road, Croydon CR0 1JN. Tel: (0181) 680 0122. (Web address: *www.enjoyillinois.com*).

- **Kentucky**: Garden Studios Suite 302, 11–15 Betterton Street, Covent Garden, London WC2H 9BP. Tel: (0171) 470 8804.

- **Louisiana**: c/o Travel & Tourism Marketing, 20 Barclay Road, Croydon CR0 1JN. Tel: (0181) 760 0377. (Web site: *www.louisianatravel.com*).

- **Massachusetts Office of Travel and Tourism**: Tel: (0171) 978 5233.

- **Michigan Information Centre**: 110 St Martin's Lane, London WC2N 4DY. Tel: (0171) 240 1422.

- **Mississippi**: c/o Lofthouse Enterprises, Suite 2, 6c Brand Street, Hitchin, Hertfordshire SG5 1HX. Tel: (01462) 4440787. (Web site: *www.gardencitynet.co.uk/lofthse/tenn.html*).

- **New England**: The Business Village, Bromhill Road, London SW18 4JQ. Tel: (0181) 874 5038/7281, or **Discover New England** on (01732) 742777. (Web site: *www.discovernewengland.com*).

- **New York Division of Tourism**: 9 Gower Street, London WC1E 6HA. Tel: (0171) 916 4111. Once in New York City dial 397 8222 for citywide information. (Web site: *www.nycvisit.com*).

- **North Carolina Tourism**: Cellnet Travel Services Ltd, 47 High Street, Henley-in-Arden B95 5AA. Tel: (01564) 794999. For a free brochure ring 0990 333 123.

- **Oklahoma**: PO Box 126, Hemel Hempstead, Hertfordshire HP3 0AZ. Tel: (01442) 214621.

- **Rocky Mountains International** (Wyoming, Montana, South Dakota): 10 Station Road, Burgess Hill, RH15 9DQ. Tel: (01444) 233224.

- **South Carolina**: 20 Barclay Road, Croydon CR0 1JN. Tel: (0181) 688 1141.

- **Tennessee**: c/o Lofthouse Enterprises, Suite 2, 6c Brand Street, Hitchin, Hertfordshire SG5 1HX. Tel: (01462) 440784. (Web site: *www.gardencitynet.co/uk/lofthse/tenn.html*).

- **Texas**: c/o Lofthouse Enterprises, Suite 2, 6c Brand Street, Hitchin, Hertfordshire SG5 1HX. Tel: (01462) 440784. (Web site: *www.gardencitynet.co/uk/lofthse/tenn.html*).

- **Virginia**: 1st Floor, 182–4 Addington Road, Selsdon, Croydon CR2 8LB. Tel: (0181) 651 4743.

More Useful Addresses

Visas and permits

- Blair Consular Service Ltd,
  9 City Business Centre
  Lower Road
  London SE16 2XB
  Tel: (0171) 252 1451

- BCL Immigration Services
  11–14 Grafton Street
  Mayfair
  London W1X 4NP
  Tel: (0171) 495 3999
  Email: bcl@workpermit.com

Packing and Overseas Removals

- Excess Baggage Company
  Units 1–17 Commercial Way
  Abbey Way Industrial Esate
  London NW10 6XF
  Tel: (0181) 965 3344
  Web site: *www.excess-baggage.com*

- Global Silverhawk Ltd
  16 Perivale Industrial Park
  Horsenden Lane South
  Greenford, Middlesex UB6 7RW
  Tel: (0181) 997 4321

- Cargo Forwarding International plc
  96 London Industrial Park
  Roding Road
  London E6 4LS
  Tel: (0171) 474 1000/7000
  Web site: *www.cargoforwarding.co.uk*
  (lists regional offices and contact numbers)

Adventure Holidays

- AmeriCan. Tel: (01892) 511894
- Ranch America. Tel: (0181) 868 2970.
- InterWest Adventures. Tel: (01444) 811991.
- Rocky Mountain International. Tel: (01225) 481088.
- River Island Expeditions. Tel: (0181) 810 4525.
- American Round-up. Tel: (01404) 881777.
- JetSave. Tel: (01342) 312033.

Magazines

- *Essentially America*
  Annual subscription £14.70 in UK from
  Phoenix Publishing & Media Ltd
  18/20 Scrutton Street
  London EC2A 4RJ
  Tel: (0171) 247 0537
  http://phoenix.wits.co.uk.esssam

Journals

- *Jobtrac USA*
  Suite 10, 29 Harper Road
  London SE1 6AW
  Tel: (0181) 461 5938

- *The Expatriate*
  First Market Intelligence Ltd
  56A Rochester Row
  London SW1P 1JU

- *Going USA*
  Outbound Newspapers Ltd
  1 Commercial Road
  Eastbourne
  East Sussex BN21 3XQ
  Tel: (01323) 412001

Further Reading

Althen, Cr., *American Ways*, Intercultural Press 1988.

Bloom, A., *The Closing of the American Mind*, Simon & Schuster, New York 1987.

Bradbury, M., *Stepping Westward*, Arena, London 1984.

Brogan, H., *The Pelican History of the United States of America*, Penguin, Harmondsworth 1986.

Brookeman, C., *American Culture and Society since the 1930s*, Macmillan, Basingstoke 1985.

Brown, H., *Working Abroad*, Northcote House, Plymouth 1986.

Burgess, A., *The Expatriate's Guide*, Neville Russell, London 1986.

Cunningham, Matthew, *Finding Work Overseas, How and Where to Contact International Recruitment*, How To Books, Plymouth 1996.

Deutsch, H. D., *Getting into America*, Hodder & Stoughton, Sevenoaks 1985.

Fleischer, R., *Applying for a United States Visa*, How To Books/ International Venture Handbooks, Plymouth 1993.

Fox, K., *Metropolitan America: Urban Life in the US 1945–1980*, Macmillan, Basingstoke 1985.

Furnell, Michael, *Daily Telegraph Guide to Living & Retiring Abroad*, Kogan Page 1990.

Golzen, G., *Working Abroad*, Kogan Page, London 1987.

Griffin, S., *Live and Work in the USA and Canada*, Vacation Work, Oxford 1995.

Griffin, S., *Work Your Way Around the World*, Vacation Work, Oxford 1990.

Grossman, S, *Have Kids Will Travel*, Christopher Helm, London 1987.

Haslam, D., *Travelling with Kids*, Macdonald, London 1987.

Hirsch, E. D., *Cultural Literacy, What Every American Needs to Know*, Vintage Books, New York 1988.

Jones, R., *How to Emigrate*, How To Books, 1994.

Jones, R., *Getting a Job in America*, How To Books, 5th edition 1998.

Lanier, P., *Living in the USA*, Intercultural Press 1988.

Leppard, D., *The Directory of Jobs and Careers Abroad*, Vacation

Work, Oxford 1987.

Let's Go: The Budget Guide to the USA & Canada 1994.

Lipinski, A., *The Directory of Jobs & Careers Abroad*, Vacation Work, Oxford (7th edition) 1989.

Lodge, D., *Changing Places*, Penguin, Harmondsworth 1975.

McFedries, Paul, *10 Minute Guide to Travel Planning on the Net*, Macmillan 1997.

McGinnis, Christopher J., *202 Tips Even the Best Business Travelers May Not Know*, McGraw-Hill 1994.

Mobil Guide series, Springfield, updated periodically.

Moss, M. and G., *Handbook for Women Travellers*, Piatkus, London 1987.

National Geographic Society *National Parks of the United States*, Washington DC 1994.

Owen, D., *High School*, Viking, New York 1981.

Potter, D. M., *People of Plenty: Economic Abundance and the American Character*, University of Chicago Press, Chicago 1954.

Reich, R. B., *The Next American Frontier*, Penguin, Harmondsworth 1984.

Rosenberg, S., *American Economic Development Since 1945*, Macmillan, Basingstoke 1985.

Ryan, D. S., *America: A Guide to the Experience*, Kozmik, London 1986.

Savageau, D. & Boyer, R., *Places Rated Almanac*, Prentice Hall, New York 1993.

Stanford, J., *Holidays and Travel Abroad*, The Royal Association for Disability and Rehabilitation (RADAR), London (6th edition) 1991.

Trudgill, P., *Coping with America*, Basil Blackwell, Oxford 1985.

Vandome, N., *How to Find Temporary Work Abroad*, How To Books, Plymouth 1994.

Wanning, E., *Culture Shock! USA*, Kuperard, London 1991.

Wicks, R. and Schultz, F., *Long Stays in America*, David & Charles, Newton Abbot 1985.

Wood, K., *Globetrotter's Bible,* HarperCollins 1995.

Other titles in the How To series:

How to Get a Job Abroad, Roger Jones (4th edition 1995)
How to Study Abroad, Teresa Tinsley (3rd edition 1995)
Passing That Interview, Judith Johnstone (4th edition 1997)
Teaching Abroad, Roger Jones (3rd edition 1998)

(See back cover for How To Books address.)

Weights and Measures

US imperial measures of length are the same as in the UK but measures of capacity are somewhat different: the US gallon is smaller than the British equivalent (1 US gallon = 0.83 UK gallon); the US hundredweight (cwt) is smaller than the British (being 100 lb rather than 112 lb); a US ton is short (2,000lb rather than 2,240 lb, whereas a metric tonne is 2,204 lb).

All imperial and US measures are gradually being replaced by metric (SI) measures, in theory if not in people's minds. As in the UK the change-over is long and drawn out, in comparison to Canada where it was short and sweet.

British visitors who think of themselves as firmly non-metric may find to their surprise that they are more metric than they thought when confronted with US measures. The author once mistook a 12 degrees weather report for 12 degrees Celsius rather than 12 degrees Fahrenheit and almost froze.

Index

GETTING A JOB IN AMERICA
How and where to find the right employment opportunities and contacts

Roger Jones

This is an essential handbook for everyone planning to work in the US, whether on a short-term vacation assignment, on secondment or contract, or on a permanent basis. Roger Jones is a freelance author specialising in careers and expatriate matters and has himself worked overseas. 'Essential for anyone who is thinking of working in the US.' *Going USA*. 'Outlines with some thoroughness the procedures a future immigrant or temporary resident would have to undertake ... For young people considering a US exchange or summer employment, the section on vacation jobs is particularly worthwhile.' *Newscheck* (Careers Service Bulletin). 'Very good value for money.' *School Librarian Journal*.

224pp illus. 1 85703 372 8. 5th edition.

WORKING ON CONTRACT WORLDWIDE
How to triple your earnings by working as an independent contractor anywhere in the world

Rod Briggs

This book is the first to explain in practical steps how to break into the lucrative world of contracting. It explains how to become a contractor yourself, how to cope with the professional, commercial and personal aspects of contracting and how to maximise the opportunities it can offer. Rod Briggs has himself worked for over 25 years as a contractor worldwide.

160pp. illus. 1 85703 429 5.

FINDING WORK OVERSEAS
How and where to contact international recruitment agencies, consultancies and employers

Matthew Cunningham

This is an essential reference guide for all overseas job hunters and recruiters. It lists more than 1,500 key recruitment agencies, international consultancies and employers, who can offer international employment opportunities. The data is presented in a consistent, clear and user-friendly format, summarising each organisation's recruitment specialities, full contact details, and work locations abroad. Matthew Cunningham is a professional corporate manpower planner.

200pp. illus. 1 85703 409 0.

GETTING A JOB ABROAD
A handbook of opportunities and contacts

Roger Jones

Now in a fifth fully revised edition, this top-selling title is essential for everyone planning to spend a period abroad. 'A highly informative book...containing lots of hard information and a first class reference section.' *The Escape Committee Newsletter.* 'An excellent addition to any careers library... Compact and realistic... There is a wide range of reference addresses covering employment agencies, specialist newspapers, a comprehensive booklist and helpful addresses... All readers, whether careers officers, young adults or more mature adults, will find use for this book.' *Newscheck* (Careers Services Bulletin). Roger Jones is a specialist writer on expatriate and employment matters.

272pp. illus. 1 85703 418 X. 5th edition.